Performance Administration

Performance Administration

Improved Responsiveness and Effectiveness in Public Service

Alan Walter Steiss
Virginia Polytechnic Institute
and State University

Gregory A. Daneke
University of Arizona

LexingtonBooks
D.C. Heath and Company
Lexington, Massachusetts
Toronto

Library of Congress Cataloging in Publication Data

Steiss, Alan Walter
  Performance administration

  1. Public administration.   2. System analysis.
3. Policy sciences.   I. Daneke, Gregory A., joint author.
II. Title.
JF1411.S73   350.007'8   79-48028
ISBN 0-669-03637-4

Copyright © 1980 by D.C. Heath and Company

Published simultaneously in Canada.

Printed in the United States of America.

International Standard Book Number: 0-669-03637-4

Library of Congress Catalog Card Number: 79-48028

Contents

List of Figures

List of Tables

Performance
Administration

1   Performance Administration: A Prologue

In the waning years of the twentieth century, public confidence in the ability of government to deal effectively with critical problems is perhaps at its lowest ebb since the founding of the Republic. Proposition 13-style referenda, anti–big-government candidates for public office, calls for a balanced federal budget, and a rejuvenation of Jeffersonian idealism may not be harbingers of a widespread popular rebellion. However, these phenomena do signal a growing concern with the apparent low correlation between government spending and effective public policies. Moreover, in some quarters, the focus of government resources on a problem may be a guarantee of failure rather than of success. It may be that policy failures often result because the issues addressed are beyond the legitimate scope of government. However, the manifest impotence of government has come at a time when more and more problems are arising in day-to-day operations and not merely in more grandiose endeavors.

The Need for a Broader Planning/Management Orientation

As E.S. Quade has observed, "We see signs everywhere of ineffective programs, wasted money, and unsolved problems. There are complaints that the solutions being proposed range from poor, at best, to counterproductive at worst."[1] Not only is the margin for error between success and failure shrinking, but many public issues appear to defy effective planning and/or management when defined in the more narrow sense. Dwindling fiscal resources, rapidly increasing clientele, relatively inflexible productivity ratios, charges of collusion between public employees and private interests, and the emergence of public unions have all contributed to increasing difficulties in the delivery of public services. New York City, Cleveland, and other major municipalities stand as glaring reminders of the widening gap between public expectations and public services. Thus, the coming era of fiscal austerity is not just a matter of less government—it is essentially an issue of better, more responsive administration of public activities.

1

The Performance Approach   .

Effective administration must be a dynamic process, involving the blending and directing of available human and physical resources in order to achieve public objectives. Its basic purpose should be to provide focus and consistency to the action programs of government. The effectiveness of such an approach must be measured by the results achieved and by the people served, that is, in terms of performance. This concept of performance suggests a melding of the management objectives of efficiency and effectiveness. Moreover, effectiveness must be measured in terms of the response time required to make adjustments when things go wrong. As a consequence, this more systematic and responsive approach to public planning and management has been labeled *performance administration.* This perspective combines the traditional approaches of public administration with contemporary concepts of systems analysis and comprehensive planning and budgeting in an attempt to achieve a coordinative process capable of yielding more rational public policies and decisions.

The following procedural definition identifies the intended scope of performance administration:

1. Establish overall strategic goals and select appropriate objectives for particular public programs or enterprises (the strategic plan).
2. Determine requirements to meet identified goals and objectives and establish the necessary procedures, operations, and/or activities to carry out the strategic plan, including a selection of the best sequence for performance (management planning and programming).
3. Determine the available resources (fiscal, personnel, materials, equipment, and time) required for public programs as a whole, and judiciously allocate these resources in accordance with some system of priorities (budgeting).
4. Schedule the entire program from the point of commitment to completion and exercise control by reacting to (and anticipating) deviations between predicted and actual performance (operations scheduling and control).
5. Monitor activities to determine whether or not reasonable, feasible, and efficient plans and programs are being produced and executed adequately, and if not, why not (performance monitoring and evaluation).

Performance administration is concerned with deciding in advance what an organization should do in the future (planning), determining who will do it and how it will be accomplished (management), and monitoring and enhancing ongoing activities and operations.

A Balanced Blend

Many of these procedural tasks presently are assigned to various sectors in the public policy-making process—planners plan; financial analysts prepare budgets; program personnel schedule and control resources for specific activities; administrators monitor and evaluate. Some of these tasks are undertaken on a grand scale, while others are fairly routine. With the increasing complexity of government operations, however, the "divisions of labor" established to deal with complexity may well become the major impediment to effective policy formulation and implementation. Unless a more comprehensive framework is created to provide guidance and coordination, the sum of the administrative parts may not be an integrated whole.

One key to performance administration is systematic thinking about both the monumental and the mundane. The somewhat artificial distinctions among planning, analysis, and management become superfluous when the impact of administrative activities on policy is considered. In general, it is the responsibility of the performance administrator to reduce uncertainty and to bring risk within tolerable bounds. The functions of performance administration must necessarily be carried out as a balanced blend between objective methods and subjective ability.

Systems Analysis:
Panacea or Pearly Pachyderm?

In recent years, concern for better government has focused on more systematic procedures for problem solving. This emphasis can be seen in public sector applications of operations research and other management science techniques, the refinement of cost-benefit and cost-effectiveness techniques, the advent of zero-base and program budgeting, and the growing attention to more orderly approaches to policy analysis and evaluation. At present, however, these disjointed techniques and remnants of more comprehensive schemes do not constitute a coherent framework for the planning and management of public policies and programs. Performance administration seeks to build the positive attributes of these procedures, while circumventing some of their shortcomings.

Evaluation of Alternative Solutions

During the late 1950s and early 1960s, systems analysis was offered as a cure-all to a wide array of public-sector problems. Emerging from the highly technical field of systems engineering, systems analysis is often associated with such people as Robert McNamara and Charles Hitch and with such organizations as the Rand Corporation. It evokes an image of high-speed computers, large-scale mathematical models, multidisciplinary teams of military strategists, and elaborate cost-benefit analyses. None of these factors, however, is essential for successful systems analysis. Systems analysis has evolved as a generic term that can be applied to any explicit, theoretical, or deductive approach to problem solving. Thus, in some cases a good systems analysis can be performed by a single individual doing some elementary calculations on a scratch pad, without once mentioning cost-benefits. Such an individual, of course, would have to apply some criteria for the evaluation of alternative solutions to the problem at hand—and herein lies the key to systems analysis.

Hitch has described systems analysis as an approach that defines and attacks problems explicitly in terms of the following elements:

1. An *objective function*—a clear identification of the goals and objectives to be sought;
2. Alternative means (or *systems*) by which the goals and objectives may be accomplished;
3. Knowledge about the *costs* or resources required by each alternative;
4. A description (that is, a *model*) of the relationships among the objectives, the alternative means of achievement, the problem environment, and the resource requirements; and
5. A *criterion* for choosing the preferred alternative that usually relates the objectives and costs in some manner.[2]

Involvement in goal identification was a source of contention in early government experiments with systems analysis. Defenders of pluralism asserted that the involvement of administrative analysts in the policy-formulation process was antithetical to disjointed, yet democratic, political procedures.[3] Meanwhile, defenders of analysis offered assurances that the systems approach would merely augment, not circumvent, traditional legislative prerogatives.[4] The debate continues.

Systematic examination of alternative courses of action is fundamental to systems analysis; equally important is the information base that may lead to the design of additional alternatives. A thorough and imaginative analysis may result in modification of the initial objectives. Thus, systems analysis is a dynamic process—as the problem unfolds through analysis, the desired solution or objective function may undergo a number of redefinitions on the basis of new information.

Systems analysis is concerned with the future—often the distant future. Because of this, the environment is one of uncertainty—an important facet of the problem that should be recognized and treated explicitly from the outset. Quantitative methods often must be supplemented by qualitative analysis. The importance of good qualitative work in systems analysis and the use of appropriate combinations of quantitative and qualitative methods cannot be overemphasized. Many of the shortcomings of systems analysis in application stem from a failure to recognize adequately this need for a balanced approach.

Asking the Right Questions

In applications of systems analysis to real-world problems, two additional elements not enumerated above are worth noting. The first—one which should perhaps head the entire list—is the need to address the right problem in the first place. The second is the need to interpret results in terms of the real-world decision environment.

As Peter Drucker has suggested, the most common source of mistakes in management decisions is the emphasis on finding the *right answers* rather than on asking the *right questions*.[5] As Drucker has observed: ". . . the important and difficult job is never to find the right answers, it is to find the right question. For there are few things as useless—if not as dangerous—as the right answer to the wrong question." [6] Similarly, Anatol Rapoport asserts that the first step in solving a problem is to state it:

> The statement usually involves a description of an existing state and desirable state of affairs where the factors involved in the discrepancy are explicitly pointed out. The success with which any problem is solved depends to a great extent on the clarity with which it is stated. In fact, the solution of the problem is, in a sense, a clarification (or concretization) of the objectives.[7]

Vague statements of the problem lead to vague methods that are, at best, only erratically successful. The more a given situation is extensionalized, the better the classification of the problem and the greater the promise of a successful solution.

Short-circuiting this stage of analysis may mean that more time must be spent later to get at the real problem. Emotional bias, habitual or traditional behavior, or a tendency to seek the path of least resistance may lead to a superficial analysis, resulting in a statement of the apparent instead of the real problem. Even an excellent solution to an apparent, but nonexistent, problem will not work in practice.

Interpretation of the Results of Analysis

Applications of systems analysis in commerce and industry, the military, and, more recently, government have been dominated by an *efficiency orientation.*

In such applications, analysis follows a fairly mathematical pattern, resolving simple "operational or optimization" problems.[8] Such problems typically involve an attempt to increase efficiency in situations where it is clear what more efficient means. Analysis often can be reduced to the application of a basic model, such as linear or dynamic programming; by the specification of parameters and constraints, the analytical model can be made to fit a wide variety of operations. An optimal solution is then obtained by means of a systematic computational routine.

In many public-decision situations, however, such analytical techniques can only assist in solving elemental components of larger, more complex problems. Such problem situations normally involve more than the efficient allocation of resources among some clearly defined set of alternatives. These problems are not solvable in the same sense as efficiency problems in which some "payoff" function can be maximized in a clear expression of what is to be accomplished. In these more complex situations, many factors may elude quantification, and it is not totally clear what "more efficient" means. The difficulty often lies, therefore, in determining what ought to be done (planning), as well as in how to do it (management).

Opponents of systems analysis assert that basically it is little more than a rather obvious, explicit, common-sense approach to problem solving that has been given a scientific aura through the use of mathematical models processed on high-speed computers. Critics argue that all too often the form of the analysis rather than the problem becomes the center of attention. In their rush to embrace more sophisticated techniques, both analysts and clients may lose sight of the main purpose of the analysis. Thus, systems analysis has become something of a white elephant in its public sector applications, that is, often it is more of an impediment to problem solving than a cure-all.

Even the best systems analysis, properly applied, has its limitations. Bad systems analysis, improperly applied, can be worse than useless. It is all too easy for the analyst to begin to believe his own assumptions, even if they are drawn out of thin air, and to attach undue significance to the results of his analysis, especially if it involves some sophisticated mathematics and much hard work. Clients may also be too easily impressed by systems analyses, especially if the results come out of computers and are agreeable or plausible and impressively presented. Other clients may be skeptical for the wrong reasons—because the results contradict their own biases rather than because of questionable features of the analysis.

The analyst and the client must both accept responsibility for the interpretation and continuous testing of analytical results in terms of real-world problems. The explicit nature of systems analysis can expose deficiencies that might otherwise go unnoticed. But systems analysis becomes a "white elephant" when analysts and clients expect more than it can provide. Systems analysis cannot guarantee against the possibility of addressing the wrong problem or of approaching it in terms of the wrong objectives, alternative systems, measures of costs, or criterion of choice. Nor does the method ensure that the results will be interpreted correctly.

Importance of Continuous Planning

In performance administration there is considerable emphasis on the role of planning as a continuous process rather than as a "one-shot optimization" at the beginning of policy formulation. Nevertheless, policies and programs are rarely executed exactly as initially conceived. Random events, environmental disturbances, competitive tactics, and unforeseen circumstances may all be obstacles to smooth implementation. There is a growing recognition that static plans, fixed targets, and repetitive programs are of little value in a dynamic society. Planning must go beyond the initial phases of policy making to include strategic planning, management planning, and operations planning and control.

Strategic Planning

Strategic planning involves identification of public goals and objectives, determination of necessary changes in these objectives, and decisions on the resources to be used to attain these objectives. It entails:

1. basic research and analysis (data collection and inventory studies, including a determination of the planning horizon);
2. diagnosis of trends and needs;
3. identification of effectiveness measures;
4. formulation of goals and objectives as definitions of the desired state of affairs;
5. analysis and evaluation of alternative courses of action;
6. the development of policies governing the acquisition, use, and disposition of public resources.[9]

Through strategic planning, *policies*—factual premises representing what can be done—are tested against *goals*—value premises representing what should be done. This should result in the incorporation of both ideal and practical elements in public policy.

In strategic planning, considerable emphasis is placed on the development of public awareness and participation in formulating goals and objectives. The focus is on the delineation of problems that must be solved, environmental threats that must be countered, and opportunities that may be profitably exploited. These problems, threats, and opportunities may be generated from within, or they may arise from the broader economic, political, technological, or natural environment. A strategic plan should be not merely an internal document but rather the result of a systematic interpretation of the socio-political environment of the community. Strategic planning provides a blueprint for translating broad intentions into specific commitments of resources needed to achieve agreed-on goals.

Management Planning

Management planning ensures that public resources are used effectively and efficiently to accomplish public objectives. It involves: (1) programming approved goals into specific program, projects, and activities; (2) designing organizational units to carry out approved programs and plans; and (3) staffing these units and procuring the necessary resources to carry out the plans. Effective management planning—sometimes called "organization and methods research" or simply "administrative analysis"—requires a continuous search for more productive ways to operate government agencies. Such planning puts the administrator in a better position to evaluate government's ability to meet its changing obligations. Ideally, management planning is the link between goals and objectives and the actual performance of public activities. Therefore management planning is necessarily closely associated with the budgetary process.

The concept of Planning Programming Budgeting Systems (PPBS) burst on the scene in the 1960s and was heralded as the "holy grail" of over fifty years of budget and administrative reform. By the early 1970s, however, PPBS had been quietly put to rest. As with many innovations introduced by dictum, there was inadequate groundwork for the full implementation of PPBS in the federal budget process, and the problem was even greater in state and local governments. Public budgeting practices are firmly entrenched, and insufficient leadership, support, and resources were invested on behalf of PPBS to overcome these traditions.

Program budgeting, a predecessor of PPBS, survived the 1960s, however, and has been accepted by various state and local governments as a more systematic process for the allocation of scarce resources. Major public goals and objectives are identified in programmatic terms, and government activities are structured and analyzed according to these objectives. Detailed item-ization of expenditures (object codes) is introduced only when it contributes to the analysis of the total system or when it is needed to determine potential impacts of marginal trade-offs among competing proposals. Furthermore, a conscious effort is made to formulate multiyear program and financial plans, analyze a wider range of program alternatives, and incorporate specific procedures for updating programs once implemented. In short, program budgeting explicitly recognizes the notion that planning and budgeting are complementary.

Operations Planning and Control

Operations are the activities or tasks that must be performed to meet the objectives of public programs. In addition to determining a desirable sequence for these activities, program managers must establish the methods, time, and costs of performing each activity. Operations planning or scheduling involves the determination of requirements for program resources and their appropriate order of commitment to ensure that specific tasks are carried out efficiently and effectively. In its more advanced forms, operations planning involves the application of such management tools as Program Evaluation and Review Technique (PERT) and Critical Path Method (CPM).

Management must be able to control a program or project from its initiation until it is completed or significantly modified to result in a new program or project. Operations control involves monitoring program activities to ensure that they adhere to a performance schedule. Control procedures should be designed so that management is called in only when the program is off schedule or otherwise potentially in trouble, a practice known as *management by exception.*

Planning/Management Information Requirements

Every administrative system, however rudimentary, should incorporate these basic planning processes. The relative emphasis among them, however, varies considerably. As a practical matter, strategic, management, and operations planning have tended to be viewed as competing processes, with no neat division of functions among the various participants. Since time is one of the scarce resources in administration, central authorities must be selective in the things they do and the elements they emphasize. This scarcity suggests that the control responsibility should be decentralized to operating levels, while strategic and management planning functions should remain centralized. However, the lack of reliable and trusted internal control systems has forced central authorities to assume many control functions, often at the expense of strategic planning.

Moreover, each of these basic planning modes requires different skills, has different informational needs, and results in different ways of handling administration. Information requirements differ in terms of time spans, levels of aggregation and detail, linkages with operating units, and the input-output foci. The apparent solution is to design an information system that can serve multiple needs. Historically, however, there has been a tendency to homogenize information structures and to rely on a single classification system to serve all administrative purposes. In general, information systems have been structured to meet the purposes of control, so that the greater responsiveness of planning and management systems envisioned by contemporary advocates of administrative reform has been almost impossible to achieve.

A principal responsibility of performance administration is to supply decision makers with three specific areas of information: (1) *autointelligence,* which provides information about the component elements of the particular organization under study; (2) *environmental intelligence,* which provides information about the broader environment within which the organization must operate; and (3) *historical data,* which brings together and analyzes the lessons of the past.[10] Incorporating the three modes of planning into the basic framework of performance administration gives explicit recognition to the range of information needed in the formulation of management-information and program-evaluation systems.

Performance Administration: Innovation or Reinvention of the Wheel?

Comprehensive approaches have come and gone, leaving behind fragmented sets of techniques that have found selective applications and misapplications. Meanwhile, practitioners and academics have refined these techniques, rendering them either innocuous and hence more palatable to administrators or so elaborate and esoteric that they are useful only in full-blown academic research.

Performance administration attempts to balance these polar pressures for utilization and methodological sophistication; a mixed bag of analytical techniques and strategies can be successfully combined in a number of permutations, applicable to a variety of situations. In these various applications, the primary focus of performance administration remains the integration of planning and management in productive harmony.

At least three categories of decisions are reflected in the procedural definition of performance administration: (1) decisions relating to problem recognition, classification, and appraisal; (2) decisions required to convert the intentions of the strategic plan into more specific programs and projects; and (3) control and monitoring decisions that assess the performance of ongoing programs and provide additional inputs in subsequent cycles of the process. The conceptual framework of performance administration draws heavily on both previously developed and emergent theories of systems analysis, strategic planning, and program budgeting. It attempts to amplify these concepts to find a coordinative mechanism that will build on their strengths while circumventing some of their shortcomings. Performance administration also borrows freely from the concepts and techniques of policy analysis and evaluation as it seeks to provide a possible stepping stone to the eventual development of a policy science.

As De Woolfson has observed: "At different times and in different places, different management systems are in vogue. Some of these systems represent real innovations; more often someone 'reinvents the wheel.' "[11] It is up to the reader to decide which of these characterizations best describes the concept of performance administration.

Notes

1. E.S. Quade, *Analysis for Public Decisions* (New York: American Elsevier Publishing Company, 1975), p. vii.

2. Charles Hitch, *Analysis for Military Decisions,* ed. E.S. Quade (Chicago: Rand McNally Company, 1964), pp. 13–14.

3. See Aaron Wildavsky, *The Politics of the Budgetary Process,* 2nd ed. (Boston: Little, Brown and Company, 1974), pp. 181–208; also "The Political Economy of Efficiency," *Public Administration Review* 26 (December 1966):292–310.

4. See William Capron, "The Impact of Analysis on Bargaining in Government"; and James Schlesinger, "Systems Analysis and the Political Process," in *The Administrative Process and Democratic Theory,* ed. Louis Gawthrop (Boston: Houghton Mifflin Company, 1970), pp. 336–371.

5. Peter F. Drucker, "The Effective Decision," *Harvard Business Review* 45(January-February 1967):92.

6. Peter F. Drucker, *The Practice of Management* (New York: Harper, 1954), p. 353.

7. Anatol Rapoport, "What is Information?" *ETC: A Review of General Semantics* 10(Summer 1953):252.

8. Note the distinction between these types of problems and what have been identified as planning problems in Kenneth Kraemer, *Policy Analysis in Local Government* (Washington, D.C.: International City Management Association, 1973), pp. 24–27.

9. Alan Walter Steiss, *Public Budgeting and Management* (Lexington, Mass.: Lexington Books, D.C. Heath and Company, 1972), chap. 9.

10. Anthony J. Catanese and Alan Walter Steiss, *Systemic Planning: Theory and Application* (Lexington, Mass.: Lexington Books, D.C. Heath and Company, 1970), p. 49.

11. Bruce H. De Woolfson, Jr., "Public Sector MBO and PPB: Cross Fertilization in Management Systems," *Public Administration Review* 36(July-August 1975):387.

2

Performance Administration and Public Policy Making: An Overview

Studies of policy making enjoy great currency in various academic disciplines, but it is often difficult to bring together these diverse contributions into anything resembling a single frame of reference. Research and teaching are unavoidably colored by individual preconceptions, as are the collective formulations of various disciplines. Practitioners are usually more concerned with discrete sets of problems, and become impatient with having to wade through a profusion of conceptual biases in search of answers to these specific problems. Definitions are further clouded by the use of terms such as *decision, judgment,* or *choice* when dealing with the policy-making process. Clear distinctions seldom are made as to the similarities and differences implicit in these terms. In short, relatively few academics and perhaps fewer practitioners have explicitly defined what they mean by policy making.

What Is Public Policy?

The concept of *policy* seems to be a typically English one. There is no precise equivalent in German, Spanish, or French—the words *politique, diplomatie,* and *ligne de conduite* are frequently used in translation—or in Italian, where *politica* means "tactful or diplomatic." The political economist Bruno Leoni tells of a Russian commander in Berlin just after World War II who was alarmed when the American and British commanders invited him to cooperate in a common "policy." He had no instructions from Moscow and was fearful of becoming involved in some sort of political agreement that would not be approved by his superiors.[1]

Levels of Public Policy

Some students of policy making have suggested that the term *policy* should be reserved for relatively high-order statements of intention and direction. Lasswell, for example, suggests that: "The word 'policy' is commonly used to designate the most important choices made either in organized or in private life. . . . Hence, 'policy' is free of many of the undesirable connotations clustered about the word political, which is often believed to imply 'partisanship' or 'corruption.' "[2] Thus, Lasswell concludes that the basic emphasis of policy analysis should be ". . . upon the fundamental problems of man in society, rather than upon the topical issues of the moment."[3]

Public policy has also been defined in behavioristic terms. In a study concerned with the identification and analysis of the values that influence public policy and decision making, Jacob and Flink define policy as ". . . an integrated program of actions which an actor (or group of actors) is accustomed or intends to undertake in response to a given problem or situation with which he is confronted."[4]

As Simon and others have suggested, serious ambiguity might be avoided if different terms were used for these different levels of policy. "Perhaps the ethical premises of management could be called 'legislative policy;' the broad non-ethical rules laid down by top management, 'management policy;' and other rules, 'working policy.' "[5] Simon notes, however, that in addition to these several kinds of policy, or authoritatively promulgated rules, almost every organization, public and private, has a large number of *practices*. These practices, although not established as orders or regulations and seldom enforced by official sanctions, are nevertheless observed in the organization by force of custom or tradition. "Often, the line between policy and practice is not sharp unless the organization follows the 'practice' (or 'policy') of putting all its policies in writing."[6]

David Easton also acknowledges these different levels of policy.[7] According to Easton, "authoritative outputs" are public decisions or policies that members of society regard, willingly or unwillingly, as binding, pre-emptive, and entitled to obedience. He adds, however, that "associated outputs" occur along with authoritative outputs but are nonauthoritative in character. Nevertheless, according to Easton, they create or moderate public support for the political system in precisely the same way as authoritative outputs. Easton also distinguishes between *output* and *outcome*. The former refers to policy decisions and their intended effects, while the latter refers to the secondary and tertiary—and often unanticipated—consequences of political outputs.

Given the apparent divergence in techniques between the policy level and the program level, some authors draw a line of demarcation between policy analysis and program analysis. Theodore Poister, for example, suggests the following distinctions:

> The term *policy analysis* generally refers to the analysis of the determinants, characteristics, and implications of public policies and programs, particularly of the relationship between the content of policies and programs and the substantive consequences and outcomes they produce. Public *policies* are guidelines for public action, prescribing in general terms the means for moving toward a desired course of events or outcome. Programs are sets of organized activities conducted by governmental institutions in pursuit of established policy objectives; they can be thought of as vehicles for carrying out policy. Thus, program analysis is a subset of the general field of policy analysis.[8]

As a subset of policy analysis, however, program analysis is not mutually exclusive. Furthermore, since the content of policies often emerges through program development, separation of these anaiytical techniques may result in a dysfunctional bifurcation.

Bureaucratic Policy Making

Bureaucracy is on trial precisely because the public is bound in countless ways by a vast array of rules and regulations made by an army of appointed administrators. To the average citizen, *bureaucracy* is an ugly word, conjuring up images of official red tape and dronelike functionaries who inhibit rather than facilitate the smooth operations of public affairs.

For many years, the predominant belief among administrative theorists was that bureaucrats were not and should not be engaged in the policy-making process. This tradition, often called the Wilsonian model, has had a significant normative influence over the years. It was Woodrow Wilson, of course, who set the tone with statements like the following:

> . . . the field of administration is as a field business. It is removed from the hurry and strife of politics; it at most points stands apart even from the debatable ground of constitutional study. It is a part of the political life only as the methods of the countinghouse are part of the life of society; only as machinery is part of the manufactured product.[9]

This theme was sustained over the years by a series of authors who emphasized the mechanistic aspects of administrative behavior. Frederick Taylor, writing just after the turn of the century, viewed the bureaucrat as a "money motivated machine," subject to performance improvements through "time and motion studies." In the 1930s Gulick and Urwick fashioned an elaborate set of performance principles based on advances in private sector management.[10] Their prescription was not unlike more recent attempts to bring systems analysis from the private to the public sector.

With the Hawthorne Studies just before World War II, serious doubt arose as to the motivations and expectations of public- as well as private-sector employees.[11] These observations about the humanistic underpinnings of administrative behavior were given theoretical substance by the recent Nobel laureate Herbert Simon. In the early 1950s, Simon launched a devastating attack on the classic models of rational and formalistic administration, ushering in an era of human-centered rather than technique-centered reform.[12]

After the turbulence of the 1960s, these humanistic theories were recast into the so-called New Public Administration, the purpose of which was to provide better conditions both within and without public organizations. In essence, it calls for more relevant administrative policy making, thereby acknowledging that administrators do indeed make policy. Moreover, it suggests an obligation on the part of the administrator to reduce "economic social, and psychic suffering."[13] However, despite the acceptance of a new normative ethic and the abandonment of the once sacred "policy-administration dichotomy," the tools and strategies of public-policy formulation still tend to mirror more traditional moorings. This theme will be explored at length as the discussion of alternative strategies unfolds. For now, it may be sufficient to say that administrative policy making remains, at best, controversial and somewhat muddled.

On the empirical side, the bureaucratization of policy making began long before the New Public Administration labeled it as such. The emphasis on professionalism in the early 1900s and the expansion of public programs during the Great Depression led to a geometric expansion of public bureaucracy. Following the New Deal, a widespread dependence on bureaucratic activity was solidified and has never diminished. Today, one out of every seven employed Americans works for a government agency. Millions more produce for and/or are financed by government. The framers of our governmental institutions did not foresee these developments, and increasingly, the perennial question of liberty versus authority is becoming an issue of democracy versus bureaucracy.

Policies made and enforced by administrative agencies constitute a body of law, usually called rules, regulations, or general orders, which public administrators promulgate or execute within authority delegated to them by legislative bodies or executive directives. The term *administrative policy* thus refers to agency rules and decisions, essentially legislative in nature, affecting private rights, obligations, and interests. When legislative bodies make laws, however, they follow prescribed, broadly predictable procedures. No parallel exists in the administrative process to govern the making of agency policies that have the force of law.

There are several reasons for the increased reliance on the administrative process. First, many legislative bodies meet for only a few months each year. Even if a legislative body met in continuous session, it would be unable to act quickly enough to respond to changing conditions. To secure the flexibility necessary for effective government action, legislative bodies at all levels have delegated to administrative agencies the authority to deal with problems as they arise.

As modern government has become big business, administrative detail has grown to monumental proportions. Much of this detail derives from the trend toward preventive legislation, usually in the form of regulation and licensing. There is little doubt that the time-consuming detailed work required by these procedures can best be performed by administrative agencies. Numerous difficulties have arisen when legislative bodies or the courts have attempted to perform such functions.

The requirement that state or local agencies be designated to administer federal grant-in-aid and revenue-sharing programs also has contributed to the expansion of administrative regulation. Such agencies often must establish specific policies needed to carry out the intent of the program.

The administrative process encourages the use of specialists and technical experts. In a complex society, economic and social problems require the attention of those who have the training, time, and facilities to remain continually informed. Legislators cannot be expected to be expert in all areas in which they must act. Although legislative bodies have made significant advances in developing and using analysis, they still depend on the bureaucracy for much of the authentic systematic thinking. For example, improvements at the federal level, such as the establishment of the Congressional Budget Office, the increased responsibility of the General Accounting Office, and the addition of analytical staff to all prominent standing committees, have obviously boosted the analytical capabilities of the Congress. Nevertheless, Congress is not set up to carry out full-blown analyses of federal programs. As congressional consultant Daniel Dreyfus sees Congress:

> . . . it does not engage in sufficient independent, scientific and orderly policy analysis accompanied by all of the accoutrements of data collecting, technical advice and comprehensive exposition of analysis. . . . [However] the circumstances of the Congressional role makes a rigorous application of policy research nearly impossible and practically unwarranted.[14]

In short, often necessity is the mother of delegation. Legislative bodies at all levels have been prompted to delegate law-making authority to administrative agencies, despite constitutional mandates stipulating that all legislative powers granted shall be vested in the legislature. The courts, in turn, have generally upheld this delegation if the legislature has fixed proper and clear standards to govern administrative discretion. The fact remains, however, that much of the legislative function, that is, the function of policy making, has shifted to the administrative process. The consequence has been a subtle but inexorable change in our system of government.

Legislative bodies have sought to retain much of their power through various oversight and review functions. Newly devised requirements for administrative analysis and evaluation provide added safeguards to administrative discretion. In other words, policy analysis is becoming a mechanism for administrative accountability.[15] Legislative bodies can spell out more clearly the intent of administrative due process through procedures embodied in program and zero-base budgeting, performance auditing, sunset legislation (that is, mandatory evaluation and termination procedures), and sunrise provisions (for example, increased opportunities for public participation in administrative decision making). They can also stipulate the types of analysis required to improve on the information provided by the bureaucracy.

Participants in Decision Making

Some individuals and groups are automatically included in decision making because of their position in the organizational hierarchy; they can claim participation as a matter of right, whether this "right" is explicit or merely a matter of general consensus. Their participation is based on inherent prerogatives associated with the office they hold. These individuals often are called policy makers to distinguish them from other participants in the decision-making process, although such arbitrary labels beg the question of who really makes policy decisions.

Other individuals or groups are included in decision making because of their technical competence and are brought into the system when special skills and information are required. Such participation, at least initially, is merely advisory and does not involve actual authority or responsibility for the decisions made. As various writers have observed, however, much more than mere expertise is implied here, since the recommendations of experts may be important in establishing the basis of a decision or policy. Thus, the line between advisory and prerogative-based participation is often blurred, and advisory participants, over time, often become "prerogative" participants.[16] As a result, they come to expect this relationship to exist in whenever their technical expertise is required. This situation is particularly evident among those who must translate policies and decisions into action programs. Management by Objectives, which will be discussed in subsequent chapters, is built on these expectations of participation in decision making.

"Agenda setters" and "communication intermediaries" also contribute significantly to the identification of issues requiring decisions and actions, as well as functioning as liaison between decision groups. As Jacobson and Seashore observe: "These liaison persons appear to be of critical importance to the conceptualization of organization in communication terms as they are in a position to influence significantly or to control the communications to and from certain groups."[17] By extension, these liaison persons can greatly influence the decision process even though they may not participate in actual decision making.

It is evident that the question of who participates in a policy- or decision-making situation depends on more than the traditionally defined dimensions of importance, comprehensiveness, and complexity of the required decision. There are also such organizational aspects as: (1) the information from which the problems and issues are formulated and the routes by which this information enters and is circulated through the organization; (2) the specialized training and experience of individuals and the distribution of these resources within the organization; (3) the orientation of the people who will be called on to carry out the decisions as well as these individuals' expectations about participation in the decision-making process; and (4) the amount of discretion and initiative granted to subordinate groups in the organization. Various writers have also suggested that major policy decisions are not always made in the upper echelons of an organization but may be the result of an accumulation of a number of lesser decisions. As Lepawsky has observed: "Administrators at all levels of responsibility are being constantly thrown into the area of decision-making, and their decisions inevitably add up to major policies in the subsequent course of events."[18]

The Evolution of Administrative Theory and Practice

The evolution of administrative theory reflects the dynamics of administrative behavior and the current significance of administrative-policy development. Administrative theory, usually more prescriptive than descriptive, often does not correspond precisely to reality, but it is generally a good indicator of the self-image of public administration. Moreover, several basic themes that recur throughout the history of administrative thought have served to shape both the professional and the ideological basis of the administrative policy enterprise.

Origins of the Policy-Administration Dichotomy

One of the most important features of the present epoch is the demise of the well-known "policy-administration dichotomy." This was the notion that the administrator merely carried out the will of the people as manifested in legislative initiatives, and had little or no direct involvement in setting policy. The roots of this supposed separation of functions can be found in the writings of the Founding Fathers. In his classic work, *Rights of Man,* Thomas Paine suggested that there are two primary functions of government—legislating, or enacting laws; and executing, or administering laws. He classified the judicial function as executive.[19] These early distinctions also are reflected in the conflict between the Federalist and the Democratic ideals of government. White notes that the essence of the American system of administration can be discovered in the balance sought between: (1) power and control, (2) the expert and the layman, (3) national versus state rule, (4) executive leadership versus legislative supremacy, (5) law versus discretion, and (6) direction versus freedom. [20]

The Jeffersonian concept of administrative decentralization and control prevailed from the time of Andrew Jackson to the administration of Theodore Roosevelt. Following the Age of Jackson and the industrial revolution, pressures for increased government participation and direction to meet critical human needs led to a multiplication of public functions and to new administrative requirements. However, this growth of government did not involve modification of the Jeffersonian ideal that the legislative branch should remain at the center of the system.

Administrative structural change is rooted in the Reconstruction period following the Civil War, a time when government functions expanded into fields requiring greater technical competence. The Pendleton Act of 1883 stated that operating efficiency would logically result from the establishment of a merit system for the allocation of jobs and other occupational rewards. This act established the basis for civil service standards and gave increased recognition to the importance of technology and the professions in government. Reform provided a motive for change and improvement in government practices; improved public management provided the means.[21] Thus, a New Hamiltonianism, as it was called, ushered in a trend toward the concentration of administrative authority in the offices of the chief executive (strong mayors, city and county managers, governors, and presidents).

The more contemporary formulations of the policy-administration dichotomy were introduced by Woodrow Wilson and Frank Goodnow in the first clear break with a priori rationalism of late nineteenth-century political science.[22] Wilson, writing in 1887 while a member of the Princeton University faculty, suggested that all government could be divided into "politics" and "administration." His conception assigned to certain units of government the functions of policy making and control, reserving for others the expert task of executing these policies.[23] This led Goodnow in his writings to reject the descriptive validity of separation of powers. The activities of government, he maintained, could not be accurately classified under the traditional triad of executive, judicial, and legislative; rather, there were in all governments two primary or ultimate functions—politics, or "the expression of the will of the state"; and administration, or "the execution of that will."[24] In making this distinction, however, Goodnow was not attempting to make concrete divisions in terms of branches of government or to equate a given operation with a given agency; he was merely differentiating behavior. He stated clearly that, although the functions of government could be differentiated in terms of policy and administration, the authorities or concrete agencies to which such government operations are entrusted could not be completely separated.

Goodnow's distinction was quickly lost, however, as other writers began to contribute to the literature of the emerging field of public administration. W.F. Willoughby, for example, attempted to give an even more distinct status to administration by not only marking it off from policy making, but also setting it up as a fourth branch of government.[25] Soon students of public administration shifted their emphasis to concrete agencies, which were assumed to carry out administrative functions, as opposed to policy-making bodies such as the legislature.

Increased Executive Initiative and Control

Writing in support of administrative and budgetary reforms, Willoughby strongly stated the case for greater centralization by noting that, while the scope of the federal government was greater than that of any multinational corporation, government was run, in effect, without a "general business manager." Furthermore, he asserted, a system in which legislative controls exist on administrative organization and action, or in which agencies are responsible directly to legislative bodies, is basically ineffective. "One may go further and say that unless this provision (that is, that of the chief executive as a general manager) does exist the whole administrative system of government must be deemed to be radically defective."[26] Willoughby also noted that under the prevailing system at the time, the president had no constitutional administrative authority; the heads of the various executive departments forming his cabinet were not his subordinates in the sense that he had any legal authority to give them orders.

Although few shared Willoughby's exact interpretation of presidential powers, a series of initiatives were launched over the next several years to strengthen executive leadership. Notable among these efforts was the Budgeting and Accounting Act of 1921, designed to correct the chaotic situation that had existed for over a century in the federal government's budgetary practices.

Charles Dawes, budget director under President Warren G. Harding, emphasized three themes as keystones of the organization of the Budget Bureau: (1) adherence to the bureaucratic model, which was part of the scientific management literature of that period; (2) frugality and cost reduction; and (3) administrative neutrality—the administrator divorced from political intrigue and serving as a specialist with professional detachment. In noting that the principal responsibility of the Budget Bureau was to save money and improve efficiency in routine business, Dawes stated that the "success of the Budget Bureau depends upon our integrity and sincerity in a determination to be non-partisan, non-political, and impartial."[27]

The Science of Administration

By the early 1920s, when the first textbooks of public administration appeared, the dichotomy between policy making and policy administration as separate functions was widely accepted. The separation-of-functions doctrine served early students of public administration well. It enabled them to distinguish and to emphasize that part of government in which they were most interested—the execution of decisions. It justified a new emphasis on the proper professional training for administrative work. More important, it lent support to the notion that, since administration is a function distinct from politics, politicians should not be permitted to interfere with administration.

During this era, the field of public administration was based on four doctrines. In addition to the notion of the separation between policy and administration, there was the doctrine that administration could be made a science, or at least could be studied in the same way as the phenomena of physical sciences. This concept led to the suggestion that the scientific study of administration would uncover principles of administration more or less analogous to the laws of the physical sciences. Such notions as "division of labor" and the "principle of specialization," which were given such prominence in the writings of Luther Gulick during the 1920s and 1930s, illustrate these efforts to discover the fundamental "laws" of administration. The fourth doctrine of early public administration was that of economy and efficiency as the central, if not the only, goals of administration. Early public administration textbooks adopted and systematized these doctrines, and this helped them to win acceptance as firm and lasting truths.

The main postulate of scientific management and economic rationalism of that period was the *minimax* strategy of minimum costs and maximum profits. This attitude spilled over into government administration; operating efficiency was seen as a universal principle applicable to all administrative situations. This emphasis was reflected in the adoption of the line-item budget, which emphasizes accountability by detailing various objects of expenditure. This assumption formed the basis for a science of administration which ". . . shall seek to straighten the paths of government, to make its business less unbusinesslike, to strengthen and purify its organization, and to crown its duties with dutifulness."[28]

Perhaps the most important work on public administration to appear in the 1930s was entitled *Papers on the Science of Administration,* edited by Luther Gulick and Lyndall Urwick. In one essay in this volume, Gulick presents the acronym POSDCORB as a mnemonic device for recalling the functions of the executive in administration: Planning, Organizing, Staffing, Directing, Coordinating, Reporting, and Budgeting.[29]

In practical terms, the focus in the 1930s tended to be on the formulation of devices for controlling the increasing number of administrative functions of government. This focus, in turn, resulted in the further prominence of the budget as a public administration tool. Program outputs were seen in terms of limited and fixed values, and the budget was used as a central control mechanism to govern inputs. The task of budgeting became that of coordinating the fiscal and organizational resources of government to assist in the performance of public agencies. Central control of spending remained, however, with the budget viewed as a safeguard against political abuse of public funds.

The Politics of Administration

From the mid-1920s until the late 1930s students of public administration were generally content with the existing conceptual structure. During the Roosevelt administration, however, the line between administration and policy began to lose whatever empirical basis it might have had. Merriam, Brownlow, Emmerich, White, Pfiffner, and others began to explore the divergence between administrative theory and practice. The label "classical theory," which Simon and March use to characterize the writings of this era, indicates its position in the study of public administration today. It remains the foundation and the legitimatizing rationale for many who practice administration. In a fundamental sense, therefore, much of the current emphasis in administrative reform is "neoclassical."

The war effort of the 1940s showed that good administration permits discretion in the use of funds. In his writings on policy and administration, Appleby observed that: ". . . legislative bodies make very general policy, and . . . administrators make policy by applying the general policy at successively less abstract levels."[30]

By the early 1950s the rigid separation of politics and administration had been almost wholly abandoned, at least conceptually. It has become proper to regard administration as a process permeated with politics—both the contest for power and the making of policy. As Norton Long has observed:

> However attractive an administration receiving its values from political policy-makers may be, it has one fatal flaw. It does not accord with the facts of administrative life. Nor is it likely to. In fact, it is highly dubious even as an ideal. Though the quest for science, mathematical precision and certainty has an undeniable psychological appeal, it runs the risk of becoming a fastidious piece of ivory-tower escapism.[31]

Politics was thus reintroduced as a vital ingredient in the study of administration. The long-held notion that administration could be developed as a science independent of policy was refuted.

Public administration is policy making, but it is not autonomous, exclusive, or isolated policy making. Since all administration and all policy making within government is political, politics is the means by which society faces issues and decides how to resolve them.

The emphasis on politics in the study of administration reached a reduction to absurdity in the late 1960s. Students of government such as Wildavsky and Lindblom, who had been concerned with accurately describing disjointed, fragmented, and incremental policy making, went on to defend such policy making as the only true path to pluralism.[32] By the early 1970s, following the ill-fated experience with Planning Programming Budgeting Systems (PPBS), these authors were suggesting that the political process logically excludes any form of systematic analysis.[33] More cautious observers of this era concluded that systematic analysis is merely a tool for improving rather than for replacing political decisions.[34] Systematic analysis will be discussed at length in subsequent chapters. Suffice it to say for now that, although some fear systems thinking as usurpation of legislative prerogatives, others see it as a useful mechanism for stimulating greater public access and expanding the social basis of administrative policy making.[35]

Other Major Cross Currents of Administrative Thinking

Many diverse trends of thought have affected the theory and practice of public administration during the seventy years that it has been recognized as a realm of inquiry. As a composite discipline, public administration has drawn on a range of sources, including psychology, political science, economics, and business administration (which is itself a compilation of diverse approaches). It is impossible to review all the ingredients in detail, but what follows is a brief overview of some of the major cross currents.

The Influence of the Human-Relations School

One influential strain in modern administrative theory has been human relations. Studies in the organizational dimensions of human relations began in the early 1920s with the research of Roethlisberger and Dickson and the subsequent efforts of the Harvard Business School. Much of this early work focused on the private sector, but public administrators were influenced by the general tenor of this approach.

In the Hawthorne studies, Roethlisberger and Dickson established the existence of a relationship among social norms, group behavior, noneconomic rewards and incentives, and worker productivity. Management must consider the importance of such factors as communications between ranks, worker participation in decision making, and democratically structured and socially concerned management techniques. It has been postulated that workers who are more satisfied with their working conditions and who have some say in setting those conditions will set goals corresponding more closely to those of the organization.

Those interested in administration as a group process shifted their attention to leadership styles in the late 1940s. Further shifts occurred: from leadership to communication, then to the dynamics of motivation, to sanctions (reward and penalty systems), and most recently to group decision making and

participation. Current manifestations of this approach are found in the
emphasis on organizational development (OD). The basic elements of OD are
expressed in a variety of popular administrative practices, including "task
team management," "sensitivity training," and "interpersonal and intergroup
cooperation" strategies, as well as in general approaches to "synergistic
leadership."[36] OD procedures also are an important component of such
systematic processes for organizational goal setting as Management by
Objectives (MBO).

Humanistic elements have had considerable influence on the New Public
Administration, which emerged from the concern for greater social relevance
in the 1960s. Most of the "Young Turks" who met in 1968 at the
Minnowbrook retreat (sponsored by the Maxwell School of Syracuse University) were thoroughly imbued with the concept of self-actualization formulated
by Abraham Maslow as a guiding principle for organizational change.[37] In this
regard, the New Public Administration developed a theme of moral responsibility in the pursuit of public policy, invoking normative premises such as
John Rawls's concept of "justice as fairness."[38]

*Public Choice: A Market Theory
of Administration*

Issues of centralization versus decentralization have been debated since the
founding of the Republic. Recently this traditional battle has been renewed as
public administrators have become enamored of both the theories and the tools
of economics. Vincent Ostrom, one of the principal exponents of economic
theory in the field of administration, has advanced the concept of *public choice*
as a challenge to the prevailing paradigm of public management, which he
labels the Wilsonian model.[39] It was Woodrow Wilson, of course, who posited
the axiomatic principles of administration that still have a strong following
today.

Ostrom and others argue that there are better responses to offset the
apparent economies of scale achieved through consolidation. The key to
public choice is that it does not begin by assuming that polycentric systems,
with dispersed levels of authority and overlapping jurisdictions, are an
inherently poor form of public enterprise.[40] The public choice model begins
with the individual and works toward Pareto efficiency, rather than the
maximum efficiency implied by the Wilsonian model. However, market
failures such as poverty and pollution that plague our urban society still seem
to demand a more centralized approach, at least in the area of resource
redistribution. Nevertheless, the market approach is a useful tool for several
aspects of resource regulation.[41]

The Central Role of Decision Making

Writing in 1945 in the tradition of Gulick and Urwick, Alvin Brown stated that, ". . . if planning is the highest of the three phases of administration . . . decision may be said to be the highest act of administration"[42] Herbert A. Simon, however, must receive credit for casting the concept of decision making in a starring role. Noting that Barnard and Stene both had pointed the way before World War II, Simon asserts that decision making is the pivotal act of administration.

Few books on administrative theory have aroused as much controversy as Simon's *Administrative Behavior,* published in 1947.[43] A second edition was published in 1957; except for the addition of an introduction, however, the text remained unchanged. In this introduction, however, Simon included a number of new concepts such as the "model of satisficing," which substantially altered the rationale of his original formulations. This led reviewers, such as Edward Banfield, to speak of "straining" and "pretense," and to conclude that it "was a better book ten years ago than it is now."[44] Banfield suggests that Simon destroyed the "rationale of the old conceptual scheme without offering any new one and without, apparently, being aware of what he has done." The crux of the objections raised about Simon's formulations is that, by separating fact and value in decision making, he produced ". . . a new and subtle version of the earlier formulation of the separation of policy and administration."[45]

Simon introduced the doctrines of *logical positivism* into the literature of administrative theory. Asserting a close connection with modern physical science, logical positivists abhor metaphysics, dismiss ethics, emphasize empiricism, and place a premium on rigorous, logical analysis. They make a sharp distinction between questions of fact ("is" questions) and questions of value ("ought" questions). Basic to Simon's formulation is the concept that the realm of value is the realm of preference, of morals or ethics, and therefore cannot be empirically verified.

In Simon's scheme, a decision is defined as a conclusion drawn from a set of premises. These premises are of two kinds:

1. *factual premises:* subject to empirical testing in order to ascertain their validity;
2. *value premises:* imperatives that are not subject to testing since they are concerned with what "ought to be" rather than with what "is."

Simon makes this distinction to clarify policy and administration by asserting that organizations are based on not one but two divisions of labor and specialization. In addition to the recognized type of horizontal specialization—a division of labor according to particular tasks—there is a form of vertical specialization in which the division of labor is based on authority rather than on work assignments. Decision making is divided in such a way that those higher in rank establish broad policy guidelines, while lower-echelon personnel administer policy by breaking it down into more detailed and specific decisions.

This separation of decision functions has met with continued objections and has led to the assertion that Simon's position is empirically unsound; in real-life decision making, fact and value are so closely related that they cannot be separated. Simon does not differ conceptually from those who argue that policy making and administration must be viewed as a continuum. Policy making occurs at many levels and these points shift as time, circumstances, and political behavior demand.[46] Simon was not attempting to defy reality, merely to distinguish among various essential components of decision-making responsibilities. He has isolated certain characteristics of the decision process, for purposes of analysis only, in an effort to develop a set of concepts that might permit empirically valid descriptions of administrative situations. Insofar as decisions lead to a selection of final goals, they may be treated as *value judgments*—the value component predominates; insofar as decisions implement these goals, they may be treated as *factual judgments*—the factual component predominates.

The Emergence of Public Management Science

One of the most powerful recent influences on public administration has been *management science* (or the management sciences—both singular and plural forms are used). Management science is a generic term encompassing various forms of systematic analysis and a variety of private-sector management practices designed to provide a more rational basis for decision making. It involves the application of mathematical and related systems approaches to the solution of relatively large-scale management problems. Often included in this eclectic field are such analytical modes as operations research, systems analysis, information theory and management cybernetics, managerial economics, cost-benefit analysis, gaming and simulation techniques, and network analysis.

Management science has contributed significantly to the improvement of management decisions in a broad range of applications. However, critics are quick to point to limitations in the capacity of management science to incorporate intangibles into its mathematical orientation, that is, political, institutional, nonrational (but real), and other nonquantifiable and value-laden factors.[47] Both critics and supporters of management science agree that these techniques are best applied where problem parameters and constraints can be identified with relatively great specificity and where objective functions are clearly defined.

These and other limitations have led some scholars and practitioners to assert that management science is inadequate for effective application to many of the complex issues in the public sector. What is needed, they conclude, is something beyond management science—something that might be called *policy science.*

In fact, the general impact of management science on public administration is the result of a blend of both rational and transrational aspects of policy. As Bruce Gates explains,

> The past three decades have made the management sciences sensitive to the many roads to useful knowledge. Unnecessary or only apparent rigor has been a prime barrier to its utilization. The utility of the management sciences in the public sector is increasingly seen as being dependent on factors once not considered within its limited purview. Successful utilization . . . will require that esoteric theories and models . . . be melded with other, less rigorous but no less valid determinants of knowledge—for example, professional ideology . . . and even popular theories.[48]

Broadly speaking, public management science might be characterized as any analytical approach designed to help decision makers identify a preferred course of action from among several alternatives. In this respect it is similar to systems analysis introduced to government through the budget structure of the Department of Defense during and after World War II. Systems analysis represents a way of looking at complex problems of choice under uncertainty, and as such it has had extensive application and utility in the field of public management.

Thus, while "analytical pragmatism is yielding to political and organizational pragmatism" in the development of public management science,[49] the road to rational decision making in the public sector still has many potholes that must be repaired before the journey can be smooth. Unfortunately, the rational model often is oversold, and advocates may offer definitions of rationality in somewhat idealized terms that leave them vulnerable to criticism.

Rationalism Versus Incrementalism

Charles Lindblom and others have pointed out that decision makers rarely face the clear-cut problems suggested by the rational model. Moreover, information is scarce and therefore expensive, and decision makers seldom are willing or able to incur the high cost of data collection for the sake of complete rationality in their decisions.

Lindblom offers the concepts of *disjointed incrementalism* and *partisan mutual adjustments* as the basis for a countertheory to the rational model. He argues that the only policy alternatives considered are those whose consequences are known incrementally—those that vary only slightly from the status quo. Human ability to foresee the consequences of government action is so limited that objectives must be approached in small, manageable steps. Since the problems confronting the decision maker are continually redefined, incrementalism allows for countless ends-means and means-ends adjustments that make the problem more manageable.[50] Most decisions, therefore, are simply marginal adjustments to existing programs; the question of the ultimate desirability of most programs arises only occasionally.

Lindblom suggests that people can coordinate with each other without anyone coordinating them, without a dominant common purpose, and without rules that fully prescribe their relations to each other. They achieve this coordination by mutually adjusting their positions from their individual partisan perspectives. Lindblom and his followers conclude that partisan mutual adjustment is a positive factor in the current system of public decision making. By dividing the organizational structure of government into interacting areas, Lindblom suggests that competition among agencies will lead to optimal decisions and actions.

The concepts of disjointed incrementalism and partisan mutual adjustment have a certain pragmatic appeal and have been embraced by both academics and practitioners in the field of public administration. Decision making under the incremental approach can be carried on with the knowledge that few problems have to be solved once and for all. Since there is no "right" solution to any given problem, the test of a good decision is that various analysts agree on it, without agreeing that the decision is the most appropriate means to an agreed objective.[52] Incremental decision making, however, is essentially remedial, geared more to the amelioration of present imperfections than to the promotion of future social goals. Many problems brought before decision makers have no precedents and therefore cannot be examined solely in terms of their incremental differences. Such problems require innovative solutions; incremental adjustments may only postpone the inevitable or may even exacerbate the problem. Unlike day-to-day operational decisions which can be corrected if the incremental approach proves wrong, more fundamental problems require strategic decisions, arrived at through a more rational approach.

Etzioni offers an alternative theory in an effort to reconcile these different perspectives. His mixed scanning approach implies that, when the decision maker has the time and information and perceives the problems to be of importance, he will pursue a more comprehensive approach; in other situations, he will "muddle through."[53]

Performance Administration and the Cross Currents

While there are strong arguments for enhancing the rationality of public decision making, there are equally valid cautions against a technocratic society and reminders of the inherent limitations of rational analysis. Opinions about the proper interface between rationality and transrationality (socio-political considerations) range across a broad spectrum of ideas and ideologies. The perspective offered here is that analysis has both rational and transrational—perhaps even irrational—aspects. The defeatist attitude that all sociopolitical issues escape rational assessment is unacceptable; moreover, although many problems lie beyond the scope of systematic analysis, the level of social complexity in itself is not necessarily the most important criterion of applicability. As Kenneth Kraemer has suggested, "The greatest potential benefit of policy analysis is in just those areas where problems are the most complex and the risks the highest, the uncertainties greatest, and the results most likely to be seen only over an extended time period."[54]

Schick has suggested that the arrival of more systematic approaches to decision making provides strong evidence of high-level dissatisfaction with status quo processes of public policy formulation.[55] Such approaches can be more effective in identifying public objectives and in measuring progress toward their attainment at a time when public confidence in government's ability to eradicate hard-core social problems is low. Reformers today call for less emphasis on the tenets of earlier government reforms and more on responsiveness, effectiveness, political responsibility, and citizen involvement. In asking: "What is our business and to whom are we accountable?" various related systems approaches may be able to restore some balance between the Federalist and Democratic ideals of government.

The concepts of performance administration outlined in this book are offered not as a substitute for the various conceptualizations that make up the cross currents of contemporary public administration, but in an effort to provide greater focus and clarity, so that these formulations may be applied more effectively in a concerted effort to restore public confidence in government.

Notes

1. Bruno Leoni, "The Meaning of 'Political' in Political Decisions," in *The Making of Decisions,* ed. William J. Gore and J.W. Dyson (New York: The Free Press, 1964), p. 94.

2. Harold D. Lasswell, "The Policy Orientation," in *The Policy Sciences: Recent Developments in Scope and Method,* ed. Daniel Lerber and Harold D. Lasswell (Stanford: Stanford University Press, 1951), p. 5.

3. Ibid., p. 8.

4. Philip E. Jacob and James J. Flink, "Values and Their Function in Decision-Making," *The American Behavioral Scientist* 5(May 1962):8.

5. Herbert A. Simon, *Administrative Behavior* (New York: The Free Press, 1965), p. 59.

6. Ibid., p. 59.

7. David A. Easton, *A Systems Analysis of Political Life* (New York: John Wiley and Sons, 1965), pp. 351.

8. Theodore H. Poister, *Public Program Analysis* (Baltimore, Md.: University Park Press, 1978), p. 1.

9. Woodrow Wilson, "The Study of Administration," in *The Administrative Process and Democratic Theory,* ed. Louis C. Gawthrop (Boston: Houghton Mifflin Company, 1970), p. 79.

10. Luther Gulick and Lundall Urwick, *Papers on the Science of Administration* (New York: The Institute of Public Administration, 1937).

11. See Fritz Roethlisberger and W.J. Dickson, *Management and the Worker* (Cambridge, Mass.: Harvard University Press, 1939).

12. Simon, *Administrative Behavior.*

13. See Todd La Porte, "The Recovery of Relevance in the Study of Public Organizations," in *Toward a New Public Administration,* ed. Frank Marini (Scranton, Pa.: Chandler, 1971), p. 20.

14. Daniel Dreyfus, "The Limitations of Policy Research in Congressional Decision-Making," *Policy Studies Journal* 4(Spring 1976):269.

15. See Gregory A. Daneke, "Policy Analysis and Bureaucratic Reform," *Southern Review of Public Administration* (June 1977):108–128; Gregory A. Daneke, *Administrative Policy and the Public Interest: An Introduction to Policy Analysis* (Boston: Allyn and Bacon, 1980).

16. For a further discussion of advisory and prerogative participation and the related concepts of structural and functional authority, see Alan Walter Steiss, *Public Budgeting and Management* (Lexington, Mass.: Lexington Books, D.C. Heath and Company, 1972), chap. 4.

17. Eugene Jacobson and Stanley E. Seashore, "Communication Practices in Complex Organizations," *Journal of Social Issues* 7(1951):33.

18. Albert Lepawsky, *Administration: The Art and Science of Organization and Management* (New York: Alfred A. Knopf, 1949), p. 74.

19. Raymond G. Gettel, *History of American Political Thought* (New York: D. Appleton-Century Company, 1928), pp. 102–103.

20. Leonard White, *Introduction to Public Administration* (New York: The Macmillan Company, 1950), p. 14.

21. Ibid., p. 18.

22. Martin Landau, "The Concept of Decision-Making in the 'Field' of Public Administration," in *Concepts and Issues in Administrative Behavior,* ed. Sidney Mailick and Edward H. Van Ness (Englewood Cliffs, N.J.: Prentice-Hall, 1962), p. 16.

23. Woodrow Wilson, "The Study of Administration," *Political Science Quarterly* 2(June 1887).

24. Frank J. Goodnow, *Politics and Administration* (New York: The Macmillan Company, 1914), pp. 1–2.

25. W.F. Willoughby, *Principles of Public Administration* (Washington, D.C.: The Brookings Institution, 1927), p. 1.

26. Ibid., p. 442.

27. Charles G. Dawes, "The First Year of the Budget," in *The Administrative Process and Democratic Theory,* ed. Louis C. Gawthrop (Boston: Houghton Mifflin Company, 1970), p. 87.

28. Woodrow Wilson, "The Study of Administration," in *The Administrative Process and Democratic Theory,* Gawthrop, p. 79.

29. Gulick and Urwick, *Papers on the Science of Administration.*

30. Paul H. Appleby, *Policy and Administration* (Tuscaloosa: University of Alabama Press, 1949), p. 76.

31. Norton E. Long, *The Polity* (Chicago: Rand McNally Company, 1962), p. 78.

32. See Aaron Wildavsky, "The Political Economy of Efficiency," *Public Administration Review* 26(December 1966):292–310.

33. Note in particular Allen Schick, "A Death in Bureaucracy: The Demise of PPB," *Public Administration Review* 32(March-April 1973): 146–157; and Ida Hoos, *Systems Analysis in Public Policy* (Berkeley: University of California Press, 1972).

34. Note the arguments advanced by William Capron, "The Impact on Bargaining in Government," and James Schlesinger, "Systems Analysis and the Political Process," in Gawthrop, *The Administrative Process and Democratic Theory,* pp. 336–371.

35. For a review of this notion, see Gregory A. Daneke, *Administrative Policy and the Public Interest* (Boston, Mass.: Allyn and Bacon, 1980), chap. 5.

36. Nicholas Henry, *Public Administration and Public Affairs* (Englewood Cliffs, N.J.: Prentice-Hall, 1975), p. 67.

37. La Porte, "The Recovery of Relevance."

38. John Rawls, *A Theory of Justice* (Cambridge, Mass.: Harvard University Press, 1964); also see David K. Hart, "Social Equity, Justice, and Equitable Administration," *Public Administration Review* 34(January-February 1974).

39. For a general overview of public choice, see Vincent Ostrom and Elinor Ostrom, "Public Choice: A Different Approach to the Study of Administration," *Public Administration Review* 31(1971); for the seminal work in this area, see Gordon Tullock and James Buchanan, *The Calculus of Consent* (Ann Arbor: University of Michigan Press, 1962).

40. See Vincent Ostrom, *The Intellectual Crisis in American Public Administration* (Tuscaloosa: University of Alabama Press, 1971); for specific arguments on metrogovernment, see Vincent Ostrom and Robert Bish,

Understanding Urban Government (Washington, D.C.: The American Enterprise Institute, 1973).

41. See Allen Kneese and Charles Schultze, *Pollution, Prices, and Public Policy* (Washington, D.C.: The Brookings Institution, 1975).

42. Alvin Brown, *Organization* (New York: Hibbert Printing Company, 1945), p. 88. The term *administrator* has generally been defined to subsume some decision-making activities. In his classic essay, Gulick cites decision making as a crucial "line" function and then defines the D in POSDCORB as "Directing, the continuous task of making decisions. . . ."

43. Herbert A. Simon, *Administrative Behavior* (New York: The Free Press, 1957).

44. Edward C. Banfield, "The Decision-Making Schema," *Public Administration Review* 17(Autumn 1957):278–285.

45. Wallace S. Sayre, "Trends of a Decade in Administrative Values," *Public Administration Review* 11(Winter 1951):5.

46. Appleby, *Policy and Administration,* p. 15; Philip Selznick, *Leadership in Administration* (Evanston, Ill.: Northwestern University Press, 1957), pp. 74ff.

47. Michael Radnor, Michael J. White, and David A. Tansik, *Management and Policy Science in American Government* (Lexington, Mass.: Lexington Books, D.C. Heath and Company, 1975), pp. 6–7.

48. Bruce Gates, "Better Policy Administration Through Management Science?" in *Public Administration and Public Policy,* ed. F. George Frederickson and Charles Wise (Lexington, Mass.: Lexington Books, D.C. Heath and Company, 1977), p. 156.

49. Ibid., p. 156.

50. James E. Anderson, *Public Policy-Making* (New York: Praeger, 1975), p. 10.

51. See Charles E. Lindblom, *The Intelligence of Democracy* (New York: The Free Press, 1965); Aaron Wildavsky, *The Politics of the Budgetary Process* (Boston: Little, Brown and Company, 1964).

52. Anderson, *Public Policy-Making,* p. 10.

53. Amitai Etzioni, "Mixed Scanning: A Third Approach to Decision Making," *Public Administration Review* 27(December 1967):309–390.

54. Kenneth L. Kraemer, *Policy Analysis in Local Government* (Washington, D.C.: International City Management Association, 1973), p. 27.

55. Allen Schick, "Systems Politics and Systems Budgeting," in *The Administrative Process and Democratic Theory,* Gawthrop, p. 392.

3

Responsibility, Responsiveness, and Performance Administration

Bu-reau-crat (byŏor'ə-krat) n. 1. A member of a bureaucracy. 2. An official who narrowly adheres to a rigid routine. 3. An inefficient muddler, primarily concerned with rules and "red tape." 4. An unwarranted intruder into the minuscule aspects of our daily lives. 5. This two-headed beast is highly unique; one head is omnipresent but not omnipotent, and the other head is usually up his/her excretory opening at the lower extreme of the alimentary canal.—bu'reau-crat'ic or i-cal adj.—bu'reau-crat'i-cal-ly adv.

The Bureaucratic Dilemma

As James Q. Wilson has suggested, the American public has built an inherently schizophrenic system of public service. On the one hand, we demand that bureaucracy be highly *responsible,* that is, follow strict rules and procedures; on the other hand, we expect bureaucrats to be *responsive,* that is, to adapt to unique situations. This is a complex dilemma; responsiveness also implies that government can remedy social ills and redress social inequities. Wilson offers the following elaborations on the nature of the bureaucratic dilemma:

1. There are inherent limits on what can be accomplished by large, hierarchical organizations.
2. The supply of able, experienced executives is not increasing nearly as fast as the number of problems being addressed by public policies and programs.
3. The only point at which very much leverage can be gained on the problem is when we decide what it is we are trying to accomplish.[1]

Even if we do not share Wilson's pessimism, we must admit that his statement of the dilemma is cogent. If performance involves serving the public well, then performance administration must be more than a handful of strategies and techniques. Almost by definition, it is a set of attitudes regarding the appropriate mix of responsibility and responsiveness in administrative policy making. In short, performance administration is a matter of *management style,* as this style influences actions and activities both within and outside the organization.

Types of Management Styles

Administration occurs at all levels in every public organization. It may be formal or informal, systematic or haphazard; its focus may be short- or long-range; it may be highly responsive to perceived public needs or it may be perfunctory; and it may involve individual actions or team efforts. In short, administration is ubiquitous in modern organizational life. (The policy-administration dichotomy is abandoned in this discussion on the grounds that this traditional distinction is unrealistic and unnecessary in modern government. The functions of both the policy maker and the policy administrator are encompassed by the term performance administration.)

It follows, therefore, that administrative leadership is situational and somewhat episodic. Each situation is a little different, and the style of management that works best in one situation may be relatively ineffective in another. It would be impractical, however, for administrators to approach each situation as if it were unique. By seeking common dimensions among the problems and situations they confront, administrators can develop procedures and responses applicable to most areas of responsibility. The attitudes they develop, however, have an important bearing on overall administrative effectiveness.

The Managerial Grid: Variations on a Basic Theme

Perhaps the best-known approach to the question of management styles is the work of Robert R. Blake and Jane Mouton in the formulation of their Managerial Grid.[2] This grid is built on two universal dimensions of human behavior: a horizontal axis represents "concern for production," while a vertical axis denotes "concern for people." Each axis is divided into nine degrees of intensity (1 is low and 9 is high), producing a total of eighty-one different areas representing varying mixes of concern for production and for people. From this grid Blake and Mouton derive five major characteristic management styles:

1. A 1,1 manager exhibits a low concern for both production and people and exerts a minimum effort to get the required work done. This approach, Blake and Mouton assert, leads to abdication of responsibility, supervisory bankruptcy, and alienation among workers.

2. The 1,9 manager devotes considerable attention to the needs of people, producing a comfortable, friendly organizational atmosphere at the expense of productive results. This approach is highly permissive in dealing with people.

3. A produce-or-perish attitude (9,1) emphasizes efficiency and arranges work conditions to minimize interference from human elements. This management style, however, motivates people to beat the system and reduces their contributions to the organization.

4. The 9,9 style is identified by Blake and Mouton as "solution-seeking" and emphasizes work accomplishment through a common stake in organizational purposes. High standards are used to achieve rigorous goals through involvement, commitment, and readiness to confront issues needing resolution.

5. In the middle of the grid is the 5,5 management style, which emphasizes accommodation and compromise. Adequate organizational performance is sought by balancing the necessities of production with the maintenance of satisfactory work morale.

A strong preference for the 9,9 style of management is evident in the writings of Blake and Mouton and in the subsequent applications of the Managerial Grid. The 1,1 style appears as the least desirable; the other three are considered less than perfect.

Michael Harmon has adopted a two-dimensional grid to describe administrative styles of public-policy formulation.[3] In his Policy Formulation Grid, policy responsiveness is depicted on the vertical axis, while the horizontal axis indicates the extent of administrative willingness to advocate policy change. The terms *responsiveness* and *advocacy,* according to Harmon, are intentionally defined in broad terms to accommodate their varying interpretations implicit in the five styles of his model. In general, *responsive behavior* is that which is accountable in some way to the democratic process by which public demands are (or might be) translated into policy. *Advocative behavior* refers to the degree of active support by administrators for the adoption of policies.

The five styles of administration defined by Harmon can be summarized as follows:

1. *Survival style* (1,1): To assure survival of their agencies, public administrators limit access of political authorities and interest groups in order to promote the efficient continuation of existing programs. The 1,1 style of administration is both nonadvocative and unresponsive.

2. *Rationalist style* (1,9): This approach focuses on public demands as legitimately expressed through elected representatives and thus avoids direct involvement in the determination of agency policies and programs. The administrator is seen as an agent of political authorities: the assumption is that all legitimate values relevant to policy formulation are expressed through voting or by elected representatives.

3. *Prescriptive style* (9,1): This approach is based on the presumption of professional expertise of administrators, who have the greatest knowledge of the problems confronting their agencies and, therefore, should be the key formulators of programs and policies. This style predominates in organizations in which there is wide latitude for statutory interpretation by administrators or in situations in which technical complexity requires particular expertise.

4. *Proactive style* (9,9): Proactive administrators participate in policy formulation both by acting as advocates of new policy and by facilitating

access of interest groups to the political and administrative systems in order to maximize their opportunities to influence public policy. In determining policy, proactive behavior implies reciprocal influence between the administrator and those to whom he is responsible.

5. *Reactive style* (5,5): The difficulty in drawing clear distinctions between policy formulation and implementation requires administrative reactivists to operate in both areas; they may regard separation of the two as ethically desirable, but unattainable. Their advocacy and responsive behavior varies according to the context within which policy questions emerge.

Like Blake and Mouton, Harmon implicitly favors the 9,9 or proactive style of administration; he suggests that although the proactive administrator cannot be sure of finding the correct answers, at least he will be likely to ask the right questions. In practice, however, the majority of managers and administrators seem to think of themselves as 5,5 types, as described by Harmon as well as by Blake and Mouton, with tendencies toward (but not total commitment to) the 9,9 style.

The Third Dimension

W.J. Reddin has added the dimension of *effectiveness* to the two axes of concern for people and concern for production developed by Blake and Mouton. This third axis forms a cube, which Reddin calls the Tri-Dimensional Grid.[4]

Reddin's approach produces four pairs of management styles, which share common levels of concern for people and production but differ according to level of effectiveness. The Deserter, for example, is ineffective not only because of his lack of interest, but also because of his impact on organizational morale. The Bureaucrat, on the other hand, is effective because he follows procedures, maintains the appearance of interest, and does not have adverse effects on morale. The Developer is effective where the Missionary is not, because he seeks to create a work environment in which his subordinates will develop commitments both to himself and to the job. The Benevolent Autocrat succeeds by overcoming the coercive nature of the Autocrat and thereby, is able to get people to do what he wants without creating resentment that might cause a decline in production. The Compromiser is ineffective in integrating factors and concerns, whereas the Executive is effective both as a motivator and as a production coordinator. Although Reddin suggests that managers adopt different styles according to their responsibilities and that organizations with particular missions have discernible characteristic style profiles, he implicitly favors one style—the Executive—over all others.

Table 3–1
Reddin's Tri-Dimensional Grid

| Concern for: | | | |
People	Production	Low Effectiveness	High Effectiveness
Low	Low	*Deserter:* Lack of interest in both task and relationships; may hinder performance of others through intervention or by withholding information.	*Bureaucrat:* Not really interested in tasks or relationships but does not make this obvious; follows rules and procedures and maintains appearance of interest.
High	Low	*Missionary:* Places harmony and relationships above other considerations; unwilling to take risks in order to get greater production.	*Developer:* Sees job as primarily concerned with developing talents of others and providing a good atmosphere conducive to maximizing individual satisfaction and motivation.
Low	High	*Autocrat:* Puts immediate tasks before all other considerations; has no concern for relationships and little confidence in others.	*Benevolent autocrat:* Concerned with both immediate and long-run tasks; skillful in creating environment that minimizes aggression, while maximizing obedience to commands.
High	High	*Compromiser:* Recognizes the advantages of being oriented to both task and relationships but incapable or unwilling to make sound decisions; ambivalence and compromise are his stock-in-trade.	*Executive:* Sees job as effectively maximizing efforts of others in relationship to the short- and long-run tasks of the organization; sets high standards for performance but recognizes individual differences.

Adapted from W.J. Reddin, "The Tri-Dimensional Grid—For Integration of Management Style Theories," *Training Directors Journal* 18(July 1964).

The Fourth Dimension

F. Gerald Brown has added a fourth criterion to the basic formulations to create what he calls the Managerial Field of Vision.[5] Brown suggests that management styles can be characterized by the level of an administrator's active involvement in four basic areas: (1) concern for tasks, (2) concern for people, (3) concern for interfaces, and (4) concern for things. Brown derives six "pure" management styles from these four factors, as follows:

1. *Concern for tasks:* The task-oriented management style has two major subvariations:
   a. The Master Craftsman leads by example, keeps up with the field, serves as a professional model for employees, and seeks interaction with the work group at a quasi-peer level.

b. The Boss excels at making work assignments and setting production expectations, carefully plans activities on a short- and medium-term basis; and places importance on schedules and performance standards.

2. *Concern for people:* The human-relations style of management emphasizes good relationships with employees and the delegation of responsibility. Such a manager supervises rather than controls and depends on a reward system that features recognition as a means of stimulating performance.

3. *Concern for things:* This style is based on the assumption that employees know what they are doing and what must be done and that the organization will operate effectively as long as the work group has what it needs to get the job done. An administrator with such a style sees his primary role as providing the best possible setting in which to accomplish the organization's objectives, including an appropriate physical environment, materials and supplies, budgets, and other resources.

4. *Concern for ideas:* This approach is characterized by a relatively low level of concern for tasks and for people. In this management style, delegation is emphasized along with the principle of "management by exception." The focus is on planning, on identification of goals and objectives, and on innovations.

5. *Concern for interfaces:* This type of manager is oriented toward individuals and groups outside the immediate work situation. He strives for good relations with other groups and for maintenance of two-way communications between the work group and the outside world.

6. *Integration of factors—The All-Together Manager:* This type of manager has learned to shift focus between thinking and doing, between technological process and the social system of the organization. The approach is objective-centered; the manager assesses the objectives and directs his energies according to what needs to be done at any given time. In short, this style embodies all the positive attributes of the other five styles.

Brown suggests that each of these management styles has its place and is an appropriate response to its own kind of situation. As with each of the previous paradigms, however, there is a composite style that incorporates most of the best features of the other approaches. According to these conceptual frameworks, public administrators should strive to be *solution-seeking, proactive, executive, all-together managers.*

Determinants of Performance Effectiveness

Administrative efforts must, at bottom, have utility and relevance to the purposes of the organization and/or the community. Even though an effort may have internal consistency a frequently cited test of effectiveness, if it contributes little or nothing to the achievement of purpose, it is obviously of limited value. Once objectives have been defined and direction established, however, the administrative process must be continually analyzed as a series of activities that can operate with varying degrees of effectiveness. In short, a critique of any administrative approach or management style must begin with an examination of its relevance to overall goals and objectives. Beyond this basic determination, however, the appropriateness of an approach must be criticized at each stage of the problem-solving and decision-making process.

The performance effectiveness of administration depends largely on how people influence each other in solving problems and making decisions; how they handle disagreements; and how they seek out facts, share information, and communicate with one another. These activities, in turn, are often a function of the basic attitudes that administrative personnel bring to their tasks. An important issue, therefore, is: What basic attitudes might a public manager adopt as he attempts to sort out information, identify goals and objectives, and carry out his principal administrative responsibilities?

The nature and quality of administration is a function of three basic sets of concerns:

1. *systemic concerns* (organizational purpose, stability, comprehensiveness, and responsiveness to the environment)
2. *concerns for risk* (including innovation and opportunity)
3. *time concerns* (time perspectives adopted in preparing for resource commitments).

A detailed examination of these three basic areas will provide a fuller understanding of the possible attitudes that public sector personnel may adopt in the performance of their administrative responsibilities.

Systemic Concerns

In every human situation, there is an inherent desire to put things in order, to establish priorities, to relate specific activities to broader purposes, and to provide mechanisms for measuring success. Three key ingredients lie at the core of these concerns:

1. *Purpose:* a concern for the relevance of specific occurrences to overall goals, objectives, and orientation. An attempt is made to place new events and objectives into a future-oriented priority system.
2. *Stability:* the desire to reduce the effects of chance or randomness in the operations of the organization. Every organization seeks to develop a set of expectations—norms, standards, rules, policies, and procedures—for

determining appropriate courses of action or for dealing with specific problems. The desire for stability is reflected in the need to establish order, sequence, and predictability; to anticipate events; and to establish procedures to deal with problems as they arise.

3. *Comprehensiveness:* concern with an organization or community as a total entity. A community, institution, or organization is a complex system with many related and interdependent subsystems—smaller units within the total entity. In order to maintain direction and stability, information from one part of the system must be linked with information from all other parts to create a comprehensive whole.

These three ingredients of concern for the system—purpose, stability, and comprehensiveness—are closely linked. In other words, the greater government personnel's awareness of the entire system, the more they can plan and work in terms of the system's purpose and stability. Conversely, if personnel do not appreciate overall purpose and goals of the system, it is difficult or impossible for them to carry out their responsibilities in a way that will maximize their contributions to the total system.

Every individual in an organization should have systemic concerns on some level—concerns for maintaining direction, achieving stability, and dealing with the total system. These concerns may be with specific *elements* or facts without parallel concern for their interrelationships, or they may be with the *total system,* with explicit recognition of the linkages among elements and subsystems. An individual may take a position somewhere between these two extremes, manifesting a concern for *events* or combinations of elements or a concern with *subsystems* or combinations of events without recognizing that they fall into a system or combination of subsystems. Thus, as shown in figure 3–1, degrees of concern for the system manifested by government personnel can be arrayed on a continuum ranging from high (positive) concern to low or negative concern (resistance to systemic considerations).

As a further illustration, consider the city manager who has been asked by downtown merchants to solve the parking problem, which they maintain has caused them to lose business. The manager might respond in several ways:

1. He might instruct the public-works director to install parking meters to promote greater turnover in on-street parking along Main Street (concern for elements).
2. He might initiate an off-street parking study to determine the feasibility of municipal parking facilities adjacent to the downtown area (concern for events or combination of elements).
3. He might launch a major thoroughfare and parking study to determine whether rerouting through traffic, in combination with one-way streets and off-street parking, would make the downtown business district more accessible (concern for subsystems).

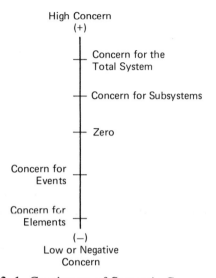

Figure 3–1. Continuum of Systemic Concerns

4. He might request that the city planner undertake a comprehensive analysis of the downtown area, including a study of the competition from outlying shopping centers, to determine the feasibility of renewal and redevelopment programs—involving both public and private investment—to make the downtown area more attractive to shoppers, to stimulate new business ventures, and so forth (concern for the total system).

The likelihood is that the solution to the problem will be found somewhere in the subsystems. However, if studies show that the merchandising practices of downtown businessmen are outdated, then a solution to the real, long-term problem may not be found in providing more parking, but rather in making changes in these practices or in the interfaces between the natural and built systems.

Concern for the total system can, of course, lead to a major digression into larger and larger systems. For example, a proposed jetport on marshland in New Jersey may at first be seen as affecting merely the surrounding local communities. But it may also be necessary to consider the impacts of diminished marsh areas on nearby fisheries or the consequences for aquifer recharge areas. Moreover, a new jetport is an integral link in the entire Boston-to-Washington transportation corridor. The level of systemic concerns obviously is a function of *boundary conditions,* discussed in chapter 6. In most cases a decision maker draws boundaries that are contiguous with his scope of authority. It may be well, however, to consider the full range of spillover effects, particularly in the early planning stages.

Concern for Risk

The concerns outlined in the previous section are associated with the maintenance or repair of a system or parts of a system. These concerns do not deal explicitly with the possibilities of innovation, change, and risk— ingredients of the second major dimension of management concerns.

Decision makers continually must consider opportunities, risks, and innovations. Sometimes the risks are personal; at other times, they affect the entire organization. From an organizational standpoint, the risks of a new policy or program generally include higher costs, reduced effectiveness, negative public reaction, and program failure. Innovation and risk taking are inevitable bedfellows. A risk is taken no matter what the decision; even the decision to do nothing involves the risk of lost opportunity. An effective administrator, whether in the public or private sector, is aware of how opportunity, innovation, and risk are interrelated and is willing to take risks appropriate to his or her level of responsibility. The ultimate decision to take risks should be based on the weighing of available *information,* the exercise of *logic,* the assessment of *uncertainty,* and the estimate of alternative *payoffs* or *gains.*

In the same way that the degree of systematic concern can be represented schematically, attitudes and assumptions regarding risk can be arrayed on a continuum, as illustrated in figure 3–2. At the right-hand (positive) end of the scale, risk is synonymous with challenge or the opportunity to develop or exploit situations in the best interests of the organization. At the opposite (negative) end of the continuum, there is strong resistance to risk. Between the positive extreme and the midpoint of the continuum (zero) lie various degrees of acceptance of risk; from zero to the negative end of the continuum there are various degrees of avoidance of risk.

Risk becomes highly significant when the probable *utility function* of a given decision is considered. This notion is illustrated in figure 3–3, based on von Neuman and Morgenstern's concept of "standard gambles" derived from probability theory and risk or decision theory.[6] When potential returns are great, the marginal utility is positive for the risk acceptor and negative for the risk avoider. The opposite is true when the potential returns are low, a result of the risk acceptor placing a higher-than-expected value on potential returns.

Since the possibility of windfall returns is slight in the public sector, the acceptance of risk has been relatively limited. However, as accelerated change makes the future increasingly uncertain, public officials will find significant

Figure 3–2. Continuum of Concern for Risk

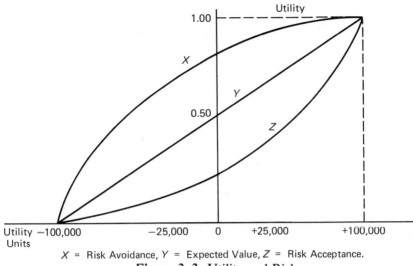

X = Risk Avoidance, Y = Expected Value, Z = Risk Acceptance.

Figure 3–3. Utility and Risk

risk involved in even simple management functions, such as garbage pickup. For example, in a case involving spot market gas purchases by the mayor of an eastern-seaboard resort community, the potential of increased tourist travel as a result of stable gas supplies was considered by the mayor to be worth the unusually high price for a bulk supply of gasoline.

The Time Continuum

Public-management personnel must be aware of various time dimensions associated with public decisions and of the commitment of fiscal resources resulting from these decisions. Some problems demand immediate solutions and have a relatively short-range effect because they focus on elements that can be altered at will if the initial decision proves incorrect. Although long-range approaches may be necessary to identify the causes and implications of such problems (and to develop strategies to prevent their reoccurrence), the urgency of these problems may demand immediate responses. Other problems, particularly those involving fixed capital investments, have relatively long-term time dimensions. Decisions associated with such projects can be modified only at considerable public expense. Thus, the time dimensions of different problems and issues may provoke different approaches along a continuum, with short-range, day-to-day dimensions at one extreme and long-range time dimensions associated with forecasting and planning at the other.

Over the past several decades, the differences between long-range and short-range decisions have become less significant. Reasons for this include: (1) increasing acceleration of social change; (2) increasing awareness of the longer-term consequences of even fairly rudimentary decisions; and (3) increasing appreciation of the interlocking, and therefore cumulative, impacts of small or incremental changes. Given the effects of time on basic management decisions, there seems to be an increased need for careful planning in order to expand the *time horizon* of parochial decision making. Although evidence suggests that planning is on the rise in the private sector, public administrators have yet to develop fully their inherent planning capabilities.[7] We will have more to say about planning, particularly strategic planning, in this and subsequent chapters.

A Paradigm of Administrative Attitudes

A descriptive paradigm, organized around the three basic sets of concerns outlined previously, may facilitate understanding of the alternative approaches to administrative concerns. Such a paradigm reflects the following key issues:

1. the extent to which administrators should be concerned with the total system, that is, organization or community;
2. the degree of risk, innovation, and opportunity that administrators should be willing to accept;
3. the extent to which administrators should take a long-range view in formulating public policies and programs; and
4. how administrators should relate these basic areas of concern in their use of facts and information.

Combining the Continua

The first step in the formulation of this paradigm, is to combine the two continua representing systemic concerns and the concern for risk, as illustrated in figure 3–4. For reasons that will become evident, the two axes have been enclosed in a circle, with the point midway between (−) and (+) on each axis (the zero point) now the center of the circle.

It is evident that a number of positions can be assumed within the circle, where attitudes of administrative personnel represent varying combinations of concern for risk and concern for the system. Thus, as illustrated in figure 3–4, it is possible to identify four quadrants of the paradigm representing different administrative approaches to these two sets of concerns.

The basic characteristics of the four quadrants can be summarized as follows.

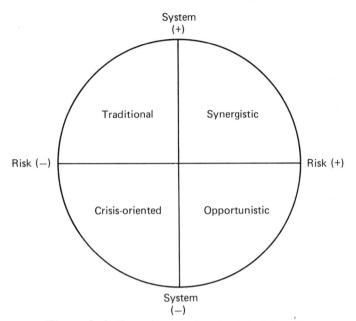

Figure 3–4. Four Approaches to Administration

1. *Traditional approach:* High concern for the system and its stability, coupled with a desire to avoid risk and innovation. In this quadrant, the concern is primarily with systems maintenance, the status quo, support for traditions and precedents, and minimization of risk and uncertainty.

2. *Crisis-oriented approach:* Low or negative concern for the system, coupled with either a desire to avoid risk or a lack of concern about risk. In this quadrant, every problem, regardless of its magnitude or its relevance to organizational purposes or growth opportunities, is treated—at the moment—as the most important job facing the administrator.

3. *Opportunistic approach:* Low to negative concern with the system and its stability, coupled with a desire to take advantage of opportunities and a willingness to accept risk. In this quadrant, organizational personnel are preoccupied with growth, exploration, and speculation.

4. *Synergistic approach:* High concern for the system (purpose, stability, and comprehensiveness), coupled with a willingness to accept risk and a desire to take advantage of opportunities. In this quadrant, a sense of total system purpose and direction is integrated with a desire for experimentation, innovation, and increased interaction with the environment or the public. Emphasis is on the long-range growth of the system.

Traditional responses emphasize stability, precedent, and control at the expense of opportunities for innovation and growth. Such an approach becomes rigid, formal, and tradition-bound. Procedures, policies, and practices developed to deal with former problems, which may be irrelevant to current problems; still are applied. These traditional practices are seen as safer and likely to succeed because, after all, they worked before. Review is resisted because it may distract from what is believed to be the basic need of the organization to stay on its current path. Any significant innovation usually is repressed. The question is not: "Where are we going and how do we get there?" but rather: "How can we stay on the previously determined course, avoid rocking the boat, control deviations from established patterns, and eliminate risk?"

Crisis-oriented responses reflect a distorted concern for stability and a strong reluctance to accept risk and innovation. Every problem is defined as ultimate and of the highest priority. Every incident is seen as an unrelated event requiring quick, firm handling. To minimize risk, administrators adopting this approach must maintain constant surveillance over situations and personnel for whom they are responsible, and must apply tight resource controls even at the expense of the overall needs and goals of the organization.

Opportunistic responses reflect a concern for innovation with little or no regard for its impact on the long-term purposes of the organization or the community. The term opportunistic here refers to individuals who react too quickly or compulsively to growth opportunities, with inadequate consideration of the total system or of the distribution of impacts. Such an individual constantly seeks new breakthroughs, especially short-term, quick-return opportunities. A typical concern is: "How can we move quickly on this opportunity?" Long-term, systemic considerations are overlooked in an eagerness to keep assets liquid and to be ready to seize any opportunity. Consequently, opportunistic administrators may take inappropriate risks or may overextend the organization on projects unrelated to overall purposes or to long-term direction.

Synergistic responses not only strike a balance between stability-direction and risk-opportunity, but also attempt to integrate these dimensions. Such responses address the overall goals of the organization or community, but system and stability are not seen as ends in themselves nor merely as means for minimizing risk. Rather, they are seen as important for maintaining a sense of direction and purpose. When growth opportunities entailing some risk arise, the synergistic administrator seeks information by which to evaluate their potential contributions to the broader system.

Addition of the Time Continuum

A consideration of the third set of concerns—those relating to the time continuum—requires an examination of the relationship of time concerns to the other basic continua (concerns for risk and systemic concerns) before

developing a composite model. As shown in figures 3–5 and 3–6, four
characteristic quadrants or attitude sets are again created by the intersection of
pairs of these continua.

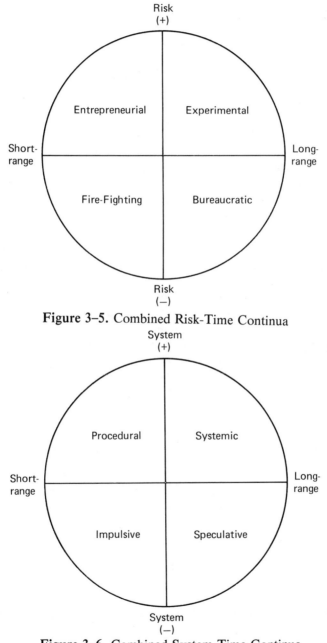

Figure 3–5. Combined Risk-Time Continua

Figure 3–6. Combined System-Time Continua

The *fire-fighting approach* (lower left-hand quadrant of the risk-time continua) characterizes individuals who see each event as a distinct, short-range problem to be contained or controlled. Such individuals are unwilling to take risks; they consider each incident as lacking precedent or antecedent; and therefore they deal with each problem without reference to long-term purpose. The concern is with solving the problem as quickly as possible, with minimal cost and risk. In the short run, this approach may be an effective way of managing certain public programs. In the long run, however, resources often are used inappropriately, unfortunate obligations are established, opportunities may be lost, and the organization is barely sustained.

Unfortunately, the fire-fighting approach is popular in public enterprises, predominating even in such a vital area as energy. For example, during the Iranian oil shortfall of 1979, the Office of Planning and Evaluation within the Department of Energy took over six weeks to come up with a "response plan." The title of this agency implies that a contingency plan would have been on the books for some time, given the declining power base of the shah.

The *entrepreneurial approach* exhibits an affinity for risk—for new opportunities—often, although not always, at the expense of long-term direction and purpose, which may be quickly abandoned (or not adopted at all) when new opportunities are detected. The primary orientation is, "How can we make a quick deal and exploit an opportunity?" rather than, "How can we determine if this is an appropriate opportunity for building toward some long-range objective?" Consequently, capital investments bearing long-term obligations may be made, with inappropriate attention to their impacts on limited resources or on long-range demands for such facilities.

The *experimental approach* characterizes those individuals who maintain an analytical attitude in their attempts to deal with risk and to exploit opportunities that may contribute to the achievement of some long-term goals. Administrators pursuing this approach seek facts and information on which to base their decisions about what to do and how best to do it. They avoid the pitfalls of both compulsive and overly rigid behavior by maintaining a long-range, purposeful outlook. However, the cost of information gathering may increase substantially the total commitments to the resolution of any problem.

The *bureaucratic approach* involves avoidance of any kind of risk or innovation, while maintaining the long-term consistency and continuity of the organization. The question is not one of applying established practices to changing situations; rather, past precedent is applied blindly. Whereas the procedural response (upper left-hand quadrant in figure 3–6) involves some concern with shifting directions within short-range limits, the bureaucratic response results in tighter control and rigidity based on blind adherence to tradition (a long-range time perspective in reverse). Bureaucratic administrators might state flatly; "There doesn't have to be a reason for it, it's just the way we always do things." Consequently, new approaches to public policy seldom are adopted, and established patterns are maintained unquestioned.

Turning to the system-time continua, it may be seen that the *impulsive approach,* like the fire-fighting response, reflects a very short-range concern for time. In addition, this response often is made by individuals who have lost touch with the overall purposes of the system. No attempt is made to limit risk or to weigh it against potential gains. The impulsive administrator responds to whatever comes along. His behavior is unpredictable since he has few internal ground rules and tends to ignore established precedent and policy. He operates almost entirely in the present; in extreme cases, he may do almost anything that comes to mind. His pattern of fiscal administration may be erratic; a spending spree at one moment and tight fiscal controls at another time.

The *procedural approach* reflects a desire to apply established policies and practices to current problems. The question asked is, "How can this present situation be handled by applying past experiences and procedures?" The procedural administrator is concerned with the maintenance of the system, but he has the focus on short-range, immediate problems characteristic of the incrementalist. He avoids long-term commitments to capital investment, and believes that as long as the next move is closely related to the past, the system cannot get into trouble. Decisions are processed incrementally within the safe boundaries of established values, policies, rules, and regulations.

The *systemic approach* reflects a concern for the total organization, for the relationship between the parts and the whole, and for long-range direction as well as short-term purposes within this longer time dimension. The systemic administrator asks: "Where are we going and how can we best get there?" Planning for a particular event, operation, or activity is carefully thought through with concern for the total system. Investment decisions are considered in terms of the long-range, comprehensive plans of the system. Information is gathered and analyzed in an effort to reduce future uncertainty. All available methods of analysis may be used to define problems and seek their solutions. However, the systemic administration may move too cautiously to meet more immediate demands.

The *speculative approach* is characteristic of individuals whose eagerness to take chances move them beyond merely opportunistic behavior to actual speculation or gambling. Although he shows little concern for the impact on the system of risk or experimentation, the speculative administrator exhibits a long-range perspective in his attitude that chances must be taken now in order to reap gains in the future. The general attitude is, "You've got to take chances if you want to get ahead, so let's give it a whirl." Indeed, the speculative administrator may attempt to create opportunities where none exist (for example, by committing fiscal resources to projects in hopes that this will stimulate investment from the private sector). As one moves further and further from any systemic considerations of goals and objectives, one moves from calculated risk, to somewhat risky exploitation, to pure speculation.

An Attitudinal Paradigm

It is evident that the quadrants in figures 3–5 and 3–6 represent paired subsets of the broader descriptive categories in figure 3–4. By combining these three basic areas of concern—systemic, risk, and time—the paradigm outlined previously can be further expanded, as shown in figure 3–7. Differences among these basic approaches can be clarified by examining the actions and attitudes generated in response to various areas of administrative responsibility, as summarized in table 3–2 and the discussion that follows.

Organizational Structure and Control

The traditional administrator seeks an organizational structure that permits the explicit definition of necessary staff functions and responsibilities, providing stability and preventing undisciplined action. The procedural administrator achieves this objective through formal rules and regulations,

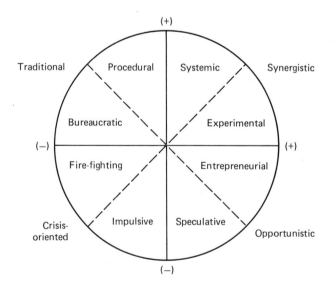

Figure 3–7. An Attitudinal Paradigm of Public Administration

Table 3–2
Profile of Attitudes toward Administrative Responsibilities

Attitude toward:	Traditional	Crisis-oriented	Opportunistic	Synergistic
Organization structure	Clear-cut chain of command; hierarchy of authority	Organization structured for trouble shooting	Formal structure avoided so as to promote flexibility	Organization structured to promote flow of communication
Controls	Close control maintained through established procedures to ensure minimum deviations	Close control to ensure that mistakes do not hurt the organization	Loose control since the staff needs to use imagination and initiative	Controls must be consistent with organization purpose—flexibility for initiative
Problem identification	Bias toward low risk, broadly defined problems; problems often stated in "how-to" terms	Problem statements with built-in action-oriented solutions	Future-oriented, but on an elemental level; tends to "take a flyer"	Reflects concern for total purpose and building in opportunities for innovation
Planning	Systematic efforts, building on established practices; planning provides control mechanisms	Impossible because of unpredictable nature of the future	Impractical since events are random; planning restricts freedom	Provides stability and sound direction; should be systematic yet flexible
Data collection	Seeks data that will cast light on deviations from predetermined patterns; detailed information to reduce risk	Focus on current problems; causes, risks, and responsibilities	Seeks data to confirm quick and easy set of solutions; reliance placed on intuition and judgment	Strong reliance on data collection and information analysis
Alternative solutions	Limited by the parameters of precedent and existing standards; low risk, "safe" solutions	Limited in number, rarely contain innovation; tend to be defensive and responsive to momentary considerations	Seeks opportunities for quick gains; focus on elements: quick solutions may work against greatest gains	Concern for long-term solutions and appropriate avenues of growth

whereas the bureaucratic administrator seeks organizational stability through a formal hierarchy of authority (the organization chart) in which each person's precise role is defined. These mechanisms are reinforced by the rewards and sanctions of the organization. Communication channels are clearly defined by the organization's chain of command and by established protocol—rules and regulations created to support the hierarchy of authority.

The crisis-oriented administrator seeks to structure the organization with accountability as the foremost issue. Staff members are likely to have specific responsibilities to identify problems, alter procedures when errors occur, and take necessary steps to "solve" problems within defined areas of jurisdiction. Since staff members are judged on the basis of ability to circumvent problems, rivalries may develop as individuals and groups vie for feasible solutions. Information is collected and communicated as current problems indicate a need to determine causes, to establish responsibility, and to identify the required action.

The opportunistic administrator avoids formal organizational structures such as job descriptions and organization charts in favor of freedom and flexibility to respond to opportunities. He collects a relatively limited amount of information, relying instead on experience, intuition, and personal judgment for solving problems and detecting opportunities. There are few organizational controls; staff members are free to use imagination and initiative in dealing with problems and are not encumbered with restrictive rules and regulations.

The synergistic administrator gives particular attention to the flow of information in the structuring of the organization. The communication system is the vital link and is structured so that the organization's resources can be quickly mobilized to handle both short- and long-range problems and opportunities. Information is collected to assist in maintaining a sense of direction and control and to provide a basis for planning ahead. Control mechanisms, however, must leave room for the exercise of initiative to guide actions relevant to perceived needs.

Problem Identification

A key issue in the identification of problems is the tendency of the problem solver to include his or her prejudices regarding the solution in the statement of the problem. For example, when a program administrator thinks of improving efficiency, he frequently states the problem in terms of reducing costs. Problem statements may have much more subtle indications of direction which nonetheless limit the number of potential alternative solutions.

A related pitfall is the tendency to couch the problem statement in terms of "how to" solve the problem. Ideally, a problem statement should not include a bias toward any particular solution, nor should it offer specific "how-to" elements. Such elements must be part of the programming effort once the specific solutions are proposed.

The primary pressure on the traditional problem solver is the maintenance of the status quo. Therefore, his or her problem statements are biased toward keeping things in line with predetermined standards or precedents. This characteristic may be seen in the expression of some "how-to" steps along with the problem statement. For example, a traditional administrator's response to a cost overrun might be, "How can we get costs back in line with established standards by reducing nonessential expenditures?"

A lack of concern for existing standards and traditions, coupled with a desire to avoid risk, leads the crisis-oriented administrator to make problem statements with built-in action-oriented solutions on an elemental level. For example, the cost-overrun problem might be stated as follows, "How can we reduce costs on operation Y of program X?" Such a problem statement includes a clear bias toward a solution, although the true problem may be outputs rather than costs.

With limited concern for the system, the opportunistic administrator tends to direct his attention toward one aspect of a given operation where growth seems possible. His problem statements show a bias toward solutions that are gain-oriented but that may not be well connected to the overall purpose of the organization.

By definition, the synergistic approach is least likely to include any predetermined indications of how the problem should be solved. In the cost-overrun example, a synergistic first statement might be, "What steps need to be taken in this situation to determine the effectiveness of our present operations?" Thus, the synergistic administrator begins with a means-ends analysis to clarify objectives and measures of effectiveness which, in turn, might lead to cost-oriented solutions. Possible solutions might also include an improvement in methods, a change in program emphasis, or a redefinition of program goals.

Orientations Toward Planning

For the traditional administrator, planning provides the organization with stable and sound direction and should involve the establishment of specific checks and balances to ensure that actions conform with existing procedures and practices. The procedural administrator is likely to give priority to the maintenance of a stable organization, whereas the bureaucratic administrator may see planning as a means of developing structures and programs to minimize risk. Thus, while their motives may differ slightly, their results often are the same—a fairly unimaginative plan (perhaps more appropriately labelled a "trend projection") which builds in linear fashion on the accumulated conditions of the past and attempts to alter these conditions only when they threaten the status quo.

In the eyes of the crisis-oriented administrator, long-range planning is impossible—a waste of time and resources—because the future is unpredictable. The organization will do all right, asserts the crisis-oriented administrator, if current situations are dealt with promptly. Risk and uncertainty associated with future conditions will be problems soon enough; there is no need to look for trouble.

Like the crisis-oriented administrator, the opportunistic administrator sees planning as impractical, since events are random and disconnected. Furthermore, planning tends to restrict freedom; action is the key to organizational success. Since both the entrepreneurial and the speculative administrator place high priority on opportunities for growth and improvement, they frequently hold that the long run can be taken care of by sensitive and creative individuals who are able to spot trends and take appropriate actions to capitalize on opportunities.

For the synergistic administrator, planning provides stability and sound direction. Although he welcomes opportunities and accepts risk as a necessary consequence of innovation, he considers sound planning to be the basis by which to evaluate opportunity and to judge the acceptability of risks. This type of administrator undertakes long-range planning in a systematic and comprehensive fashion, while allowing sufficient flexibility for innovation. In short, the planning emphasis of the synergistic administrator is on the maintenance of sound direction, while building a basis for organizational growth.

Collection and Analysis of Data

The pressures on the traditional administrator and the way in which problems are stated lead to the collection of data that will cast light on deviations from standards or predetermined pathways. When there is a cost problem, for example, data may be collected to indicate why expenditures are varying from the established budget. If there is a gap in expected performance, the tendency is to see how that performance contrasts with a written job description. As a consequence of his preoccupation with minimizing risk, the traditional administrator often collects a great deal of data systematically; often, bureaucratic organizations have floundered in the "syndrome of data collection" in which the assemblage of detailed information becomes an end in itself.

Most of the energy of the crisis-oriented administrator is devoted to action rather than to information gathering or analysis. The paradox is that when action is impossible, such an administrator may become preoccupied with surveillance and careful scrutiny of all kinds of detailed data on an elemental level in an effort to avoid or reduce risk.

The opportunistic administrator tends to collect little data, and the data that are gathered is oriented toward gains rather than toward a full analysis of possibilities. The sequence and ordering of data are unimportant since the opportunistic administrator is primarily seeking a basis for action.

The critical data issue for the synergistic administrator is relevance. This focus largely dictates the amount, nature, and sequence of data collected. The synergistic administrator seeks information which will shed light on general direction and provide guidance for long-term course corrections. Clearly, the traditional and synergistic administrators are apt to collect more data and to be more concerned with comprehensiveness and overall objectives. However, the traditional administrator's orientation away from risk means that he tends to collect the same kinds of data as the crisis-oriented administrator.

Selecting Alternatives

To a large extent, the pressures on the administrator, the way the problem is stated, and the types of data collected predetermine the range of alternatives that emerge. Traditional and crisis-oriented administrators seldom include opportunities for significant breakthroughs or innovations as potential decisions. The opportunistic administrator tends to include breakthrough strategies, but often deals only with pieces of the total problem; he frequently ignores preventive measures that might yield better solutions than gain-oriented initiatives.

In his effort to keep the organization on track, the traditional administrator rarely pursues the possibilities offering the highest payoff; rather, he is inclined to look for safe solutions—to compromise between maximum and minimum possibilities. His choices may be greatly influenced by what has worked in the past, although the very fact that something has worked in the past may be a good indication that it will not work as well in the future; the perpetuation of past solutions may be a major part of the problem.

Elemental solutions oriented toward dealing with immediate problems and reducing risks often appeal to the crisis-oriented administrator. Such solutions, however, often are inappropriate in terms of the one thing he is most worried about—survival.

The opportunistic administrator tends to select the alternative that promises the quickest gain at an elemental level. Paradoxically, the temptation to choose the quickest solution may work against the desire for the greatest gain, if gain is measured in terms of total organizational purpose.

The synergistic administrator seeks to optimize the process—to choose the higher payoff when calculated risk is appropriate to that payoff. Low risk per se is not a goal; rather, calculated risk, based on careful analysis of alternative payoffs, is optimal. The synergistic administrator identifies the decision-making process as a key component in establishing and maintaining sound direction toward overall objectives. While every decision involves a certain amount of intuition, this factor is limited by the array of alternatives under consideration. A given solution might "feel" good to an experienced person, providing that solution is set forth in the decision array. In the early stages of problem solving, therefore, synergistic administrators are concerned with uncovering data, risk probabilities, and potential opportunities so that personal knowledge, sensitivity, and intuition can more appropriately be brought to bear on the ultimate decision.

Selection of an Approach to Administrative Responsibilities

Ultimately, any decision must be analyzed in terms of its effects. Although the picture painted here clearly favors the synergistic approach, there are many administrative situations in which judgment, sensitivity, imagination, and intuition may be more effective tools than the emphases of the synergistic approach. An opportunistic administrator, in the right place at the right time, may produce a higher payoff for the organization. Similarly, a crisis-oriented or traditional administrator, in the right place at the right time, might take the appropriate steps to avoid a serious problem.

Guidelines for Selection

A number of guidelines may be applied in selecting an appropriate administrative approach to a particular situation. Among these are considerations of the estimated gain or loss, severity of the problem, the frequency with which the problems are encountered, and the spillover effects of decisions.

In any decision situation a key question is: "How much is the additional information to be derived from further study worth?" Frequently, the amount of time and energy required will be greater than the potential gains. Accordingly, there may be no point in working through to a "best" solution in a synergistic fashion; traditional or even crisis-oriented responses may yield a quick solution that will suffice, since the consequences are not great. An administrator operating initially in the synergistic quadrant may consciously decide to adopt alternative approaches if the potential gain from experimentation and fact finding is limited, or if the costs (and hence the potential loss) of such additional data collection are high.

Gain or loss often is affected by the *severity* of the problems encountered. Severe problems may require a relatively quick solution to avoid further adverse effects on the system, or they may involve complications that prevent the identification of a "best" solution. The phrase "real and immediate threat" is a good test of the severity of the problem; when this test is met, a crisis-oriented response may be required. Applying such an approach, however, should not preclude a long-term search for causes, experimentation with new methods, and development of new procedures.

If a problem is encountered frequently, then considerable potential gain may result from a search for the "best" solution—one that could be applied whenever the problem arose. If the problem is encountered infrequently, it may or may not warrant the detailed fact finding and analysis of synergistic behavior. An infrequently encountered problem, however, may be the first manifestation of a generic problem that will occur regularly in the future. Guidelines for dealing with such problems are outlined in subsequent chapters.

Many aspects of a decision affect gain or loss, although often obscurely; these are the spillover effects. A decision with a spillover effect is one that has significant impact beyond the immediate situation in which it is made. Such decisions and their effects are inevitable when administrators fail to consider appropriate aspects of the total system. Thus a single act, intended to have limited impact, may spill over into other areas and become an even more costly headache.

Organizational Implications

The discussion of this paradigm has focused until now on its application in understanding the attitudes and motivations of individual administrators. Any organization is merely the sum of the individuals who work in it; therefore, many organizations can be characterized by the prevailing attitudes manifested in one of the four quadrants of this paradigm. The classes of problems that confront an organization (or units within a larger organization) may contribute to the particular manifestations of attitudes and responses. Regulatory agencies, for example, tend to be more traditional (bureaucratic or procedural) in their orientation, whereas developmental agencies may adopt an opportunistic approach.

In addition, this paradigm may be used to trace the evolution of an organization. Many new organizations are created in response to a particular problem or opportunity. Once the crisis is past or the opportunity has been seized, the organization may be dissolved. More often, the organization continues, moving to the next stage in its development. Crisis-oriented organizations may seek new opportunities, whereas opportunistic organizations may seek to solidify their gains by adopting more systemic concerns, that is, by manifesting more synergistic attitudes. Long-range goals and objectives may be defined and specific steps taken to formalize the organizational structure. Eventually, synergistic organizations tend to become more traditional in their perspective unless specific efforts are made to counter this tendency. Rules, regulations, and practices designed to support systemic concerns may become more rigidly codified, limiting the flexibility to respond to new opportunities. Risk may become less of a challenge and more of a threat. Depending on the demands that affect the organization, the emphasis of the traditional approach on the status quo may be inappropriate as an organizational response. As problems arise, administrators may lose their overall sense of purpose and respond to new situations in a crisis-oriented fashion, seeing traditional responses as inappropriate but attempting to avoid risk. As new situations become more frequent and intense, the crisis-oriented organization may be unable to survive and may be replaced by a new organization or a significantly modified one.

In short, the evolution of many organizations can be described as a counterclockwise cycle through the four quadrants of the paradigm. This is not to say that all organizations complete this cycle. There may be conscious efforts to stabilize the organization in one of the quadrants or attempts to reverse the direction as the organization slips from quadrant to another. Since the traditional or bureaucratic mode is most stable (least subject to volatile shifts in direction), many public organizations settle in this quadrant, emphasizing systemic concerns and avoiding risk.

Summary and Conclusions

In the literature of public administration, the administrative or management process often is depicted as a set of procedures applicable to all situations; the message seems to be that there always is one best way to manage. In this discussion, the focus has been on a variety of approaches to public administration. The approaches followed by individual administrators may vary, depending on their attitudes, assumptions, and concerns. The development of this paradigm, built around three basic sets of concerns, is an attempt to show how particular administrative responses come about. Although it is obvious that the synergistic approach is considered most effective in terms of the dimensions outlined in the paradigm, the best approach for an administrator to take in any particular situation is the one most appropriate in terms of the relative importance of, and interrelationship among, a number of factors.

The problem-solving and decision-making process can be considered as a series of open loops of subsystems which contribute to the totality of the organization. In effect, every decision predetermines the degrees of freedom presented for the next decision. Viewed as a social system, any organization is continually influenced by a series of small decisions that accumulate to produce a decision-making climate. This climate involves a set of parameters that to some extent determine the range of alternatives available for future decisions.

In terms of the criteria by which an organization is evaluated, its success or failure may be determined by things that happened sometime in the past. To paraphrase John Gardner: Decisions which are made today will probably not have their true impact for five years. In industry, for example, today's profits are often the result of decisions made three to five years ago regarding new product development, selection of personnel, marketing strategies, and a wide range of operating and financial choices. When things are going well within an organization, it may be assumed that good decisions currently are being made when, in fact, the organization is benefiting from good decisions made several years ago. The assumption that the good things happening now reflect current wise decisions may be both false and dangerous. The statement frequently made that corporate profits are impossible without change and innovation can be applied as well to nonprofit organizations, except that the term effectiveness must be substituted for the word profit—effectiveness in terms of the public organization's capacity to handle problems and to deal with its mission in an efficient and effective manner.

Notes

1. James Q. Wilson, "The Bureaucratic Problem," *The Public Interest* (Winter 1967):3–9.

2. Robert R. Blake and Jane S. Mouton, *The Managerial Grid* (Houston, Texas: Gulf Publishing Company, 1964).

3. Michael Mont Harmon, "Administrative Policy Formulation and the Public Interest," *Public Administration Review* 29(September-October 1969): 483–491.

4. W.J. Reddin, "The Tri-Dimensional Grid," *Training Directors Journal* 18(July 1964):9–18.

5. F. Gerald Brown, "Management Styles and Working with People," in *Developing the Municipal Organization,* ed. Stanley P. Powers et al. ‚(Washington, D.C.: International City Management Association, 1974), pp. 69–83.

6. John von Neuman and Oskar Morgenstern, *Theory of Games and Economic Behavior* (Princeton, N.J.: Princeton University Press, 1947).

7. See Brita Schwartz, "Long-Range Planning in the Public Sector," *Futures* 9(1977): 115–127.

4 Improving Administrative Performance Through Policy Analysis And Evaluation

Many books and articles in the contemporary literature of the social and behavioral sciences contain the terms *policy analysis* or *policy evaluation,* or both, in their titles. Unfortunately for the student trying to get some grasp on these generic concepts, there are no good definitions of policy analysis or policy evaluation. Or perhaps it should be said that there are no good *short* explanations of what these concepts involve. As Wildavsky has observed: ". . . policy analysis, with its emphasis upon originality, imagination and foresight, cannot be simply described."[1] Generally, the immediate effect of all one-sentence definitions of policy analysis and evaluation is mental paralysis rather than enlightenment.

The Role of Policy Analysis and Evaluation

The concepts and procedures of policy analysis and evaluation play an important role in performance administration. Encouraged by the successful use of these techniques over the past two decades, some authors have suggested that policy analysis and evaluation can and should be extended to a science of policy making. It is much too early, however, to say whether or not a full-blown policy science will emerge. Nevertheless, it is important to understand the potential contributions of policy analysis and evaluation to improved administrative performance.

Systematic Problem Solving

Since policy analysis and evaluation are difficult concepts to pin down, it may be prudent to begin with a generic definition. Robert Lane suggests that policy analysis seeks ". . . answers to the question: What happens when we intervene in the social system this way rather than that way?"[2] Implicit in this terse definition is the notion that policy implies human decisions, normally with reference to government intervention, although Lane acknowledges that intervention may be by some other social or economic institution in either the public or the private sector. The phrase "this way rather than that way" implies that policy analysis involves a comparison of alternatives—that it involves a choice, even if the choice is to do nothing. By reference to the "social system" Lane seems to be excluding technological choices that have few human consequences. In expanding his own definition, however, Lane suggests that ". . . one of the virtues of policy analysis is that it reveals the latent human consequences of many seemingly innocent decisions. . . ."

Another rather generic definition of policy analysis is that it is a "scientific" or "systematic" approach to problem solving. This theme dominates the current literature on policy analysis and evaluation. Kenneth Kraemer, for example, suggests that policy analysis, compared with most decision-making aids, is a more formalized and systematic process to help public officials choose a desirable course of action.[3]

Many systematic interpretations of policy analysis make a point of reminding the reader that analysis and evaluation are merely tools for augmenting professional judgment. E.S. Quade, for instance, maintains that:

> In a broad sense policy analysis may be defined as any type of analysis that generates and presents information in such a way as to improve the basis for policy-makers to exercise their judgment. . . . [I]t implies the use of intuition and judgment and encompasses not only the examination of policy by decomposition into its components but also the design and synthesis of new alternatives.[4]

In spite of the increased emphasis on the tools of analysis, some students of public policy prefer to maintain a broader definition, similar to that which emerged several years ago under the rubric of policy science. A principal proponent of this point of view is Yehezkel Dror, who contends that the problem boundaries of policy analysis should include:

1. considerably more attention to the political aspects of public policy making;
2. a broader conception of policy making, beyond the narrow view of decision making mainly in terms of resource allocations;
3. greater emphasis on creativity, innovation, and the search for new policy alternatives;
4. extensive reliance on qualitative methods;
5. more emphasis on futuristic thinking; and
6. a less rigid, yet systematic approach that recognizes the complexity of means-ends interdependence, the multiplicity of relevant criteria, and the partial and tentative nature of every analysis.[5]

Developers and promoters of the tools approach freely admit that they have relatively little concern with the broader sociopolitical elements of public policy. Yet these elements often have the profoundest implications for the practicing analyst and the public official. This broader perspective must be explored along with the more pragmatic aspects of policy analysis in our study of performance administration.

Description Versus Prescription

Although the term policy analysis covers a wide variety of studies, analyses, and research, it has customarily been reserved for the more formal and systematic applications, the product of which is likely to be a set of conclusions or recommendations supported by a written report. As Quade observes, however, the same term is generally applied both to the process and to the product of that process. Thus, policy analysis produces policy analyses. Dror cautions, however, that policy analysis can take one of two major forms: (1) descriptive and (2) prescriptive.[6]

Sharkansky illustrates the descriptive approach when he asserts that policy analysis involves the *study* of government actions, with a primary concern for explanation rather than prescription.[7] The emphasis of Sharkansky and his colleagues is on comparison—on a search for economic, social, and historical, as well as political and governmental, characteristics to aid in understanding the policies that public officials choose. Such research seeks to build theories about policy; policy recommendations are subordinate to description, analysis, and understanding.

The line between description and prescription, however, is not clear, nor need it be made explicit. Several authors, in fact, dismiss this distinction as spurious. Charles Rothwell, in his foreword to *The Policy Sciences,* one of the most influential early books in the field, suggests that policy "... is a body of principles to guide action. The application of policy is a calculated choice—a decision to pursue specific goals by doing specific things."[8] Rothwell suggests that the formulation and execution of policy usually involves four steps: (1) clarification of goals, (2) an exhaustive evaluation of the situation(s) to be met, (3) the selection of a course of action by weighing the probable consequences of various alternatives, and (4) the determination of optimum means for carrying out the action decided upon. He concludes, "Since the situation to be met is normally not static but involves a complex of moving forces, policy and action are, in effect, a design to shape the future by exerting influence upon trends that flow from the past into the future."[9] Policy analysis, therefore, involves an examination of this process and has the potential to contribute to each of the four steps identified by Rothwell.

Evaluation: Looking at Process or Impacts

As Rothwell's procedural definition suggests, the terms analysis and evaluation often are used interchangeably. Cost-benefit analysis, for example, may be referred to as an evaluation, because it is used to project the outcome of a particular decision or set of decisions as a means of choosing among different policy alternatives. Some authors have suggested that the term evaluation be reserved for an assessment of the effectiveness of policy decisions, that is, an after-the-fact form of analysis. As David Nachmias points out, however, policy evaluation can refer to both process and impacts assessments. Nachmias explains that:

> *Process evaluation* is concerned with the extent to which a particular policy or program is implemented according to its stated guidelines. The content of a particular public policy and its impact on those affected may be substantially modified, elaborated, or even negated during its implementation. . . . *[I]mpact evaluation* is concerned with examining the extent to which a policy causes a change in the intended direction. It calls for delineation of operationally defined policy goals, specification of criteria of success, and measurement of progress toward the goals.[10]

The type of evaluation most valuable in performance administration is actually a blend of these two approaches. It is important to point out, however, that the concern for impacts inherent in performance administration cannot await the long-term, "scientific" studies often associated with impact assessments. This point will be discussed in detail in chapter 11. For now it suffices to say that process evaluations have been the most useful to the program manager and public decision maker.

This interpretation of evaluation coincides with the procedural definition offered by Joseph Wholey and his colleagues. Evaluation: "(1) assesses the effectiveness of an on-going program in achieving its objectives; (2) relies on the principles of research design to distinguish a program's effect from those of other forces working in the situation, and (3) aims at program improvement through program modification (as contrasted to the formulation of a new policy)."[11]

In defining evaluation, a distinction must be drawn between evaluation and other forms of managerial assessment, such as the *post-audit examination*. A conventional post-audit assesses the legality, fidelity, and propriety of financial transactions and ensures that expenditure ceilings are not exceeded. It is not really an evaluation, since it tells the policy maker or program manager relatively little about the accomplishments of the program or project under investigation. It deals with inputs, not outputs. Furthermore, conventional post-audits tend to look backward in an attempt to place blame. Evaluations, on the other hand, are or should be primarily forward looking, helping management decide what to do next.[12]

The concept of a *performance audit* has emerged in recent years in an effort to extend the traditional audit of financial operations to encompass the degree of achievement of management objectives. A performance audit includes three elements: (1) financial and compliance—the traditional aspects of the conventional post-audit; (2) economy and efficiency—identification of inefficiencies and uneconomical practices, including inadequacies in management information systems, administrative procedures, and organizational structure; and (3) program results—determination of whether the desired results are being achieved, whether the objectives established by the legislature or other authorizing body are being met, and whether the agency has considered alternatives that might yield desired results at lower cost.[13]

The procedures of policy evaluation closely parallel those of policy analysis. If a sound analysis is conducted before the initiation of a specific public program, the basic framework for evaluation should be well established. The objectives of the program or policy to be evaluated must be identified, measures of effectiveness developed, and criteria for comparison determined. The available alternatives are then investigated, data are gathered, and costs and other consequences are estimated. There are always at least two alternatives—to continue an existing program or to terminate it. Evaluation contributes to the analysis of these alternatives as well as providing a basis for improving ongoing operations.

Wholey has pointed out some of the problems with evaluations: "From the point of view of decision-makers, evaluation is a dangerous weapon. They don't want evaluation if it will yield the 'wrong' answers about programs in which they are interested."[14] In such situations, political pressures often override the empirical evidence available from the formal evaluation. On the other hand, policy makers sometimes ask pertinent questions for which evaluators cannot provide timely answers at reasonable cost. Consequently, the policy maker may return to intuitive methods for making critical choices or may move in an incremental fashion at times when bolder action is required to deal effectively with problems. As Wholey has observed: "Valid, reliable evaluation is very hard to perform and can cost a lot of money. Evaluators have real problems in detecting causal connections between inputs and outputs—and in doing so in timely enough fashion to be useful to decisionmakers."[15] A further problem arising from cost constraints is that such evaluations often are one-shot rather than continuous efforts, or are carried out on the basis of such a small sample that insufficient information is available regarding the wide variations possible in program costs and performance.

A parallel distinction must be made between programmatic and organizational effects. It is necessary to decide whether the program or the organization responsible for the program is to be evaluated. A program may be evaluated in terms of its effectiveness and costs, but an organizational structure should not be evaluated solely on the basis of its success in operating a particular program. As Quade observes, an organization should be judged not by an initial program failure, but by its capacity to learn from failure and to improve the operation of the program.[16]

In spite of these pitfalls, systematic attempts to ascertain the positive and negative impacts of programs and policies are becoming a vital part of the public administrator's responsibilities, and are central to the concepts of performance administration. The objective of such evaluations should be not merely to grade existing programs and policies with a view to eliminating the worst ones but more importantly, to provide an effective basis on which to improve those worthy of continuation.

Summary Definitions

Policy analysis can be seen to be a systematic process involving the delineation of pertinent problems and issues, the clarification of relevant goals and objectives, the identification and comparison of available alternatives (often requiring the design and synthesis of new alternatives), and the determination of the optimum resources necessary to attain the desired goals and objectives. Although policy analysis may be descriptive or prescriptive, its basic aim is to develop guidelines to assist public policy and decision makers in exercising their judgment regarding commitments to action.

Evaluation involves an assessment of the effectiveness of ongoing and proposed policies and programs in achieving agreed-on goals and objectives and an identification of areas needing improvement through policy or program modification (including the possible termination of ineffective programs). Such evaluations must identify and take into account the possible influence of external as well as internal organizational factors on the overall effectiveness of the policy or program.

The Quest for a Policy Science

Practical applications of policy analysis and evaluation have emerged from two main streams of activity over the past two decades: (1) the national defense and space exploration programs, and (2) the continuous efforts of state and local governments since the 1920s to improve public planning and management practices. The conceptual concerns of the social and behavioral sciences regarding policy inquiry also reflect several other general trends in these disciplines and in related fields, including: (1) the emergence of a general systems theory and the application of systems analysis to a wide range of phenomena; (2) the acceptance, at least in some quarters, of the concept of government policy as applied social science and of government programs as social experiments; (3) the development of social indicators (increased quantification of social variables); and (4) the general struggle for greater relevance in the traditional social science disciplines. Both conceptual and practical changes have been accelerated by the development of cybernetics and of greater information-exchange capacity. Finally, in recent years there has been increased emphasis on government responsiveness, effectiveness, and accountability. All these factors have contributed to the quest for a more scientific and systematic approach to the formulation and implementation of public policy.

Elements of the Policy-Science Movement

Before exploring further the current quest for a policy science, it may be helpful to put this quest into perspective by tracing briefly some of the factors that have helped to draw social and behavioral scientists into the arena of scientific policy making.

Government Policy as Applied Social Science. This profound component of the policy science movement can best be summarized by reference to the recommendations of four books and two national conferences held in the early 1970s. The four books are *The Behavioral Sciences and the Federal Government* (Washington, D.C.: National Academy of Sciences, 1968); *Knowledge Into Action* (Washington, D.C.: National Science Board, 1969); *The Behavioral and Social Sciences: Outlook and Needs* (Washington, D.C.: National Academy of Sciences, 1969); and *Federal Evaluation Policy: Analyzing the Effects of Public Programs* (Washington, D.C.: Urban Institute, 1970). The conferences include the Symposium on Applying Knowledge from the Behavioral Sciences to Social Legislation Programs and the Conference on Social Research and Foreign Affairs, both held in Washington, D.C. in October 1970. Recommendations emerging from these sources share the premise that public policy is an intervention in the social system. These authors and conference participants assert that this premise implies a greater role for social scientists in public policy making. While some of these recommendations may seem self-serving, they do highlight the increased awareness on the part of social and behavioral scientists of their potential contributions to and responsibilities for influencing the course of public policy at all levels of government.

Applied General Systems Theory. Policy inquiry has drawn much from the theory and application of the general systems approach. To begin with, many forms of policy inquiry borrow the basic systems model (described at length in later chapters). Also, most policy analysts have adopted the notion that a change in one set of specified elements of a mutually influencing network of elements (a system) can be seen to effect a specifiable change in the other elements. As Radnor has observed: "Inspired by general systems theory (and at the moment it has little more to give us than inspiration), we derive the notion of hierarchies of enveloping and overlapping systems with varying degrees of inter-system linkages."[17] In attempting to create a theory or metascience of all systems, general systems theory holds the potential for providing theoretical underpinnings for a science of the management of complex open systems—a policy science.

Improvements in available technology—particularly advances in modeling, simulation, and analytical techniques involving relatively large, complex systems—has broadened the application of systems analysis and operations research to situations where "approximate solutions" can be used.[18] Such solutions permit the use of decision makers' opinions and other "soft" variables as basic data inputs. These techniques are increasingly applicable to policy- and decision-making problems in "fuzzy" environments "in which the goals and/or constraints . . . constitute classes of alternatives whose boundaries are not sharply defined."[19]

It is essential to point out, however, that many of the techniques currently applied in government are systematic in name only. That is, they are aids to problem solving or alternative selection that do not necessarily involve an appropriate consideration of the broader system and its environment.

The Social-Indicators Movement. This trend in policy inquiry emerged in the early 1960s. Social indicators became a watchword with the Ford Foundation's funding of "urban observatories" at various universities, NASA's funding a major study of social indicators by Raymond Bauer and others,[20] and the continuing work by such social scientists as Otis Dudley Duncan, Philip Hauser, Albert Biderman, and Bertram Gross,[21] all contributing to a growing recognition of the need for more definitive social measures to monitor the impact of public policies and programs. The traditional interest of social scientists in the type of data provided by the census, the concern of economists with masses of self-generated data bases, and the needs of government for increasingly sophisticated data also played an important part in the social-indicators movement.

Likert concludes, however, that although social scientists have produced a great deal of statistical information regarding the *state* of the system—for example, population data, price indices, measures of the level of business activity, and so forth (descriptive data)—they have been far less successful in building an adequate knowledge base as to the *nature* of the system (a conceptual model or general theory relevant to contemporary society).[22] This conclusion leads to an important question about the social indicators movement: How can the adequacy of social measures be assessed if social scientists lack sufficient prior knowledge to guide them in determining what should be measured?

There have been countless efforts to develop singular generalizations and partial theories about any number of selected and presumably coherent areas of contemporary society.[23] The task of the theorists is to construct a body of logically interrelated propositions adequate for explaining behavior in some particular aspect or segment of the system. However, the task does not necessarily include the effort to fit each of these partial theories into a larger logical and consistent whole. What remains ambiguous is the relationship between such partial theories, an area that has formed an intellectual no-man's-land.

While social indicators are still largely descriptive, the greater comprehensiveness of these efforts provides a significantly broader base upon which to build prescriptive recommendations. As Bauer suggests: ". . . the system of indicators must be broader than the range of effects postulated if only to determine what the range is." Thus social indicators strive to ". . . take as a point of departure those values, goals, and features of the society that we consider important in assessing the state and direction of the society."[24]

The Cybernetics Revolution. The sophisticated concern for improved information exchange, arising out of the field of cybernetics and made possible by the computer, has played an important role in the current movement of policy analysis and evaluation toward a policy science. The term cybernetics is derived from the Greek word *kybernētikē,* which means, literally, the art of steersmanship. Plato used the word often, both in the generic sense and in the metaphoric sense of the art of guiding men in society—the art of government. The modern science of cybernetics grew out of the work of Norbert Wiener and his colleagues at MIT during World War II. The purpose of cybernetics is to develop a language and technique that not only can deal with the general problems of communication and control but also may find ". . . the proper repertory of ideas and techniques to classify their particular manifestations. . . ."[25] From the outset Weiner envisioned cybernetics not so much as a discipline in itself but rather as a framework for the observation of real-world phenomena.

Cybernetics promotes a new, more dynamic way of thinking, with emphasis on adaptive and evolutionary systems. Complex policies and decisions often are contingent, dynamic, and subject to changing circumstances. Cybernetics offers a set of methods, the potential application of which can be useful in solving problems that occur in virtually every type of human decision.

One of the principal missions of cybernetic theory is to explore the qualitative as well as the quantitative aspects of information. Information and communication flows are essential ingredients of policy formulation. If communication, as Bavelas and Barrett have suggested, is more than a secondary or derived aspect of any organization but is in fact a basic process from which other functions derive, then Wiener's thesis that man can control his environment through the control of information and communication becomes an important premise for the development of a policy science.[26] As Wiener asserts:

> The existence of Social Science is based on the ability to treat a social group as an organization and not as an agglomeration. Communication is the cement that makes *organization.* Communication alone enables a group to think together, to see together, and to act together. All sociology requires the understanding of communication.[27]

To this the postscript might be added that such understanding is also of paramount importance in policy analysis and evaluation.

A New Sense of Public in Public Policy

Another movement with profound implications for policy analysis and evaluation is that of *public involvement* or *citizen participation,* terms that often are used interchangeably. Traditionally, key decisions affecting the development of a community or state have been made in legislative chambers and political caucuses or through public referenda; full discussion by the electorate of the range of possible choices is not feasible. Or the public may be informed of a decision only after specific alternatives have been selected (for example, through the mechanism of a public hearing). If serious objections emerge to the decision or to the relatively narrow range of possible alternatives, implementation might be blocked through a variety of means, including judicial action. Public-agency staffs often are frustrated by such "public obstructionism" because they have spent considerable time and effort in the development and technical evaluation of programs. Traditionally, many technicians view such obstructions as an inevitable outcome of informing the public about plans and programs.

A new era of public involvement was mandated in the early 1960s in connection with the War on Poverty. Most public programs involving federal funds, as well as many state-funded programs, now require that efforts to increase public awareness and involvement begin in the initial stages of policy analysis, that is, with the definition of problems and the identification of goals and objectives, and that these efforts remain active at key points throughout the process. In this way, the different publics (various interest groups) can inform public officials and administrators of their viewpoints, goals, and preferences among alternative solutions proposed for particular problems or issues.

It is important that factual and attitudinal information flow into communication channels early enough in the policy-analysis process to permit its consideration in the technical deliberations, as well as in the examination of policy issues. In this way, the needs and concerns of various groups can be considered, a broad set of alternatives can be presented to and evaluated by the public, and decisions about the best course of action or choice among alternatives can be made with the greatest hope of equity. In addition, programs of public awareness and involvement facilitate compromise and agreement among the various interest groups by helping to clarify objectives and identify alternatives to be considered by decision makers.

Merely having an opportunity to participate is not enough, however. In our complex society, people may not heed the opportunity unless they are mobilized. Therefore, programs of public awareness and involvement must also include efforts to generate interest and active involvement early in the policy analysis process.

Public-awareness and involvement programs are not without their drawbacks, however. Such programs may require substantial time and effort on the part of technical specialists—time and effort that many professionals feel could be more appropriately applied to the identification of alternatives and the refinement of plans and programs. The obvious counterargument is that the time and effort spent in the early stages may mean the difference between success and long delays when various interest groups become aware of pending decisions and apply countermeasures to subvert commitments. In this political era, with public confidence at a low ebb, the cumulative results in terms of increased support for public decisions provides an overriding motivation for such involvement programs.

Some see citizen participation as a counterthrust to the greater centralization often associated with more systematic decision-making theory and practice. To be effective, a science of policy must include a fully articulated role for public involvement and participation.

Policy Science: Supradiscipline or Collection of Partial Theories?

Harold Lasswell, more than any other individual, has been identified with the efforts to formulate a policy science to provide a more systematic basis for the development and clarification of policy alternatives.[28] Lasswell's early writings, however, did not provide a definition of the specific contributions that traditional theories might make to the further articulation of this new field.[29] Building on the foundations of management science, Michael Radnor, David Tansik, Yehezkel Dror, and others have attempted to identify the concerns and the methodological approaches that might serve as a basis for this new supradiscipline.

After a thirty-year crusade, many are skeptical about the future of policy science. As Horowitz and Katz observe: "Lasswell's idea of a 'science of policy making' has largely given way to a *de facto* operational view that because of the fragmentation of power the social scientist is primarily concerned with facts, while the policy makers are concerned primarily with the strategies necessary to implement desired legislation rather than social goals as a whole."[30] If the twain shall never meet, is there any real hope that policy science will emerge above the level of a collection of interesting partial theories?

Lasswell, in his more recent writings, also seems to acknowledge the threshold on which his conceptualizations now stand, as suggested by the title of his 1971 book, *A Pre-View of Policy Sciences.* Lasswell asserts that ". . . the policy sciences are concerned with knowledge *of* and *in* the decision processes of public and civic order."

> Knowledge *of* the decision process implies systematic, empirical studies of how policies are made and put into effect. When knowledge is systematic, it goes beyond the aphoristic remarks that are strewn through the "wisdom" literature of the past. The systematic requirement calls for a body of explicitly interconnected propositions.[31]

According to Lasswell, the insistence on empirical criteria to specify that general assertions are subject to the discipline of careful observation is a fundamental distinction between science and nonscience. In this, Lasswell and his followers may be approaching the trap that has ensnared many of their brethren in the social sciences.

It often is assumed that the formulation of *normative theory*—theory that deals with what ought to be rather than merely analyzing what is—has no place in the practical and factual world of social scientists. This position stems partly from the popular misconception that scientists must be concerned with facts alone. Facts are safe to deal with; they seem definite, certain, unquestionable, and self-evident. The formulation of normative theory is assumed to be in the realm of the philosopher. Scientific investigation, therefore, is conceived largely as the summation of accumulated facts on a given subject. Even this function is considered relatively restrictive, since facts often are thought to "speak for themselves." Social scientists frequently make the false assumption that if only enough facts can be gathered, the answers will become obvious. However, as Huxley has observed: "Those who refuse to go beyond fact rarely get as far as fact."

An examination of what scientists actually do when they engage in research makes it clear that normative theory and empirical knowledge are not diametrically opposed, but inextricably intertwined. To be scientific is to be very much concerned with both theory and fact. Theory identifies the major orientation of a science by defining the kinds of data to be abstracted. It offers a conceptual scheme according to which relevant phenomena are systematized, classified, and interrelated. Theory is used to summarize facts into empirical generalizations and systems of generalizations and to identify gaps in the present state of knowledge.

What then are the partial theories that lie at the foundation of policy science, setting it apart from other disciplinary pursuits? Lasswell asserts that: "The emphasis on *decision process* underlines the difference between policy sciences and other forms of intellectual activity. By focusing on the making and execution of policy, one identifies a relatively unique frame of reference, and utilizes many traditional contributions to political science, jurisprudence, and related disciplines."[32]

Comparison with Other Decision Technologies

Various proponents of policy science have attempted to explain this emphasis on the decision process by comparing it with other analytical techniques that assist in decision making, such as systems analysis, systems engineering, and operations research. Systems analysis is limited in many of its applications by certain assumptions, including its emphasis on quantifiable, deterministic variables and on economic rationality, and its restriction to conditions of risk as opposed to those of uncertainty. Acknowledging that in attempting to become operational policy science will also be faced with its own set of "unrealistic assumptions," Michael Radnor asserts: "The development of useful and operational models will be a critical testing point for policy science."[33] In formulating such models, Radnor suggests, the policy scientist might fairly adopt the basic framework of systems analysis as a point of departure. Presumably, policy-science models would address perceived shortcomings of systems analysis—that is, they would accept nonrational decision processes, examine nondeterministic or stochastic variables, deal with uncertainty, provide explicit mechanisms for the search for new alternatives, and so forth.

Systems engineering has a well-developed technology to describe the functioning of systems, using sets of fairly complex mathematical equations. Its applications, however, have been limited for the most part to closed physical systems. Proponents of policy science have concluded, therefore, that systems engineering as a field of study is fundamentally irrelevant to the further development of policy science. This conclusion provides an additional insight into the types of problems and issues that form the focus of policy science—those which emerge from the open system characteristics of public policy making.

In its early years, operations research was heralded as "the fundamental and final solution to management decision-making requirements." Attempts were made to optimize large systems, and operation researchers were welcomed in the inner circles of top-level decision and policy making. Over time, however, the focus of operations research shifted to more narrowly-defined problems that were more amenable to its mathematical orientation and techniques. "Operations research analysts . . . backed down to those small and middle-sized problems that provided them with the relatively easier opportunities for demonstration of quick, measurable results—the 'gold-plucking' period."[34] More recently, operations researchers have again turned their attention to the problems of large, complex systems. Radnor has suggested that, "Policy science today speaks much like operations research of yesterday. One cannot help but suspect that unless its advocates are willing to learn from the experience of operations research, policy science will suffer a similar fate."[35]

The success of policy science in application, as contrasted to theory, will depend in large measure on how well its operational techniques and methodologies can serve the decision needs of top-level officials. The general models of systems analysis and operations research may provide a point of departure, but the identification and measurement of certain key variables—especially those related to criteria for success (objective functions)—will constitute, prima facie, the most difficult obstacles for the policy scientist. In seeking to identify these key decision variables, policy scientists must adopt more extensive and creative search procedures that go beyond the comparison of easily identifiable alternatives. They must also recognize that ". . . the organization consists of a cybernetic system in which, therefore, not only do strategy decisions determine structure, but also structure influences strategy and activities create structure.[36] Such recognition would lead logically to a rejection of the top-down or essentially Weberian model of organizational decision making and to the acceptance of an interactive model that deals explicitly with the contributions of operational levels of management in policy making.

Together with Michael Radnor and David Tansik, Michael White suggests that the future of policy science might be viewed in terms of its *diffusion, dispersion,* and *differentiation.*[37] By diffusion White means the spread of policy science within peer-group organizations and institutions, while dispersion refers to the dissemination of principles and techniques of policy science among organizations with differing levels of sophistication in their application. The projected trend of differentiation is somewhat disconcerting, since this phenomenon has contributed significantly to the failure of management science to fulfill its initial potential as a set of unifying techniques for improved decision making.

From Theory to Practice

Any recognition of the potentialities of a thoroughgoing set of policy sciences pales amid the accomplishments and the utility of the management sciences. The issue thus becomes one of moving from a basis of solid accomplishments into a realm of further contributions. Or, in the words of Yehezkel Dror, "enhancement steps" need to be developed that will facilitate a transition from management science to policy science.[38]

Enhancement Steps

To build on the accomplishments of policy analysis and evaluation toward a policy science or sciences, it is necessary to contruct a conceptual set that expresses the main dimensions of policy analysis, its methodology for dealing with policy problems, and its main modes for developing preferable policy alternatives. As a starting point, Dror has identified five fundamental concepts—megapolicies, value sensitivity, operational code assumptions, political feasibility, and policy analysis networks.[39]

Megapolicies are "master" policies that determine the basic assumptions and main guidelines to be followed in the development of more specific policies. Megapolicies may: (1) involve pure or mixed strategies; (2) be incremental or innovative; (3) focus on high- or low-risk situations; (4) involve comprehensive approaches or seek breakthroughs at specific points in the system (what Dror calls the "shock dimensions"); (5) be adopted by sequential decisions or worked out in advance as an extended strategy; (6) involve concrete goals or define future options; (7) set "approach" or "avoidance" goals, that is, positive goals to be achieved or situations to be avoided; and (8) evidence various time preferences that go beyond the traditional assumptions of positive interest rates and discounting of the future.

To overcome the weaknesses of management science, and of some contemporary applications of policy analysis and evaluation, policy science must include both advanced methodologies for handling value issues and substantive inputs from applied ethics and political philosophy. While Dror suggests *value-sensitivity testing* as a technique for handling value issues, other approaches include early involvement of the public in decision making (as discussed previously) and techniques for reducing the level of bias in policy-analysis processes (for example, the use of multi-iteration Delphi techniques). These latter techniques will be discussed further in chapter 7.

The notion of *operational code assumptions* also addresses the issue of decision biases. This approach offers mechanisms by which the behavior of various actors in policy-decision situations can be simulated and predicted. Applications of such techniques have been somewhat limited.[40] In the development of a policy science, however, these techniques require greater sophistication, especially in terms of the basic assumptions on which such operational codes are formulated and applied. Built-in biases, stereotyping of responses, and other shortcomings of these techniques must be eliminated; and a wider range of alternative explanations of actual organizational behavior must be identified.

Policy analysis is particularly concerned with prediction of the political feasibility of specific policy alternatives. However, current efforts to determine the readiness of systems to adopt policies and programs often are based on too narrowly defined constraints and may ignore the capacity of human efforts ". . . to overcome apparently insurmountable barriers and to achieve not only the improbable but the apparently impossible."[41] Estimates of political feasibility are provisional and sometimes must be taken as a challenge rather than accepted as an absolute constraint. In formulating the basis for systemic planning, Catanese and Steiss conclude that:

> The problem with contemporary planning practice is that goals and objectives tend to be a "mixed bag" of varying performance levels. Minimum standards of service, maximum community aspirations, optimal conditions, and utopian goals are all lumped together. If these goals, standards, objectives, aspirations, and so forth could be more rigorously stated so that it would become clear as to the level of generality or specificity attached to them, it would provide a more meaningful basis for alternative evaluation.[42]

Catanese and Steiss recommend the determination of goals and objectives at various levels—maximal, minimal, optimal, and normative—and the formulation of four distinct plans reflecting these four levels. A normative plan embraces goals and objectives that may lie outside the currently defined parameters of political feasibility. In implementing such a plan the focus would be on the adjustment of these parameters rather than on merely accepting these constraints as givens. A maximal plan seeks to identify certain "key levers"— problems and opportunities to which resources can be applied to maximize achievement (that is, to resolve problems and capitalize on opportunities). Such a plan is undertaken in full recognition that in the short run, other factors may show relatively little improvement or may even become more dysfunctional. An optimal plan seeks to distribute resources more or less equally among all factors so that some improvement will be realized in all areas. A minimal plan is the least effort that must be made to maintain the status quo. It may produce little measurable improvement but is considered unlikely to make the situation worse.

In formulating public goals and objectives as part of the policy-analysis process, comprehensiveness becomes a primary concern. It is imperative to take into account the possible goals of diverse groups and individuals and to deal with all aspects of a given policy area. At the same time, specific safeguards are necessary to minimize the undue influence of personal biases that may influence goal statements by the analysts. In the absence of commensurate quantitative statements commonly found in systems analysis and operations research, however, policy analysts frequently encounter difficulties in their efforts to present objective, coherent, and meaningful studies of discrete policy issues.

What is needed, therefore, is a concise conceptual framework that can incorporate mechanisms for clear identification of existing or potential areas of value conflict, as well as an explicit articulation of the various alternative assumptions and uncertainties. Dror suggests that such a framework can be provided by a *policy analysis network,* which he defines as "... a morphological breakdown of a policy issue into a set of interrelated subissues in a form conducive to a decision-making program.[43] Steiss suggests a similar set of tools for the identification and analysis of value conflicts through what he calls the *multidimensional goal matrix* and *multiple policy matrix.*[44] The purpose of the goal matrix is to identify subsets of opposing interests by stating goals in more precise and action-oriented terms. The policy matrix then arrays alternative responses on a continuum of means, ranging from long-range, general, and educational objectives to more immediate, specific, action-oriented programs. Explicit tradeoffs among conflicting goals are identified in policy or program terms.

A particularly valuable aspect of these approaches is their attention to the interaction and potential conflicts among goals and objectives, as well as the impact that fulfillment of one goal may have on the possibility of fulfilling others. Such analyses should provide a full explication of assumptions, value and goal elements, uncertainties, predictions, and program methods. Moreover, multiple policy alternatives should be fully examined and the main interconnections with other issues and systems identified. Such analyses should remain open-ended to permit a search for additional alternatives and a possible redefinition of the problems and issues.

Quis Custodiet Ipsos Custodes?

Ultimately, the emergence of a policy science or sciences depends not only on the policy analyst's better understanding of the system, but also on the system's better understanding of the policy analyst. Public policies and programs have been analyzed for centuries, usually without noticeable impact, even when the analytical techniques were sound and the resulting recommendations well-founded. To lead to action, suggestions for improvement must not only reach the right people but must also gain their attention. Even then there is a danger that the recommendations will be neutralized by adjustments elsewhere in the system before their influence can be felt.

The concepts of policy analysis and evaluation appear to have gained the attention of enough public officials to be considered important additions to the repertoire of public administration. To be effective, however, policy analysis and evaluation must become integral to the policy-making process at all levels of government.

Our democratic, representative form of government does not make it easy for policy makers to take advantage of analysis in making political and social decisions. Although public officials may appreciate the advantages of an analytical approach, they also must face the realities of politics. Even if they themselves are not politicians, they depend on politicians. If politicians fail to produce (or at least appear to produce) what their constituents demand, their time in office may be short. Decisions, therefore, often depend more on what is politically feasible than on what is analytically sound.

It has been suggested that a primary purpose of introducing analysis into the public policy arena is to eliminate politics from decision making. If this is so, such efforts are not only doomed from the outset, but are actually undesirable. "To try to eliminate politics and bargaining from public decision making in a nation that guards its freedom from authority is not only impractical but unappealing. Impractical because no policy decision can be based on analysis alone, divorced from consideration of political values; unappealing because it would imply a surrender of authority to analysts."[45] Thus the question: *"Quis custodiet ipsos custodes?"* Who shall guard the guards themselves?

This chapter has been an examination of the emerging concepts of policy analysis and evaluation in an effort to explore the roots and the first few feet of the policy science "beanstalk." It remains to be seen whether this stalk will become strong enough to bear the weight of those who wish to climb above the present limitations of policy analysis techniques to the realm of a science of policy making. Meanwhile, there should be concerted efforts to strengthen the gains achieved to date, to support and maintain policy-analysis capabilities where they exist, to increase staff capacities for analysis through recruitment and education programs, and to develop a further appreciation among policy makers of what analysis can and cannot do.

Notes

1. Aaron Wildavsky, "Rescuing Policy Analysis from PPBS," *Public Administration Review* 29(March-April 1969):189.

2. Robert E. Lane, "Integration of Political Science and Other Social Sciences Through Policy Analysis," in *Integration of the Social Sciences Through Policy Analysis,* ed. James C. Charlesworth (Philadelphia, Pa.: American Academy of Political and Social Science, 1972), p. 71.

3. Kenneth L. Kraemer, *Policy Analysis in Local Government: A Systems Approach to Decision Making* (Washington, D.C.: International City Management Association, 1973), p. 21.

4. E.S. Quade, *Analysis for Public Decisions* (New York: American Elsevier Publishing Company, 1975), p. 4.

5. Yehezkel Dror, "Policy Analysts: A New Professional Role in Government Service," *Public Administration Review* 27(September 1967):200–201.

6. Yehezkel Dror, "General Policy Science," in *Policy Studies in America and Elsewhere,* ed. Stuart S. Nagel (Lexington, Mass.: Lexington Books, D.C. Heath and Company, 1975), p. 3.

7. Ira Sharkansky, "The Political Scientists and Policy Analysis," in *Policy Analysis in Political Science,* ed. Ira Sharkansky (Chicago, Ill.: Markham Publishing Company, 1970), p. 1.

8. C. Easton Rothwell, foreword to *The Policy Sciences: Recent Developments in Scope and Method,* ed. Daniel Lerner and Harold D. Lasswell (Stanford, Calif.: Stanford University Press, 1951), p. ix.

9. Note a similar definition by Austin Ranney, "The Study of Policy Content: A Framework for Choice," in *Political Science and Public Policy,* ed. Austin Ranney (Chicago, Ill.: Markham Publishing Company, 1968), p. 7.

10. David Nachmias, *Public Policy Evaluation* (New York: St. Martin's Press, 1979), p. 5.

11. Joseph S. Wholey et al., *Federal Evaluation Policy: Analyzing the Effects of Public Programs* (Washington, D.C.: The Urban Institute, 1970), p. 1.

12. Quade, *Analysis for Public Decisions,* p. 225.

13. U.S. General Accounting Office, *Standards for Audit of Governmental Organizations, Programs, Activities, and Functions* (Washington, D.C.: U.S. Government Printing Office, 1972), p. 2.

14. Joseph S. Wholey, "What Can We Actually Get from Program Evaluation?" *Policy Sciences* 3, 3(1972):361–369.

15. Ibid., p. 362.

16. Quade, *Analysis for Public Decisions,* p. 235.

17. Michael Radnor, "Management Science and Policy Science: Transition or Integration?" in *Management and Policy Science in American Government,* ed. Michael J. White et al. (Lexington, Mass.: Lexington Books, D.C. Heath and Company, 1975), p. 301.

18. E.H. Bowman, "Consistency and Optimality in Managerial Decision Making," *Management Science* 9(January 1963):310–321.

19. R.E. Bellman and L.A. Zadeh, "Decision Making in a Fuzzy Environment," *Management Science* 17(December 1970):141.

20. Raymond A. Bauer, ed., *Social Indicators* (Cambridge, Mass.: MIT Press, 1967).

21. Otis Dudley Duncan, *Toward Social Reporting: Next Steps* (New York: Russell Sage Foundation, 1969); Albert D. Biderman and Elizabeth T. Crawford, eds., *Social Role of the Social Sciences* (New York: John Wiley and Sons, 1969); Bertram M. Gross, "The State of the Nation: Social Systems Accounting," in Bauer, *Social Indicators,* pp. 154–271.

22. R. Likert, "The Dual Function of Statistics," *Journal of the American Statistical Association* 55(1960):1–7.

23. *Singular generalizations* apply to limited types of behavior or events at a given time and place. *Partial theories* relate to some aspects of behavior in a system, less than the whole but greater than a singular or isolated fragment, which experience or intuition suggests are related in a significant manner. For a further discussion of partial and general theory, with particular reference to urban society, see Alan Walter Steiss, *Urban Systems Dynamics* (Lexington, Mass.: Lexington Books, D.C. Heath and Company, 1974).

24. Bauer, *Social Indicators,* p. 2.

25. Norbert Wiener, *The Human Use of Human Beings* (New York: Doubleday Anchor Books, 1954), p. 17.

26. Alex Bavelas and Dermot Barrett, "An Experimental Approach to Organization Communication," *Personnel* 27(1951): 368.

27. Norbert Wiener, cited in Karl W. Deutsch, *The Nerves of Government* (New York: The Free Press of Glencoe, 1963), p. 77.

28. The concept of policy sciences was first proposed in 1951 by Lasswell in *The Policy Sciences: Recent Developments in Scope and Methods,* ed. Daniel Lerner and Harold D. Lasswell (Stanford, Calif.: Stanford University Press, 1951).

29. For a further discussion of this point, see Vincent Ostrom and Philip Sabetti, "Theory of Public Policy," in Nagel, *Policy Studies in America,* pp. 37–49.

30. Irving L. Horowitz and James E. Katz, *Social Science and Public Policy in the United States* (New York: Praeger, 1975), pp. 3–4.

31. Harold D. Lasswell, *A Pre-View of Policy Sciences* (New York: American Elsevier Publishing Company, 1971), p. 1.

32. Ibid., p. 1.

33. Radnor, "Management Science and Policy Science," p. 299.

34. Ibid., p. 302.

35. Ibid., p. 303.

36. Ibid., p. 304.

37. Michael J. White, "Problems and Prospects for Management Science and Policy Science," in *Management and Policy Science in American Government,* ed. Michael Radnor, Michael J. White, and David Tansik (Lexington, Mass.: Lexington Books, D.C. Heath Company, 1975), pp. 13–15.

38. Dror, "General Policy Science," p. 279.

39. Ibid., pp. 280–281.

40. Alexander George, "The Operational Code: A Neglected Approach to the Study of Political Leaders and Decisionmaking," *International Studies Quarterly* 13(June 1969):190–222.

41. Dror, "General Policy Science," p. 278.

42. Anthony J. Catanese and Alan Walter Steiss, *Systemic Planning: Theory and Application* (Lexington, Mass.: Lexington Books, D.C. Heath and Company, 1970), p. 37.

43. Dror, "General Policy Science," p. 279.

44. Alan Walter Steiss, *Public Budgeting and Management* (Lexington, Mass.: Lexington Books, D.C. Heath and Company, 1972), chapter 9.

45. Quade, *Analysis for Public Decisions,* p. 271.

Systems Thinking and the Foundations of Performance Administration

In the past several decades, there have been rapid scientific advances in the development of new techniques of analysis and tools for complex problem solving. New professions and academic disciplines—including the overlapping and complementary fields of communications engineering, systems engineering, computer science, information theory, cybernetics, operations research, systems analysis, and management science—emerged as byproducts of World War II and the subsequent defense and space programs. These disciplines have found widespread application in business, industry, and the military. Fundamental to all these fields is another intellectual theme that is particularly applicable to a more complete understanding of complex operations and processes of public policy making. That theme is *general systems theory*.

The Systems Concept

The idea of general systems is vital to performance administration, both as a way of looking at complex phenomena and as a foundation for useful methodologies. As a cognitive window on reality, systems thinking attempts to expand one's vision, directing attention toward a more comprehensive overview of the problems. Such an overview focuses not only on root causes, but also on the complex interrelationships that constrain the development of effective solutions. In this era of growing quality-of-life concerns, such as social and environmental concerns, administrators can ill afford to rely on limited or closed-systems perspectives. A more systemic outlook is a necessary, although not sufficient condition of performance administration.

Systems Perspectives

General systems theory is not so much a rigorous explanatory theory as a way of isolating certain important aspects of reality and relationships among these components. It is a shorthand way of looking at the world that also provides a framework within which apparently distinct sets of phenomena can be united. Systems thinking is a wholistic approach that seeks to discover least common denominators such as net energy or quality of life that can facilitate necessary tradeoffs between natural and manmade systems.

These underpinnings often have been lost in the various applications of systems theory. Systems thinking as a basic approach has taken diverse and sometimes counterproductive paths. In his survey of the general systems literature of the early 1960s, Young found no less than nineteen distinct conceptual interpretations.[1] Some common perspectives include: (1) a conceptual framework that is common to several academic disciplines and/or intellectual processes; (2) a method of scientific and systematic problem solving; (3) a theory of complex organizations; (4) a tool for designing and improving information and/or management structures; and (5) a means for the analysis and design of complex servomechanisms.

The systems concept presented in this discussion, therefore, is somewhat stipulative. Moreover, it is essential to point out that the view of systems presented here is fairly generic and thus not readily reducible to any particular application of systems thinking, such as cost-benefit analysis or any other currently fashionable technique of systems analysis. However, an understanding of a systems perspective such as outlined herein is necessary for effective application of any of these analytical techniques.

A Basic Process Model

A system can be defined as any physical or conceptual (real or cognitive) entity composed of interrelated parts. This widely held definition is so broad that it includes virtually any set of interdependent activities, events, or things. A computer, for example, is a system composed of interrelated parts and functions such as data-receiving and data-emission elements, control elements, a memory bank, and a processor. An automobile engine is a system that uses several resource inputs (air, gasoline, oil, and electricity); has a structure composed of pistons, valves, sparkplugs, a crankshaft, and so forth; and has certain measurable performance outputs. A community is a system composed of many structural units—primary groups, economic units, government, religious and educational institutions, and so forth—that interact according to certain rules of conduct—(laws, norms, mores, contractual agreements, and so forth—) in order to achieve certain basic objectives or functions, that is, to meet certain human needs and wants.

These diverse examples of systems have several characteristics in common. The fundamental components of the general systems model are identified diagrammatically in figure 5–1. Generally speaking, any system can be seen as a conversion mechanism, through which certain inputs are converted into outputs. This conversion mechanism operates through a series of definable processes or sets of procedures (the dynamic aspects of a system), and every system has an identifiable structure (an arrangement of interrelated component parts) that describes how these processes are organized, both in a

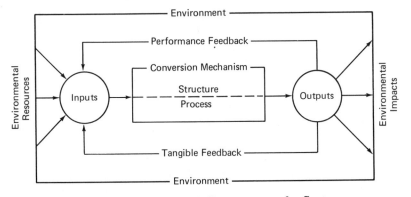

Figure 5–1. Fundamental Components of a System

formal, hierarchical sense and in an informal sense. If it is a material system, it maintains a short-term steady state; that is, the system reacts to changes in the environment in whatever way necessary to maintain its identity and stability.

Systems operate in a larger environment or as subsystems of some larger system, and they require certain resource inputs from other systems in this environment. Initially, these environmental inputs are governed by the availability of certain resources— technology, money, personnel, information, and so forth. Processes within the conversion mechanism act on the resources to produce a set of outputs. These outputs, in turn, are related to the goals and objectives of the system—what the system is designed to do. Moreover, outputs may have significant impacts on other systems in the broader environment. System outputs can take two forms: (1) tangible products (goods and services), and (2) a level of performance. Both aspects have feed back in the system as a whole and provide new inputs in subsequent cycles. Tangible outputs determine, in part, the availability of resources for the next cycle. Performance level (how well the system has functioned) provides some indication of the need for adjustments in processes or structure in order to enhance performance.

From Closed to Open Systems

From the foregoing there would seem to be little that is new about general systems theory or the more systematic approaches to problem solving derived from this theoretical framework. Systems have long been studied in the natural sciences—physics, chemistry, and biology. In fact, systems thinking is the foundation of the "hard" sciences.

Until recently, however, the approaches employed in the natural sciences have focused on parts and processes operating in closed systems, that is, systems studied in isolation from their larger environment. Closed systems have been defined as: (1) systems in which "there is no import or export of energies in any of its forms such as information"[2] and (2) systems "characterized by a lack of matter exchange with their environment."[3] Closed systems involve deterministic interactions; that is, they often represent one-to-one correspondence between the set of initial states and the set of final states.

Since it is isolated from the environment, a closed system or state-determined system (a special type of closed system) is more easily defined in mathematical terms. The state of such a system can be described by clearly perceived variables, and an equation connecting these variables constitutes a static theory of that system. For example, if a quantity of gas is confined in a container, mechanically and thermally isolated from its environment, then eventually the temperature and pressure inside the container will become uniform. The gas will constitute a system in equilibrium, that is, a system persisting in a single state in which there is a predictable balance between inputs and outputs. The state of this system can be described completely by three quantities: volume, pressure, and temperature. For a given gas, these three quantities are connected by a characteristic equation such that if two of the quantities are known, the third can be inferred.

A static theory says very little about how the system will respond if its equilibrium is disrupted; it merely posits equilibrium as a juncture of key variables. A dynamic theory, on the other hand, deals with successive states or transactions of the system.

Many systems cannot be separated from their environment in this abstract, controlled fashion; they may interact continuously with other systems in their environment and experience processes that are reversible. For example, living organisms and their organizations survive in a continuous inflow and outflow with their environment in which various components are built up and broken down. Such systems never exist in a state of equilibrium, in the chemical or thermodynamic sense, but are maintained in a so-called *steady state.* Such systems seek stability rather than equilibrium. A system that receives inputs from the environment and/or acts on the environment through outputs is called an *open system.* The essential problem has been to develop a mode of analysis that would permit the organization of relations resulting from the dynamic interaction of the functional and structural aspects of an open system and of the system as a whole with its larger environment.

Systems and the Unification of Science

One of the most important contributions of general systems theory is that it offers a single vocabulary and a unified set of concepts suitable for representing diverse types of systems. General systems theory reveals a number of interesting and suggestive parallels between different disciplines and provides a common language that can be used to make discoveries in one field more useful to other disciplines. It also offers a method for scientific investigations of complex systems that often defy analysis unless they are subdivided into simpler component parts. For understanding relatively simple systems, systems techniques may provide no obvious advantages over those long in use. It is primarily in the analysis of more complex systems that the methods of general systems theory reveal their full potential.

Although general systems theory has yet to realize its fullest potential—the unity of science—it does provide an atmosphere that promotes the quest for commonalities. The unity of science can take many paths; Peter Caws had identified three major possibilities: (1) unity as a reduction to a common basis; (2) unity as a synthesis into a common system; and (3) unity as the construction of an encyclopedia.[4]

Unity as reductionism (or the development of a single descriptive language or a single set of scientific laws) has had relatively little success, because of its obvious tendency toward oversimplification. However, such theorists as Howard T. Odum, with his concept of "net energy," have provided useful common denominators for understanding complex interactions. As Odum correctly points out, energy in its various forms is the most fundamental ingredient of both natural and human systems.[5]

Unity as synthesis has been a more powerful theme in the development of systematic observations. This concept holds that a common set of scientific inquiries exists that can be applied to a number of unique phenomena. The synthetic concept also follows closely behind the reductionist observations in attempting to develop symbiotic relationships among heretofore unique phenomena. Critics contend that this trend, and, for that matter, all attempts at general systems theories, lead to isomorphic distortions—a failure of the model to represent reality, particularly social reality.[6]

This point is well taken; however, while it may be important to maintain a difference-of-kind distinction between social and physical systems at the phenomenological level, it is considerably less fruitful to demand such a distinction at the level of epistemology. If the basic approach is sufficiently elementary, it may have a range of applications of various degrees of complexity. Operations-research techniques are especially prone to iso-morphic distortions. And yet, if requisite conditions and/or exogenous factors are described accurately, these techniques can be applied to a number of economic and social as well as physical phenomena.

Encyclopedic unity entails the classification and comparison, where applicable, of observations from unique disciplines. Over the years, this approach has prevailed in general systems theory. Boulding describes general systems as "the skeleton of science." Recognizing that an optimum degree of theoretical generality seldom is achieved in any particular science, Boulding points out that general systems seeks a theory of "practically everything" and that "all we can say about practically everything is almost nothing."[7]

Nevertheless, Boulding and others have continued to search for something additional to say, and in so doing have kept alive the dream of a unity of science.

Policy-Making Systems

Various social and political analysts have adopted, wholly or partially, the basic concepts of the general systems model as a descriptive framework for public-policy research. The notion of systems that guides performance administration, however, is essentially prescriptive. Unlike various exploratory efforts at applying systems theory to policy processes, no claims of descriptive accuracy are made or required here. It is hoped that it will be shown that the utility of systems thinking does not rely on empirical verification of the various grandiose theoretical exercises of the past several decades. Nonetheless, since these theory-building efforts provide clues to policy improvement, some of the major contributions of these efforts will be discussed in this section.

Environment, Stress, and Ultrastability

The systematic study of policy-making systems essentially has involved attempts to distinguish among *policy inputs* (demands, available resources, constituency support, and so forth), the *policy-making process* (that is, the conversion mechanism), *policy outputs* (for example, service levels, regulations, and controls which are affected by or arise from the actions of government), and *policy impacts* (the effects that public services have on a population and the responses of the public to policy outputs). In some cases, the *environment* also is discussed. As Sharkansky has observed: "Several features of the economic, social, and political environment of a jurisdiction can influence the kinds of policy decisions which officials make, and they can influence the translation of policy into outputs and impacts."[8] The environment is a source of many influences that create and shape the conditions under which the policy-making system must operate. This environment may also be the principal source of stress on the system.

The concept of *disturbance* has been adopted by Easton as a means of identifying those influences from the total environment which act upon the policy-making system so that it is different after the stimulus from what it was before.[9] In systems terms, a disturbance may be defined as any event or occurrence that threatens to drive a system outside the set of states that defines its region of stability. All systems, to maintain stability, must have the capacity to respond to environmental disturbances that impinge on them. These responses, when coupled with the system, block the disturbance so that the system remains within its stable region. This response mechanism is called a *regulator,* and its essential role is to maintain stability—to keep the system within a desired stable set of states. In systems terms, the regulator must be capable of reducing the level of entropy or disorganization within the system that is brought about by a disturbance.

Not all disturbances are dysfunctional; some may favor the persistence of the system by amplifying some of its positive aspects. Other disturbances may be neutral.

Stress occurs when external or internal disturbances push the system beyond its capacity for effective response. Something happens in the environment—for example, widespread disorganization in the society and disaffection from the prevailing political system arising from a severe economic crisis. In such a crisis, public authorities may consistently be unable to make decisions, or may make decisions that are no longer accepted as binding by a significant portion of the society. Thus, authoritative allocations of values become impossible, and the society may well collapse for lack of a political system that can fulfill these vital functions.

This is an extreme example, in which stress leads to the eventual demise of the political system. It must be recognized that the stress-producing disturbances often do not disrupt the system completely. Stress is present, but the system persists in some form. Even in a severe crisis, it may be possible for public officials to make some decisions and to attain enough support for these decisions to resolve some of the problems, at least temporarily.

The fuel shortages of the late 1970s provide a graphic example of this type of stress. Odd/even sales, gas rationing, shifts in fuel allocations, efforts to encourage oil companies to produce more gasoline and heating oil, and other minor adjustments temporarily served to deflect the potentially debilitating stress on the system. The longer-term implications of this stress remain to be seen, however. In systems terminology, these stress reductions involve the Law of Requisite Variety, that is, the selection of an appropriate set of regulators to offset an identifiable set of disturbances. These regulators are the system's defense mechanisms.[10]

Most social institutions or subsystems have developed the characteristics of *ultrastability;* that is, they can readily adapt to change with only slight adjustments in their patterns of activity.[11] No system or subsystem can survive environmental disturbances so great as to be considered extirpating. Up to this threshold, however, systems are "machines for survival," and they do indeed survive. It is important to any society, of course, that its social institutions have such solidarity. Although this ultrastability may impede social reforms, it is what gives the prevailing social system its strength. Society would be constantly on the threshold of chaos if its institutions could be toppled under pressure from anarchists or maniacs, or even through the incompetence of the individuals responsible for the operations of the system. Witness the instability of many social institutions after a military coup.

Inputs: Demands and Support

As previously stated, systems operate in a larger environment or as subsystems of some larger system, and they require certain inputs from other subsystems within this environment. In this context, an input can be defined as any event external to a given system that alters, modifies, or affects the system in any way. The concept of input relationships among systems in the same environment implies that such systems are linked in some fashion so that outputs of one system may become inputs of another.

This broad definition of inputs includes virtually every parametric event or condition in the system's environment. As a more manageable concept for policy-analysis purposes, inputs may be seen as *demands* and *supports* (commitments of resources) by individuals, groups, or the community as a whole that are intended to influence or alter public policy. A demand has been defined by Easton as: "... an expressed opinion that an authoritative allocation with regard to a particular subject matter should or should not be made by those responsible for doing so."[12] A demand does not necessarily reflect the value preferences of the demand maker. In fact, demands may be used to conceal true preferences, as when a program is promoted for the purpose of generating support for some other, unexpressed course of action. A example of this phenomenon is the adoption by a suburban community of zoning regulations or architectural controls. The expressed motive may be something like "maintenance and promotion of sound principles of orderly community development;" the real motive is more likely to be maintenance of high property values, the exclusion of young families with children, or to keep out other "undesirables."

In a relatively simple social system such as a small town the inputs to policy making may be informal and interpersonal.[13] The only political resources required are friendship, access, and time. In larger systems, the input process may be highly impersonal and institutional. Political parties, elections, interest groups, and even mass demonstrations may dominate the process.

Expressed demands are not the only demand inputs to the policy-making process. Demands may arise from dysfunctional conditions in a given situation without taking the form of expressed opinions. Such conditions may be interpreted from within the system as constituting demand inputs, even though in the larger environment they have not been identified or verbalized as such.

A demand may be narrow, specific, and relatively simple; or it may be general, vague, and complex. Demands may be expressed as specific grievances associated with a particular situation; or they may be generalized— pleas for better government, for more vigorous fiscal policies, for the alleviation of poverty and social injustices, and so forth. Such generalized demands seldom include proposals for specific courses of action, although they may embody ill-defined, all-encompassing programs. Expressed demands may be directed toward specific individuals or groups in the policy-making system, or may be ubiquitously oriented. However, every expressed demand carries with it a set of expectations concerning the responses that should come from the system.

Unexpressed demands also arise from a variety of sources and assume multifaceted characteristics. As with expressed demands, they are evidence that someone within the policy-making system recognizes the existence of unacceptable conditions. In other words, before demands can gain entry as inputs into the system, they must be sensed as demands.

It is also necessary to distinguish between demands that do not influence policy making (either because they are not recognized as demands or because they are below the system's threshold of tolerance) and those demands that are actually taken into the system and acted upon. Inputs undergo a screening process that determines the actual intakes into the policy-making system.[14] This process filters out demands for which no further action is to be taken at present, as well as those that can be handled through programmed decision mechanisms—regulatory devices that activate some predetermined response. Easton offers important observations concerning the possibility of inputs deriving from internal sources, which he calls "withinputs." These influences on policy making will be discussed more thoroughly in terms of "systems expectations," since they often differ from externally derived inputs.

As with demands, the types of *supports* that serve as inputs to the policy-making system can be divided into two general categories: overt manifestations and covert support. Political analysts refer to various measures of support when they speak of a political leader who has succeeded in winning the approval of a key group, or of a policy that has failed for want of sufficient backing. Such statements imply the existence of indexes by which support can be identified and measured, however imprecise and impressionistic the notion of measurement may be.

Typically, a variety of activities are taken as indicators and/or measures of overt support: the number of persons belonging to an organization, the regularity with which members perform their obligations, contributions to organized political parties, and so forth. Indicators of negative support or opposition, include evidence of open hostility—boycotts, breaches of laws, riots—and expressions of preference for other systems through countercultures, separatist movements, or emigration. Further hard data might be expressed in terms of the ratio of deviance to conformity, the prevalence of violence, the size of dissident movements, the amount of money spent for security, and so forth.

There is a significant measurement problem, however, in constructing a single overall index of support, although many political actors place some reliance on opinion polls. Most of the items listed above refer to past or current supportive activities; it may be necessary to make subjective inferences to determine probable future supportive behavior.

Inside the "Black Box": The Conversion Mechanism

Social institutions have been labelled functional subsystems of the larger social system because they are designed to carry out certain functions necessary to the continued operation of the society or important segments thereof.[15] The components of most functional subsystems are characterized by complex sets of internal relationships. Consequently, occurrences within these subsystems may be unintelligible to an outsider; appropriate credentials are needed to gain admission to the activities within the functional subsystem. This feature of functional subsystems has led to the suggestion that they are esoteric—understood by or meant for only specially instructed or initiated individuals.[16]

Labelling functional subsystems esoteric does not imply that they are closed systems, only that they tend to be self-organizing and self-regulating. Among the inputs to a functional subsystem are the various clientele groups, that is, members of the general public for whom the social institution was designed to serve and to whose demands and supports it must respond. For the most part, however, these clientele groups have little effect on the structure or processes of the functional subsystem. Whatever else happens, the functional subsystem goes on; it is powerfully organized to maintain its own internal stability, thereby ensuring its survival. The operations within the functional subsystems that produce this survival behavior are social mechanisms, including the socialization to a particular belief structure and a complicated set of conventions, norms, values, rules, and regulations that all contribute to the development of systems expectations on the part of insiders.

The conversion mechanism of the policy-making system—its structure and processes—exhibits these esoteric and ultrastable characteristics. To the outside observer, adjustments made by policy-making systems may seem to require few if any alterations in the characteristics for which change is sought—a measure of the extent to which policy-making systems have developed regulatory devices to maintain their ultrastability, devices that go well beyond Lindblom's notion of partisan mutual adjustment.[17]

A further point relates to the expectations of those who participate in the system. An important step in seeking an acceptable policy decision is to make a reconnaissance of these expectations. One of three conditions is likely to exist: (1) the expectations of participants within the system are in accord with the proposed course of action, in which case an acceptable policy has been found; (2) the expectations are ambivalent to the proposed policy; or (3) the expectations are hostile to the proposed policy. In the latter two cases, some means must be devised to divert the hostile attitudes and to engender support for the proposed policy. If no acceptable means are found, internal demands will be heightened, necessitating a further assessment of the proposed policy and the possible selection of new or different courses of action.

This process of modification and compromise is somewhat akin to what has been identified as "accommodating to the power structure." The more neutral notion of *systems expectations* contains explicit recognition of the role of the internal structure of the policy-making system, and provides a basis for analysis that is adaptable to both the power-elite and pluralistic approaches to policy making. The term "expectations" can include all these factors, both internal and external to the system.

Outputs of the Policy-Making Process

The question: "What are the outputs of a policy-making process?" may seem so rudimentary as to negate its asking. Obviously, the outputs of policy making are policies and the program commitments necessary to carry out these policies. However, as Sharkansky has observed,

> Powerful elements in the environment may have a telling influence on outputs. Or different elements of policy may work at cross-purposes to each other. It is therefore necessary to measure outputs independently of policy and test the assumed relationships between them.[18]

Easton has identified two types of policy outputs, authoritative and associated.[19] Authoritative outputs are binding decisions, laws, decrees, regulations, orders, and judicial decisions made by recognized authorities in the policy-making system. Associated outputs—decisions and actions that accompany formal outputs—perform a similar function in creating or alleviating supportive stress on the system but are not binding in the same sense as authoritative declarations. An example of an associated output is an ideological statement, such as an assertion in support of nationalism, that is designed to influence the way in which authoritative statements are received.[20] Such assertions are not binding, but they do play an important role in inducing members of the society to tolerate or accept authoritative outputs more readily. When such assertions take on a more formal character, as in the president's State of the Union message or the inaugural addresses of governors, these associated outputs have clear policy implications. The objective of such messages may be that of explanation and information. Frequently, however, they represent efforts to gain acceptance for subsequent authoritative outputs.

Both authoritative and associated outputs can take two forms: verbal or written statements and performance. As illustrations of the performance mode of associated outputs, Easton suggests the examples of favors granted to selected individuals who support to authoritative outputs and of special benefits that accrue to external participants as a consequence of authoritative outputs.

While the distinctions are somewhat blurred, the important point is that policy outputs are not limited to laws or regulations that represent binding commitments on the part of the political system. To focus only on the traditionally defined examples of policies is to overlook a critical realm.

Impacts and Feedback

To understand fully the implications of outputs, it is necessary to look at the *impacts* or *outcomes* of systemic activities. As Easton explains: ". . . an output is the stone tossed into the pond and its first splash; the outcomes are the ever widening and vanishing pattern of concentric ripples."[21] The consequences—the outcomes—may involve a long chain of causation traceable to the initial outputs. The function of policy evaluation is to discern the consequences or impacts of policy decisions.

The evaluation of impacts provides the *feedback* phase of the systems model. In this sense, feedback involves: (1) the policy output as stimulus, (2) the response to this stimulus by the affected groups (acceptance or rejection, support or opposition, and so on), (3) the information feedback arising from the response and flowing back to the system, and (4) the output reaction—the modification of the initial output as a reaction to the response from the originators of demands and the sources of systems support.

The concept of feedback is central to the general systems model. In its simplest form, feedback is the kind of communication an actor receives from a live audience. If the audience is enthusiastic, the performer will react with similar enthusiasm. There is, in a sense, a closed circuit of communication between the performer and the audience, with a continuous interchange of information. Essential to feedback is the notion that the flow of information has reciprocating effects on behavior. Thus, the term *loop* is frequently used in connection with the concept of feedback. This circular pattern involves a flow of information to some point of action, a flow back to a point of decision with information about the action, and then a return to the point of action with new information and perhaps instructions for modifications. With perfect feedback—a rarity—the desired output is attained by self-regulation; the input is adjusted automatically by the output.

Feedback may be either negative or positive. A classic example of an application of negative feedback is found in James Watt's governor for the steam engine, usually regarded as the first manmade feedback mechanism. Positive feedback is built into the structure of the modern turbojet engine. The greater the output or thrust at the rear of the engine, the greater the speed, leading to greater intake at the front and again to greater output. Input and output chase each other in an endless spiral of positive feedback, and the only method of controlling the process is to limit the fuel supply.

Positive feedback is potentially dangerous and must always be under some form of control. If positive feedback gets out of control, it leads to *runaway,* either toward zero or toward some maximum. Stanley-Jones has observed that a system that is "running away" under the influence of positive feedback has broken free from the monitoring or stabilizing influences of negative feedback and cannot be restored to normal except by active external intervention.[22]

These phenomena can be illustrated through the processes associated with social disorganization, as characterized by Thomas and Znaniecki:

> During periods of social stability this continuous incipient disorganization is continuously neutralized by such activities of the group as reinforce with the help of social sanctions the power of existing rules. The stability of group institutions is thus simply a dynamic equilibrium of processes of *disorganization* and *reorganization*. This equilibrium is disturbed when processes of disorganization can no longer be checked by any attempts to reinforce the existing rules. A period of prevalent disorganization follows, which may lead to a complete dissolution of the group.[23]

One of the first symptoms of social disorganization is a breakdown of harmony among social groups and institutions and the emergence of conflicts among societal mores and norms. Under such conditions, individuals and organizations must choose one set of mores over others in order to control conflict. When the mores of one group are opposed to the standards of another, a disastrous internal breakdown may result, particularly if the leaders of the political system are unable or unwilling to make the difficult decisions needed to restore order. Social disorganization feeds on itself, exhibiting the characteristics of a runaway system influenced by positive feedback. As an example, social analysts cite the prevalence of these characteristics of social disorganization in Germany following World War I. Some analysts have suggested that at the height of the Vietnam controversy the United States was on the threshold of a similar "runaway" crisis.

Social stability can be reestablished only when one set of conflicting interests is subjugated or when other accommodations can be worked out whereby the social organization regains a consistency of objectives. As

Thomas and Znaniecki observe, social disorganization may be countered before it reaches its upper limits ". . . by a new process or reorganization of the decaying organization, but in a production of new schemes of behavior and new institutions better adapted to the changed demands of the group; we call this production of new schemes and institutions social reconstruction."[24]

While this discussion of social disorganization has tended to focus on society as a whole, it should be evident that the phenomenon of runaway positive feedback is also found in individual social groups and institutions. In any system, the elements of control or self-regulation must be accomplished through the mechanism of feedback. The behavior of the system may be modified on the basis of information about actual performance as measured against established criteria—goals and objectives—basic to the well-being of the system. If these criteria are ill-defined, or if the feedback is unclear, mixed, or misunderstood, then the system may operate erratically, vacillating between negative and positive feedback. For this reason, it is critical that goals and objectives be clearly defined and that appropriate mechanisms exist to monitor system performance so that feedback about programs and policies can be properly interpreted.

Contributions of the General Systems Model

General systems theory offers a unified set of concepts that can be applied to many different types of systems. General systems theory reveals a number of suggestive parallels among various disciplines and provides a common vocabulary through which discoveries in one field can be readily transferred to other disciplines. It also offers a method for the investigation of complex systems that often defy analysis unless they are subdivided into simpler component parts. General systems theory rejects the vague intuitions that arise from mechanistic or organismic analogies from simple systems; the attempt, instead, is to build a more rigorous discipline. In this process, general systems theory not only provides generalized strategies applicable to a variety of special cases, but also gives important insights into the potential for broader applications.

As we will attempt to demonstrate in the following chapters, the general systems model provides a useful focus for the organization of various conceptual and analytical techniques that provide the basis for performance administration. Adoption of such systems thinking will not guarantee the transformation of policy analysis and administration from an art to a science. However, such a frame of reference should provide a more comprehensive understanding of the potential applications of the strategies and techniques of performance administration.

Notes

1. O.R. Young, "A Survey of General Systems Theory," in *General Systems,* ed. Ludwig von Bertalanffy and Anatol Rapoport (Ann Arbor, Mich. Society for General Systems Research, 1964), p. 63.

2. A.D. Hall and R.E. Fagen, "Definition of System," in *Modern Systems Research for the Behavioral Scientist,* ed. Walter Buckley (Chicago, Ill.: Aldine Publishing Company, 1968), p. 86.

3. N. Botnavinc, "The Wholeness of Living Systems and Some Biological Problems," in von Bertalanffy and Rapoport, *General Systems,* p. 93.

4. Peter Caws, "Science and Systems: On the Unity and the Diversity of Scientific Theory," *General Systems,* vol. 13 (Ann Arbor, Mich.: Society for General Systems Research, 1968), pp. 3–12.

5. Howard T. Odum and Elisabeth Odum, *Energy Basis for Man and Nature* (New York: McGraw-Hill Book Company, 1976).

6. Note, for example, David Berlinski's entertaining criticism of applied systems in *On Systems Analysis* (Cambridge, Mass.: MIT Press, 1977).

7. Kenneth E. Boulding, "General Systems Theroy—The Skeleton of Science," *Management Science* 2(1956); 197–208.

8. Ira Sharkansky, *Policy Analysis in Political Science* (Chicago, Ill.: Markham Publishing Company, 1970), p. 66.

9. David A. Easton, *A Systems Analysis of Political Life* (New York: John Wiley and Sons, 1965), p. 22. This book and Easton's prior work, *A Framework for Political Analysis,* provide the most comprehensive and controversial "systems model" for political analysis.

10. This principle is developed by Ross Ashby in *An Introduction to Cybernetics* (New York: John Wiley and Sons, 1963). For examples of this concept in reference to urban problems, see Alan Walter Steiss, *Models for the Analysis and Planning of Urban Systems* (Lexington, Mass.: Lexington Books, D.C. Heath and Company, 1974), chaps. 2 and 10.

11. See Stafford Beer, "The Cybernetic Cytoblast: Management Itself," *Progress in Cybernetics,* vol. 1 (London: Gordon and Breach Science Publishers, 1970), p. 71.

12. Easton, *A Systems Analysis of Political Life,* p. 38.

13. Arthur Vidich and Joseph Bensman, *Small Town in Mass Society* (Princeton, N.J.: Princeton University Press, 1958).

14. Anthony J. Catanese and Alan Walter Steiss, *Systemic Planning: Theory and Application* (Lexington, Mass.: Lexington Books, D.C. Heath and Company, 1970), pp. 307–309.

15. For a further elaboration, see Steiss, *Analysis and Planning of Urban Systems,* chap. 9.

16. Beer, "The Cybernetic Cytoblast," p. 72.

17. Charles E. Lindblom, *The Intelligence of Democracy: Decision Making through Mutual Adjustment* (New York: The Free Press, 1965), p.3.

18. Sharkansky, *Policy Analysis in Political Science,* p. 65.

19. Easton, *A Systems Analysis of Political Life,* pp. 352–353.

20. Ibid., p. 358.

21. Ibid., p. 352.

22. D. Stanley-Jones, "The Role of Positive Feedback," *Progress in Cybernetics,* vol. 1 (London: Gordon and Breach Science Publishers, 1970), p. 251.

23. William I. Thomas and Florian Znaniecki, *The Polish Peasant in Europe and America,* vol. 4 (Boston: Richard G. Badger, 1918), pp. 3–4.

24. Ibid., p. 4.

Systems Thinking and Policy Enhancement: from Description to Prescription

The literature of political science and public administration is largely descriptive in tone. However, such basic concepts as systems persistence, input-output relations, regulatory mechanisms, and feedback imply a basis for policy enhancement. The real thrust of systems thinking, therefore, is prescriptive. The general systems model facilitates a more comprehensive yet elemental perspective on the complex and manifold processes of policy and decision making. This shift from descriptive to prescriptive applications is a major line of demarcation between political science and policy analysis. The border, however, is conspicuously unguarded.

Policy Making as a Multistage Process

Early applications of systems thinking to sociopolitical phenomena, although innovative and interesting, were merely elaborate apologies for the status quo—case studies of systemic stability.[1] As a result, these case studies provide relatively few insights into policy or decision maing as a *process.*

Those who seek to improve public policies and decisions must understand the system as an integrated *multistage process.* As Roscoe Martin and his colleagues conclude in their studies of public policy:

> . . . decisions do not eventuate from single, individual choices but from a flow of choices. . . . A series of acts are involved in a decision to take or not to take a particular public action. It will prove useful to examine the process. . . .[2]

Simon and March suggest a three-stage process, beginning with a *disaggregation* of the problem to permit the solution of the parts; this is followed by a *search stage,* which may be physical, perceptual, or cognitive; and finally by a *screening stage,* in which the items identified in the search stage are examined to see if they qualify as possible solutions or components of solutions to the problem at hand.[3] Simon and March acknowledge that the elementary components of policy and decision making are characterized by a good deal of randomness and that the sequence of these steps is somewhat arbitrary. Running through the policy- and decision-making process, however, are two elements that give it structure and permit it to yield a relatively well-organized product. These elements are: (1) the broad procedural programs recognizable in most problem-solving situations; and (2) the substantive programs, that is, the structuring of the process that reflects the structure of the problem.

Understanding Policy Inputs

As a rule, the policy process becomes more orderly and identifiable at the stage in which alternative solutions are formulated and considered. Nevertheless, the earlier stages, in which the problem is first defined and the demands for policy decisions are identified and categorized, require equally systematic approaches. As Northrup so aptly pointed out: "One may have the most rigorous of methods during the later stages of investigation but if a false or superficial beginning has been made, rigor later on will never retrieve the situation."[4] Therefore, in considering policy making as a multistage process, it is necessary to begin before the stage at which a decision-demanding situation exists.

A system under study may be set apart from its broader environment, but many aspects of this environment nevertheless have important impacts on the system. They enter the system as inputs and, as noted in chapter 5, take the form of demands and supports. Before demands can enter the system, however, someone within the system must recognize the conditions giving rise to the demands as being out of phase with acceptable conditions with the desired state of the system.

It is this perception of a demand that sets the policy-making process in motion. Very often, this perception is merely a sense of uncertainty or doubt that exists because the constituent elements of a segment of the broader environment are unsettled or not unified. As Dewey has observed: ". . . it is the very nature of the indeterminate situation which evokes inquiry to be questionable . . . to be uncertain, unsettled, disturbed."[5]

This concept of uncertainty is a positive one, meaning more than a mere subjective sense of absence or deprivation. The uncertainty that exists stems from a particular uncertain objective situation.[6] Objective observations of the situation do not coincide with the definition of what should be, a concept that may be either subjectively or objectively defined.

Examining this stage of uncertainty in terms of an individual's response to an indeterminate situation, Blanshard has suggested that the immediate stimulus to reflection or thought is the appearance of "[a]n island . . . demanding union with the mainland; we must bridge the gap, but are at a loss how to do it; tension arises, and from that tension, reflection."[7] Here again the concept of *stress* or tension is suggested as a motivating force in decision making, provoking action to return the system to a steady state in which stresses and tensions can be resolved, at least temporarily.

In psychological terms, the gap between the "island" and the "mainland" of thought is a gap in the conceptual structure of an individual or individuals, brought about by awareness of an uncertain situation. The gap is alien to the present conceptual framework; therefore, the policy- or decision-making process is initiated to seek a resolution of these conditions.

Administrative personnel often are called on to appraise various aspects of the system and to identify any elements in the broader environment that may be potential disturbances to this system. This role is analogous to that of a regulator that acts as an early warning device against conditions that threaten to drive a system out of its stable region.

Beyond this initial stage, the role of the professional may vary depending on the trajectory that the policy-making system assumes. Consequently, this stage of the process often is overlooked or considered to be outside the actual process. Such a view, however, unduly rationalizes the policy-making process and leads to distorted conclusions. A clerk who recognizes a discrepancy in sales procedures that has caused reduced profits, and who brings this situation to his superior's attention, may not participate in the final policy decision to make major modifications in sales operations. Nevertheless, this change in the system came about through the clerk's initiative.

Screening Demands to Determine Intakes

Once a situation has been identified as uncertain or potentially uncertain, there are four possible responses, each involving a different degree of commitment to the policy-making process (see figure 6–1). The first possibility is to disregard the uncertain situation; that is, to decide to do nothing about it. This is the likely response when the demand (input) is below some threshold of tolerance. If, for some reason, such as time, cost, or effort, this response is invoked, the process will be cut short. For the purposes of this discussion, we have no further interest in such negative behavior.

The second possible response is to identify further the uncertain situation as one that can be handled through programmed decision mechanisms. This would suggest that the system contains some kind of memory bank in which these programmed decision mechanisms are stored and against which uncertain situations are tested to determine if an appropriate programmed decision exists. Again, the process is cut short by the application of a programmed response.

If either of the two remaining possible responses is invoked, the process moves to the next stage—that of *classification and definition*. Inputs are screened to determine the actual intakes into the system and to filter out those demands for which no further action will be taken at present and those which can be handled through programmed mechanisms. The individuals responsible for this screening are analogous to the "gatekeepers" in Easton's conceptual schema.

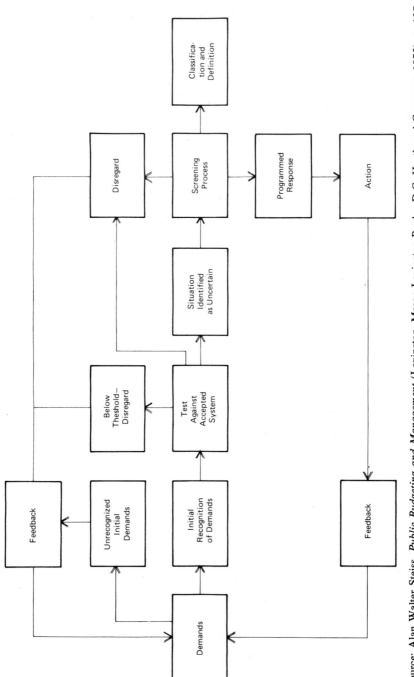

Source: Alan Walter Steiss, *Public Budgeting and Management* (Lexington, Mass.: Lexington Books, D.C. Heath and Company, 1972), p. 127. Reprinted with permission.

Figure 6–1. The Stage of Uncertainty and Doubt and the Screening Process

The Classification and Definition Stage

Although uncertainty is essential to an initiation of the policy-making process, it is not sufficient to create a problematic situation, that is, one for which policy makers are likely to seek alternative responses. As Dewey has stated, the uncertain situation ". . . becomes problematic in the very process of being subjected to inquiry."[8] Analysis does not begin with the uncertain or unsettled situation—that is anticipatory to analysis—but is initiated with the identification of a problematic situation in which a problem implied in the uncertain situation is made more explicit.

Like Dewey, Northrup emphasizes the importance of the problematic situation by asserting that decision making must begin with an analysis of the situation that generates the problem.[9] The analysis of the problem must come first, because such an analysis guides the investigator to the facts needed to understand the situation clearly and to select the elements necessary in the formulation of a policy decision. Similarly, Rapoport asserts that the first step in solving a problem is to state it:

> The statement usually involves a description of an existing state and desirable state of affairs where the factors involved in the discrepancy are explicitly pointed out. The success with which any problem is solved depends to a great extent on the clarity with which it is stated. In fact, the solution of the problem is, in a sense, a clarification (or concretization) of the objectives.[10]

Vague statements of the situation lead to vague methods, the success of which is erratic and questionable. The more a given situation is extensionalized, the better the classification and the greater the promise of a successful solution.

The first question to be asked about an uncertain situation is: "Is this a symptom of a fundamental problem or merely a stray event?" A generic problem can often be handled through the application of a programmed response, but the truly exceptional event must be handled as it is encountered.[11]

Strictly speaking, a distinction can be made among four, rather than two, different types of problem sets. First, there is the *truly generic event,* of which the individual occurrence is only a symptom. Most of the problems confronting a political system fall into this category. As a rule, such generic situations require adaptive decisions. Frequently, programmed decision mechanisms are applied to the symptoms of a generic problem. Until the generic problem is identified, however, significant amounts of time and energy may be spent in the piecemeal application of programmed decisions to the symptoms without ever gaining control of the generic situation.

The second type of occurrence is one that, although unique in the given system, is actually *generic.* For example, when a city must choose a location for its municipal airport, this is a nonrecurrent or unique situation as far as the present community decision makers are concerned. But it is, of course, a generic situation that has occurred in other cities in the past. There are some general rules for deciding on the best location for this facility, and for these the policy makers can turn to the experiences of others.

The third possible classification is the *truly unique situation.* Here, the event itself may be unique or the circumstances in which the event occurred may be unique. For example, the huge power failure of November 1965, which plunged northeastern North America into darkness, was a truly exceptional event according to first explanations. On the other hand, the collision of two airplanes miles from any air terminal is a unique situation, not because airplanes do not run the danger of collision, but because of the unique circumstances under which the event occurred.

The fourth type of event confronting the decision process is the *early manifestation* of a new generic problem. For example, both the power failure and the collision of the two airplanes turned out to be only the first occurrences of what are likely to become fairly frequent events unless generic solutions are found to certain problems of modern technology.

General rules, policies, or principles can usually be developed or adapted to deal with generic situations. Once the right policy has been found, all manifestations of the same generic situation can be handled fairly pragmatically through the adaptation of the rules or principles to the concrete circumstances of the situation. In short, such problems can be handled through *adaptive decision making.* The unique problem and the first manifestation of a generic problem, however, often require greater innovation in the search for a successful solution. Figure 6–2 illustrates the relationships between these four categories and the two fundamental dimensions of *availability of rules and principles* for dealing with such problems and the *frequency of encounter* of these situations.

By far the most common mistake in problem solving is to treat a generic problem as if it were a series of unique events. The other extreme, that of treating every problem incrementally (that is, treating a unique event as if it

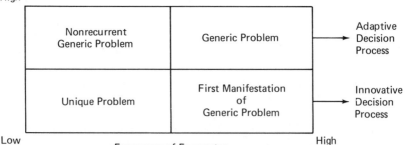

Figure 6–2. Basic Categories of Problems Demanding Decisions

were just another example of the old problem to which the old rule should be applied) can have equally negative repercussions.

The role of the experienced administrator is to avoid incomplete solutions to partially understood problems. The technical expertise of those closest to the situation should be used to classify the problem; once a problem has been classified, it is usually relatively easy to define. There is a further danger in this step, however, that of finding not the wrong definition, but a plausible but incomplete one. Safeguards against an incomplete definition include checking it against all the observable facts and discarding it if and when it fails to encompass any of these facts.

The outcome of the analysis of a problem should be a clear definition of that problem. If the problem cannot be stated specifically, preferably in one interrogative sentence including one or more objectives, then the analysis has been inadequate or of insufficient depth. Emotional bias, habitual or traditional behavior, and the human tendency to seek the path of least resistance may contribute to a superficial analysis. This type of analysis usually is followed by a statement of the "apparent" rather than the "real" problem.

Identification of Constraints and Boundary Conditions

The next major step in the policy- or decision-making process involves the clear specification of what the policy decision must accomplish. Six basic questions must be answered:

1. What are the existing or potential constraints to an effective solution?
2. What objectives must be met?
3. What are the minimum goals to be attained?
4. What measure(s) of efficiency can be used relative to each of the objectives?
5. What standard(s) can be applied for the evaluation of possible courses of action?
6. What definition of "most effective" is to be applied in judging the possible solutions to any given problem sets?

These questions aid in the establishment of *boundary conditions,* the set of factors that define the "field" within which a feasible solution can or should be found. When techniques of operations research, such as linear and dynamic programming, can be applied, boundary conditions can be identified clearly and given numerical values. In most public-policy situations, however, the identification of boundary conditions may be difficult.

Nevertheless, this stage is crucial: a policy decision that does not meet the boundary conditions is worse than one that incorrectly defines the problem. It is all but impossible to salvage policy decisions that start with the right premises but stop short of the right conclusions. Furthermore, clear thinking about boundary conditions is essential for recognition of when to abandon a given course of action. Policy failure often results from the inability of policy makers to recognize a subsequent shift in goals and objectives that makes a formerly "right" decision suddenly inappropriate. In the words of Peter Drucker: ". . . unless the decision maker has kept the boundary conditions clear, so as to make possible the immediate replacement of the outflanked decision with a new and appropriate policy, he may not even notice that things have changed."[12]

Often policy decisions are made in which the specifications to be satisfied are incompatible; for example, achievement of goal A through a prescribed course of action may preclude the achievement of goal B, or at best make this achievement highly unlikely. This dilemma represents a classic case of failure to identify boundary conditions fully and clearly. Similarly, a policy decision often involves a gamble or calculated risk. This type of decision, which may work if nothing whatsoever goes wrong, often emerges from something less rational than a gamble—a futile hope that two or more clearly incompatible specifications can be fulfilled simultaneously.

Determining boundary conditions requires a clear view of organizational and community goals and objectives. Even with active public involvement, however, public goals are often too vague to establish boundaries. What is required is some mechanism for translating these overall goals into specific program objectives and for testing identifiable boundary conditions against the more general goals. In deterministic decision situations, such mechanisms generally are available. In stochastic situations, the majority of public-policy situations, such mechanisms are difficult to develop and apply. The best device continues to be experience, coupled with a careful delineation of the problem and the associated objectives. The adoption of systematic procedures, such as those embodied in the concept of strategic planning, can aid significantly in this delineation. The concept of strategic planning will be discussed in further detail in chapter 9.

Formulation of Alternatives

It is imperative that several alternatives be developed for every problem situation. Otherwise there is the danger of falling into the trap of false either-or proposition. This danger is heightened by a tendency to focus on the extremes in any problem situation.

Alternative solutions are the only means of making conscious the basic assumptions concerning a given situation, thereby forcing an examination of their validity. Alternative solutions are no guarantee of the right policy decision, but an examination of alternatives can guard against the making of a

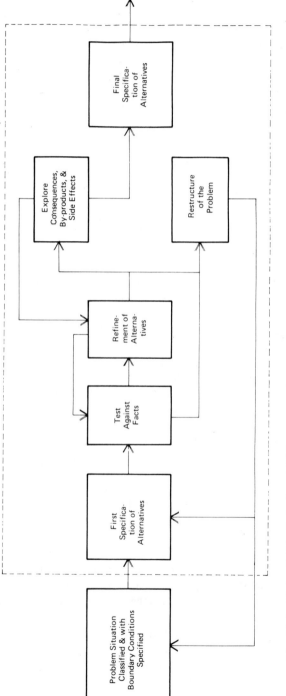

Figure 6–3. The Formulation of Alternatives

Source: Alan Walter Steiss, *Public Budgeting and Management* (Lexington, Mass.: Lexington Books, D.C. Heath and Company, 1972), p. 135. Reprinted with permission.

decision that would have been seen to be wrong if the problem had been thought through more carefully.

As shown in figure 6–3, alternative approaches to a given policy-demanding situation differ according to the level of reflection reached. At first they are relatively vague; but as the alternatives posed direct further observation, they become more suitable for resolving the problem. As alternatives become more appropriate, observations likewise become more acute. Perception and conception work together: the former locates and describes the problem, while the latter represents a possible method of solution.[13]

The next step is to develop an understanding of the possible consequences, byproducts, and side effects associated with each of the suggested policy alternatives. This examination consists of identifying the implications of particular courses of action in relation to other aspects of the system. This formulation leads to a proposition: If such and such a relation is accepted, then we are committed to such and such other courses of action because of their membership in the same system. A series of such intermediate examinations leads to an understanding of the problem that is more relevant to the policy-demanding situation than was the original conception.

Thus, the examination of suggested policy alternatives for operational fitness involves an investigation of their capacity to direct further observation aimed at securing additional factual material. This examination may result in the rejection, acceptance, or modification of ideas in an attempt to arrive at more relevant alternatives. The possible range of alternatives will vary with the problem; it must be recognized, however, that policy alternatives are in part a function of the data and concepts at one's disposal. When these are sufficient, fruitful alternatives are likely to emerge.

One possible alternative is always that of taking no action at all. This alternative seldom is recognized as a decision, although it is no less a commitment than any specific positive action. An unpleasant or difficult decision cannot be avoided merely by doing nothing. The potential consequences of a decision not to act must be clearly spelled out. A careful consideration of the alternative of doing nothing leads to a fuller examination of the traditional ways of doing things, approaches that reflect past needs rather than those of the present.

Frequently an impasse is reached in the search for policy alternatives. In such cases, restructuring the problem may lead to new insights into possible alternatives. Problem restructuring involves the manipulation of the elements of the problem; for example, it may involve a change of viewpoint, or a permissible modification of objectives, or a rearrangement of other problem elements. Further discussion of these points is reserved for chapter 9, in which the process of alternative formulation and evaluation is examined in detail.

The Search for a "Best" Policy

Only after a number of alternatives have been formulated and evaluated is it possible to determine the "best" policy decision. There is seldom one and only one appropriate course of action. More likely, there will be several possible alternatives, any of which might solve the problem, or a number of alternatives that fall short of perfection for different reasons.

Depending on the general class of decision sought—adaptive or innovative—there are two basic methods for finding the "best" policy. Since adaptive decisions merely require that the selected course of action meet minimal expectations sanctioned by the system, and do not require the substitution of new expectations, the best alternative can be selected on the basis of relatively simple criteria (see figure 6–4). The selected policy alternative should provide satisfactory solutions to the problem, thereby alleviating pressures created by the demand, while creating a minimum disturbance of established expectations. No single policy alternative may satisfy these conditions; it may be necessary to combine elements from several alternatives to achieve an appropriate solution.

There are several criteria that may be useful in seeking the best policy decision in situations requiring innovation. These criteria deal with such issues as: (1) uncertainty, (2) risks and expected gains, (3) economy of effort, (4) timing of alternatives, and (5) limitations of resources.

Most policy situations requiring an innovative response involve major conditions of *uncertainty*. In such cases, therefore, analyses of alternatives must provide for explicit treatment of uncertainty. Several techniques, applicable under varying circumstances, have been developed for this purpose. Since the problems of uncertainty are so crucial to effective innovative decisions, a major section of chapter 9 will be devoted to these strategies and techniques.

The *risk* associated with each proposed course of action must be weighed against the *expected gains.* There are several reasons for using the terms *risks* and *gains* here rather than the more conventional concepts of costs and benefits. Any public policy decision represents a choice of one alternative over others. Efforts to convert the positive and negative aspects of any alternative into dollars and cents, however, frequently result in too narrow a frame of reference. The concept of costs associated with public policy means something more than that which shows up on a profit-and-loss statement. In developing a cost-benefit analysis, items often are omitted because they are "intangibles." Many of these intangibles are important risks that may seriously affect the outcomes of the policy decision. Assessment of benefits, on the other hand, frequently involves a form of double accounting. Direct benefits, for which dollar figures can be derived, are often counted again in terms of more indirect

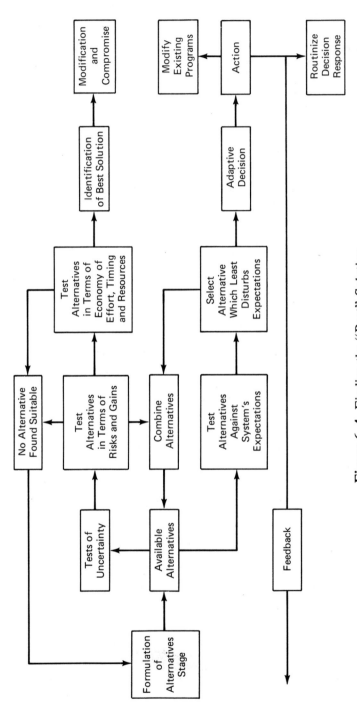

Figure 6-4. Finding the "Best" Solution

benefits. In arriving at a net-gains figure, therefore, such indirect benefits must be discounted in order to avoid an unrealistic assessment.

There is no riskless action nor even riskless nonaction. What is important, however, is neither the expected gain nor the anticipated risk but the ratio between them. Every alternative should be evaluated on this basis. The value of such an analysis lies not in the end result but in the process pursued in arriving at this result.

The third criterion involves an assessment of the *economy of effort,* that is: Which alternative will give the greatest results with the least effort? As Drucker has observed, decision makers often use an elephant gun to chase sparrows or a slingshot against forty-ton tanks.[14] Grandiose schemes have many hidden risks which, if carefully considered, would reduce the economy of effort. Similarly, solutions that fail to produce optimal results may result in a series of incremental policies that in the long run will involve a higher expenditure of effort.

The fourth criterion is concerned with the *timing* of the possible policy decision. If the situation is urgent, the preferable course of action may be one that dramatizes the policy decision and demonstrates that something important is happening. If, on the other hand, long, consistent effort is needed, a slow start that gathers momentum may be preferable. In some situations the policy decision must be final and must immediately inspire those involved to seek a new set of goals and objectives. In other situations, the first step is most important; the final goal may be shrouded in obscurity for the time being.

Timing decisions often are extremely difficult to systematize; they may elude analysis and depend on perception. There is one guide, however: whenever a public policy requires a change in vision to accomplish something new, it is best to be ambitious, to present the complete program and the ultimate aim. When a policy necessitates a change in people's habits, however, it may be best to take one step at a time, to start slowly and modestly, to do no more at first than is absolutely necessary.

The final criterion deals with the *limitations of resources* and is closely related to the notion of *systems readiness.* A basic problem of policy making in both the public and private sectors, is to achieve a balance in the programs and allocations of resources that will ensure a systems readiness in the short-, medium-, and long-term futures. Achieving this objective requires flexibility in confronting a wide range of competing possible actions.

Perhaps most important as a resource are the personnel who will be called upon to execute the decision. A less-than-optimal policy should not be adopted simply because the competence to do what is required is lacking. The "best" policy should always lie between genuine alternatives, one that provide adequate solutions to the problem. If such solutions demand greater competence, skill, and understanding than is available, then provision must be made to raise the capacity of those who must implement the programs associated with the "best" solution. All too often substantial investments in public programs are made without adequate consideration of the training of personnel to carry out the requisite activities effectively.

Converting an Acceptable Decision into Action

An effective policy maker begins with what is "right" or "best" rather than what is "acceptable" or "possible," precisely because he will invariably have to make compromises in the end. If the alternatives are limited to those that are prejudged to be acceptable, important aspects are likely to be overlooked. This approach may obviate any chance of coming up with an effective solution, let alone the right answer. This observation is related to the specification of boundary conditions: what will satisfy these constraints is not clearly known, the policy maker will be unable to distinguish between an appropriate and an inappropriate compromise, and may end up giving away more than necessary in order to gain an acceptable decision.

After the best policy has been identified, the first step in seeking an acceptable decision is to review the expectations of the system (see figure 6–5). Unlike the adaptive decision process, innovative policies usually require alteration and modification of expectations. Therefore, a careful appraisal must be made of the expectations, both internal and external to the system, that must be accommodated by the decision. This self-examination process, as Gore has suggested, often produces internal stress and tensions.[15] If such internal demands arise, a means must be devised to respond to them and to engender support for the proposed actions.

Converting the policy decision into effective action may be the most time-consuming step in the process. Yet a policy will not be effective unless a commitment to action has been built into it from the start. In fact, specific steps for carrying out a decision are someone's responsibility, no decision has been made. Until this is accomplished, the policy is only a good intention.

The flaw in many policy statements is that they contain no action commitments; they fail to designate specific areas of responsibility for their effective implementation. Converting policy into action requires answers to several distinct questions: (1) Who has to know of the policy decision? (2) What action has to be taken? (3) Who has to take it? and (4) What must the action be so that those who have to do it can do it? The first and last of these questions are often overlooked, with dire consequences.

As previously noted, the action must be appropriate to the capacities of those who will have to carry it out. Such action commitments are even more important when a policy's effectiveness requires people change their behavior, habits, or attitudes. Not only must responsibility for the action be clearly assigned, but also the standards for accomplishment and the incentives

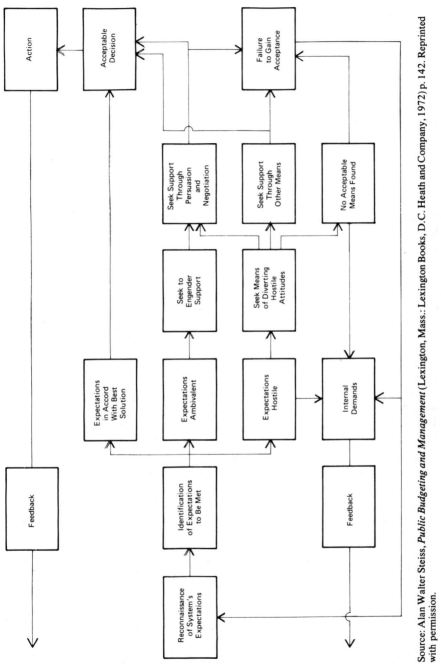

Figure 6–5. Achievement of an Acceptable Decision through Modification and Compromise

Source: Alan Walter Steiss, *Public Budgeting and Management* (Lexington, Mass.: Lexington Books, D.C. Heath and Company, 1972) p. 142. Reprinted with permission.

associated with the proposed action must be identified or modified at the time the policy is introduced.

Policy/Program Maintenance

Successful implementation and maintenance of policies and programs is rapidly emerging as the most challenging task of the public administrator. Not only is the margin for error between success and failure shrinking; but increased public demands, shorter effective lifespans of government programs, and rapid technological change have combined to make program-management responsibilities more difficult and intractable. Policy and program maintenance have heretofore been divorced from policy formulation and relegated to the realm of program administration. This artificial bifurcation, however, is no longer valid, if in fact it ever was.

Timely analyses of *implementation feasibility* should identify problems associated with carrying out particular programs or activities. These problems should be linked to and reflected in the criteria used in selecting alternatives. Assessing implementation feasibility involves a projection of the political, social, and organizational constraints associated with the set of program options under consideration. Unfortunately, all too often inadequate consideration is given to these constraints early in the policy formulation process, with disastrous results when efforts to implement the selected alternative are initiated.

Policy and program maintenance involves the allocation of program resources to specific tasks and the continuous monitoring of performance to ensure that these tasks are carried out efficiently and on schedule. It may also entail the strategic renegotiation of programs and policies as a consequence of information feedback about program impacts and results. A number of *network analysis and scheduling techniques,* developed in the private sector, can be applied in providing oversight to vital program functions. These techniques permit the breakdown of broad programs into more manageable tasks, which can then be scheduled and allocated necessary resources. In the process, the critical path—the sequence of events or activities that controls the overall program duration—can be identified and monitored through the concept of management by exception.

Feedback

Feedback, intentional or unintentional, occurs at many stages in the process. Much of this feedback is internal and results in the recycling of a particular stage in order to achieve further refinements and modifications. Feedback affecting the entire system generally occurs at two points: (1) after the policy decision has been made and action programs have been initiated; and (2) whenever internal demands are created within the system. In both cases, new demands or inputs may be generated, causing a recycling of the total system.

After a decision has been reached, information monitoring and reporting are particularly important in order to provide continuous testing of expectations against actual results. Even the best policy decision has a high probability of being wrong; even the most effective one eventually becomes obsolete. Failure to provide for adequate feedback is one of the primary reasons for persistence in a course of action long after it has ceased to be appropriate. Although the advent of the computer has made it possible to compile and analyze large quantities of feedback data in a relatively short time, it must be recognized that computers can handle only abstractions, which are reliable only when constantly checked against concrete results. As Drucker has observed, unless decision makers build their feedback around direct exposure to reality, their decisions may result in a sterile dogmatism.[16]

A basic aspect of the policy-making process is the development of a predictive capacity within the system to identify changing conditions that might necessitate modifications in selected courses of action. Controls should be developed for a given solution by:

1. Defining what constitutes a significant change for each variable and relationship that appears as a component in the policy decision;
2. Establishing procedures for modifying the screening devices to detect the occurrence of such significant changes; and
3. Specifying the tolerable range within which the policy can be modified if such changes occur and beyond which new solutions must be sought.

The information gained through feedback is a central component in the application of these controls.

Iterations and "Do-Loops"

Although the preceding prescriptive model is presented in eight distinct stages, it would be misleading to assume that real-life problems are obliging enough to permit an easy, logical sequence of attention. As Joseph Cooper has observed:

> [Problems] conceal their true nature so that halfway down the path of a decision you may find that you must retrace your steps for a new beginning. Or you may have alternatives for decisions presented to you which, in your belief, are not the only and best possible courses. This, too, will send you back to the beginning.[17]

Policy alternatives are seldom created by moving in an orderly sequence from the first stage to the last. It is not uncommon for new alternatives to occur from time to time while data are still being collected. Moreover, in a complex situation different phases of the process may develop at different rates. For example, the stage of alternative formulation may be reached for one aspect of a complex problem, while other parts of the same problem are still at the stage of definition and analysis. Thus, in a complex, difficult problem situation, various stages may appear simultaneously in different aspects of the same problem. Nevertheless, it is necessary to approach the patterns of policy making stage by stage in order to analyze the process adequately.

This systemic framework for policy and decision making will be examined in increasing detail in succeeding chapters. Although the concept of performance administration embraces more than the formulation of policy decisions, this process is central to the responsibilities of performance administration; it serves as the mainstream from which other tributaries can be explored. The various analytical currents evident in this stream will also be examined in detail.

Notes

1. A classic in this category is *The Civic Culture* by Gabriel Almond and Sidney Verba, which marvels at the ability of political systems in the United States to persist.

2. Roscoe C. Martin et al., *Decision in Syracuse: A Metropolitan Action Study* (Bloomington, Ind.: Indiana University Press, 1961), p. 318.

3. Herbert A. Simon and James G. March, *Organizations* (New York: John Wiley and Sons, 1958), pp. 178–179.

4. Filmer S.C. Northrup, *The Logic of the Sciences and the Humanities* (New York: The Macmillan Company, 1947), p. 1.

5. John Dewey, *Logic, The Theory of Inquiry* (New York: Holt, Rinehart, and Winston, 1938), p. 105.

6. Ibid., pp. 105–106.

7. Brand Blanshard, *The Nature of Thought,* vol. 2 (London: George Allen & Unwin 1939), pp. 63–64.

8. Dewey, *Logic, The Theory of Inquiry,* p. 105.

9. Northrup, *The Logic of the Sciences and the Humanities,* p. 29.

10. Anatol Rapoport, "What Is Information?" ETC: *A Review of General Semantics* 10(Summer 1953):252.

11. Peter F. Drucker, "The Effective Decision," *Harvard Business Review* 45(January-February 1967):95.

12. Ibid., p. 95.

13. Robert W. Morell, *Managerial Decision-Making* (Milwaukee, Wisc.: The Bruce Publishing Company, 1960), p. 22.

14. Peter F. Drucker, *The Practice of Management* (New York: Harper and Brothers, 1954), p. 363.

15. William J. Gore, *Administrative Decision-Making: A Heuristic Model* (New York: John Wiley and Sons, 1964), pp. 80–101.

16. Drucker, "The Effective Decision," p. 95.

17. Joseph D. Cooper, *The Art of Decision Making* (Garden City, N.Y. Doubleday and Company, 1961), pp. 15–16.

7 Problem Definition and Performance Administration

A basic tenet of performance administration is that the overall effectiveness of public management should be measured by the results achieved (outputs), and particularly by the ability to make appropriate adjustments in policies and programs when problems arise. Since public policies seldom are executed exactly as conceived, early warning systems must be developed to alert officials and managers to impending problems and issues.

Problem Awareness

A problem cannot be solved until it is recognized as a problem. Many organizational and community activities are judged according to a set of standards either formally established by persons in authority or instinctively perceived by the participants. Recognition of a problem often accompanies an awareness that a situation is exhibiting a noticeable departure from these standards or norms. This perception of a situation as being out of phase with some set of acceptable conditions sets the problem-solving process in motion.

With the acceleration of social change, the ability to perceive problems has become tantamount to a survival instinct. Often such perception is merely a sense of uncertainty or doubt that exists because the constituent elements of some segment of the broader environment are unsettled. The sensing of problems may also follow orderly, predetermined processes, with the sensors attuned to particular anticipated deviations. The concept of *management by exception,* supported by a management-information and program-evaluation system, is designed to provide this systematic approach to problem identification. However, a common shortcoming of such systematic approaches is their inability to detect the unanticipated.

Problem awareness can occur in several ways. Raybould and Minter, for example, suggest an important distinction:

> When the unsatisfactory performance becomes intolerable, we have the "sore thumb" situation—you don't have to go out and look for it; it will eventually find you. . . . At the other end of the scale lies the hidden problem. The organisation is running smoothly, employees do what is expected of them, and a satisfactory level of profitability is maintained. All these factors may well conceal a number of problems. Or some trifling and quite obvious problems may divert attention from a much more fundamental menace.[1]

When a problem reaches the obvious proportions of a "sore thumb" situation, it may have devastating consequences for the organization or community. For this reason, considerable effort should be devoted to finding and resolving problems or potential problems before they reach this crisis level. This search is at the core of the administrator's mission, since management personnel are presumed to have the skill, the training, and above all the responsibility to identify areas that need improvement.

Casual versus Systematic Approaches

Some people can walk into an organization that seems a model of effortless efficiency, quickly size up the situation, and discern that, despite outward appearances "something is rotten in the state of Denmark" or the contemporary equivalent. This instinctive ability cannot be taught in the classroom; it can be developed only by constant practice and experience in looking for certain clues. Those who have this ability usually do well as management consultants.

The *casual approach* to problem identification may consist of little more than having a gift for talking with people. A good program manager, for example, should have an intimate knowledge of the organization and the procedures associated with each program. His management style may focus on developing good employee relations through the delegation of responsibilities and the use of a reward system that features: (1) recognition as a means of stimulating performance, and (2) the provision of a good work atmosphere conducive to maximizing individual satisfaction and motivation.[2] He should also have a clear grasp of the overall project or program objectives as a result of observing the work in some detail and thinking at length about the special requirements of each principal task. In short, he should know more than anyone else about what is going on in the project or program.

If he is a good listener, able to interject the right stimuli at suitable points in the conversation, he should be able to pick up early warning signals of present or future difficulties. No one person with whom he talks is likely to pinpoint problems accurately and objectively; personal bias is usually a factor. However, by seeking comparative opinions, the manager can test and refine what he initially perceives as the emerging problems and issues. This piecing together of problems may be best accomplished by informal conversation in which the topic is introduced naturally, rather than by direct questioning. Eventually, the manager should be in a position to assert with confidence that there is or is not a problem. Chances are that if there is a problem someone else will have an inkling of it. The manager's job is to provide the impetus to establish whether the problem is real or just a personal grievance.

The *systematic approach* is based on a more careful analysis of data. Standards of expected performance must be identified and periodically revised so that comparisons can be made of performance indicators within one program area or between areas, and significant deviations can be isolated for special study. This comparison can be undertaken in various ways, often governed by local circumstances and judgment. It may be possible, for example, to break down the major components of all costs associated with an ongoing program or project. The analysis can then be focused on the largest cost factors on the grounds that they are potentially the most significant areas in which to make improvements. Alternatively, an initial estimate might be made for each cost factor as to the feasible or expected percentage of improvement, and then the various cost areas can be analyzed in order of magnitude.

Frequently the real problem can be identified only by breaking down the problem into its component parts so that parallel subproblem analysis can proceed. Solving the parts of the problem, however, may not provide an optimal solution to the total problem unless the relationships among the subparts are fully understood. A general study of the organization also may be necessary, not to lead to specific improvements but to reveal problem areas and to provide a basis for more specific improvement-oriented studies.

Problem Categories

These various approaches to problem identification suggest the existence of several broad problem situations or categories, including the following.

1. The *improvement problem* is the most typical and most common problem situation in which present performance is measured and found to be unsatisfactory. A certain desired level of performance is accepted as the target, and the task becomes one of finding the means to move from the present to the desired level of performance.

2. The *objective problem* involves a general dissatisfaction with the current level of performance; however, the nature and direction of the desired state (the objective) is unclear or unknown. The problem is to determine the appropriate objectives and to discover ways of achieving them.

3. The *deviation problem* takes two basic forms: either the desired objective is normally achieved most of the time and the problem is to maintain performance at this level; or a given level of performance is sustained most of the time, but occasionally a significantly higher level is achieved. In the latter case, the problem is to determine why this improved performance occurs, and how it can be made to occur more regularly.

4. The *potential problem* is an anticipation of what might go wrong in the future once a planned level of performance is established. This problem

category often is handled by "what-if " analyses, that is, simulations of future conditions to examine the potential impacts of environmental and organizational changes.

5. The *evaluation problem* is one of choosing among alternatives when several courses of action are open to an organization, all of which hold the promise of better levels of performance than those currently attained.

6. The *knowledge problem* involves a dissatisfaction not with the existing physical situation but with a lack of information. Not knowing and wanting to know may be just as real a problem as not being able to achieve identified objectives.

Each type of problem calls for different analytical techniques; only limited results can be expected from conventional applications of procedures in a "cookbook" fashion. All too often, the systematic approach is reduced to very particular methods, such as those associated with operations research, in search of a problem. The successful administrator must have a thorough understanding of the problems; must develop his or her judgments regarding the appropriate tools for the job; and must know how to adapt available analytical tools to different problem situations. In short, the performance administrator must focus on problems rather than on techniques.

A plausible but incomplete definition of the problem can be more dangerous than a wrong definition. If the problem cannot be stated specifically, then the analysis has not been of sufficient depth. Even an excellent solution to an apparent problem will not work in practice if it is the solution to a problem that does not exist in fact.

This assertion brings the discussion back to the crux of problem awareness—a proper understanding of what exists, coupled with a vision of and a belief in a more desirable situation. Problem awareness is not simple discontent; it requires also the belief that change is possible, that the problem deserves to be taken seriously. As Raybould and Minter have observed, "The condemned man, his last appeal rejected, awaiting execution on the morrow, appears to have a problem. He hasn't really, because, within the constraints, there is no possibility of solution."[3] In some cases, the political or social constraints are so profound that a solution does not seem possible. In spite of the current emphasis on government as the "resource of first resort," many problems may be beyond the scope of legitimate government activity. A good analyst, however, will not draw the parameters of activity too tightly.

Attitudes Toward Problem Situations

The attitudes that the administrator brings to a problem situation often have a significant effect on its successful resolution. For many, the experience of confronting a problem is a prelude to gloom and despair: tedious work lies ahead, and their peaceful lives have been disrupted.[4] Even those who enjoy the challenge of problem solving may still view the process fundamentally as one of returning to a relatively safe and acceptable level of normality—of getting back to some comfortable point of equilibrium.

Such attitudes are negative, or at best, neutral. The successful administrator, however, must view problem situations not merely as necessitating a return to a prior point of equilibrium, but also as providing opportunities to be exploited. Problem recognition should imply a commitment to initiate, accept, and support change. The solution to the problem is likely to involve an expenditure of resources and a relaxation of many previous constraints. Therefore, performance administrators should not confine their efforts to clearing up the mess, but should also attempt to discover how to gain maximum advantage from the opportunities inherent in the problem situation.

Attitudes and objectives must change during each phase of the problem-solving process. At the outset, an *analytical* posture is necessary, since the main concern is with seeking and analyzing factors that give rise to the problem. The next phase begins with the *isolation* and understanding of the problem, coupled with a *deduction* of the nature of the tasks required to achieve a solution. A *creative* phase follows, in which information is examined and manipulated in order to generate a conceptual framework within which alternatives can be formulated. Once potential alternatives have been identified, judgment and measurement must be applied to *evaluate* and, subsequently, to *choose* the most acceptable course of action. Different techniques are needed to attain the objectives of each phase and to engender the appropriate attitudes or mental sets for each of these problem-solving or decision-making tasks.

Brainstorming and the Delphi Technique

Organized *brainstorming* sessions can be of considerable assistance in problem definition and analysis. Such sessions form the foundation of such loosely systematic procedures as Management by Objectives (MBO). MBO is an attempt to create an open atmosphere in which personnel at all levels are encouraged to add innovative ideas and critical suggestions. Along similar lines, Opportunity Analysis attempts to raise the enthusiasm and morale of those involved and to engender more positive attitudes toward problem situations. Periodic sessions are held to discuss the current status of the organization in terms of the opportunities that may be presented.

Although many ideas generated in brainstorming sessions may not be relevant to the more pressing requirements of problem situations, an effective administrator cannot afford to overlook any possibilities in a preoccupation with mere remedial solutions. Such sessions should be fairly unstructured, freewheeling, and unconstrained. All ideas should be recorded no matter how "extreme" they may appear. Each individual associated with the problem situation should be involved. The administrator may wish to appoint a member of the project team to serve as the session facilitator so that his own opinions will not bias the discussion or result in premature closure. This permits the administrator to adopt an observer's role and avoid undue influence on the flow of ideas. Efforts to refine, combine, and assign priorities to the ideas derived from brainstorming should follow only after the subject has been thoroughly discussed and all participants have had an opportunity to express themselves.

Ideas about problem situations also can be elicited and refined through the use of the *Delphi technique*. This technique involves a series of interrogations, usually through questionnaires, using a panel of well-informed individuals. The Delphi approach is characterized by three fairly elementary concepts: anonymity, controlled feedback, and statistical group responses.

Anonymity is maintained by means of formal modes of communication, such as questionnaires. The free exchange of brainstorming is replaced by a formal exchange of information under the control of a steering group or exercise manager. Responses are not matched with respondents and the identity of participants may not be revealed until the end of the exercise. In this way, the psychological drawbacks of unstructured face-to-face confrontations are avoided. After each iteration, information is fed back to the participants so that they may use it to revise their earlier responses and possibly modify their attitudes toward the problem situation. Irrelevant or redundant material may be eliminated to sharpen the focus in subsequent iterations. Participant opinions tend to converge with feedback after several iterations. A statistical index rather than forced unanimity is used to represent the group response. The assumption is that this approach reduces the pressures of conformity and allows the opinion of every participant to play a role in the final determination of categorical responses.

A *modified Delphi approach* involves the use of a questionnaire or its equivalent in combination with a series of one-to-one interviews. The initial questionnaire is designed to elicit a wide range of ideas about the problem. These ideas form the basis for a more structured interview with each of the participants. A second round of interviews may be conducted to test out any ideas that emerge from the initial interview sessions. The interviewer must be skillful to avoid biasing the responses in the application of this approach. Insights into the attitudes that different participants may bring to the interview sessions also are important to the interviewer.

Other Problem Dimensions

It has been suggested that problem situations can be categorized acording to a broad classification scheme rooted in the origins of the problem. It also is possible and desirable to delimit problem situations according to several other characteristic dimensions. Among these are:

1. *systemic concerns:* the impact of problems on organizational purpose, stability, and comprehensiveness;
2. *time perspectives and systems readiness:* the orientation adopted in preparing for resource commitments and the responsiveness of the problem-solving system to change;
3. *demand patterns:* the nature of the affected clientele and implications in terms of the structure of the problem-solving system and the cost of reaching decisions;
4. *risk and uncertainty:* the degree to which problems require long-range solutions that involve an uncertain future;
5. *externalities and intersystem transfers:* the direct and indirect benefits and costs that accrue from problem situations.

The first three dimensions form the basis of the discussion in the remainder of this chapter. The dimensions of uncertainty and risk and systems externalities will be examined in detail in chapter 8, which focuses on applications of problem-analysis techniques derived from economic decision theory.

Communication of Systemic Concerns

Administrators seldom deal directly with problem situations. Rather, they deal almost exclusively with *information* about the problem. Decisions, therefore, must satisfy not actual conditions, but information about these conditions. Thus, problem solving depends on communication for its success and often for its very existence. As Bavelas and Barrett have observed, "The goals an organization selects, the methods it applies, the effectiveness with which it improves its own procedures—all of these hinge upon the quality and availability of the information in the system."[5]

Every problem has some impact on the organization or system in which it arises—on the organization's ability to achieve purposeful directions, maintain stability, and remain comprehensive in its functions. Problems must be placed in the context of the overall goals and objectives of the organization and the assigned priorities of problem resolution, based on perceived impacts on these objectives. It is important, therefore, that organizational goals and objectives—systemic concerns—be communicated, and that some consensus be attained throughout the system. Efforts to determine the appropriate level at which to address problems within the system often are highly dependent on an understanding and acceptance of the operational objectives and broader goals of the organization.

The primary or initial problem impact may be at the subcomponent or elemental level. An office or bureau may be faced with rapidly shifting demands for services, inefficient service delivery, case loads that exceed available resources, and so forth. Initially, these problems may be seen as particular to that subcomponent of the organization, although in reality they may be merely symptoms of much broader issues that have extensive consequences for the total system. Efforts to ameliorate the problem at the subcomponent level may cause these broader implications to be overlooked, with detrimental effects. The situation is further complicated by the human tendency to suppress any information that might make the subcomponent unit look bad; subordinates may even distort information so that it appears to be good news to their superiors.

The exchange of information within an organization can also be complicated by the division of labor and job specialization. As Thompson has observed, the demand for adequate communication of information among specialists often overloads the more formal communication channels, resulting in the creation of specialist communication channels and the development of specialized languages and useful shorthand categories for classifying large amounts of information.[6] Such technical jargon, however, often loses it "meaning" as it is transmitted upward in the problem-solving process. As a consequence, problem perception may be distorted at the higher levels of the organization.

Since it is often extremely difficult to communicate about intangible and nonstandardized objects, message distortion is common in organizational communication. Problem-solving situations, therefore, require conscious efforts to develop mechanisms for handling less objective communication contents. As Cyert and March observe:

> Any decision-making system develops codes for communication about the environment. Such a code partitions all possible states of the world into a relatively small number of classes of states. . . . Thus, if a decision rule is designed to choose between two alternatives, the information code will tend to reduce all possible states of the world to two classes.[7]

Such rules for the codification of information inputs, however, frequently introduce additional distortions.[8]

From a somewhat broader perspective, such systematic biasing of message content may not always be dysfunctional to the problem-solving process. In experimental situations, Allport and Postman found that transmitted messages ". . . tended to grow shorter, more concise, and more easily grasped and told," and that there was ". . . selective perception, retention, and reporting of a limited number of details from a larger context."[9] In other words, the messages often were sharpened. To the extent that this selection process reflects the broader systemic concerns of the organization, the resulting transmission of information may improve problem identification. But if these systemic concerns are omitted or ignored, the consequence of this short-circuit may be wasted time and effort dealing with symptoms rather than root causes of problems.

Omissions and inaccuracies may increase the ambiguity of messages, and since ambiguous messages are open to multiple interpretation, the receiver may attach more agreeable meanings to them. Thus, although ambiguity may cause slippage between the sender and the receiver, such slippage may also promote consensus and agreement. If this agreement is based on misunderstanding or misinterpretation of the information, however, the real problem may go unattended.

Recognition of the importance of communications in problem-solving situations has led to the development of more systematic reporting and information-transfer systems. These systems constitute the memory banks of the organization, in which information is stored. Information is not subject to the laws of conservation of matter and energy—it can be both created and wiped out, although it cannot be created from nothing nor destroyed completely. The memory bank of the problem-solving system is a repository for programmed decisions, for information concerning past experiences, for information by which "right" decisions are tested for their acceptability, and so forth.

Three specific areas of information serve as data inputs to an organization's memory bank: (1) *auto-intelligence,* which provides information about the particular organization and its components; (2) *environmental intelligence,* which provides information about the broader environment within which the particular organization must operate; and (3) *historical data,* which brings together and analyzes experiences from the past. These three areas provide the basis for a more complete articulation of the systemic concerns of any problem situation.

As an organization is divided into specialized subunits, these units must use communications to coordinate their output. An organization can be conceptualized as a configuration of communication patterns that connects individuals and collectivities of varying sizes, shapes, and degrees of stability and cohesiveness, and thereby establishes patterns of contact among individuals and groups. Thus, effective communication of information can be considered the warp and woof of the problem-solving process.[10]

The Time Dimension

Time is often the quintessence of the problem-solving process. Although many problems may require long-range approaches to identifying their root causes and formulating appropriate strategies to prevent their recurrence, the urgency of these problems may create pressure for more immediate responses. Such problems must be approached on two fronts: (1) a comprehensive analysis to examine the long-term implications for the organization, and (2) the development of satisficing solutions to alleviate the more immediate concerns generated by these problems. Other types of problems may also demand immediate or frequent solutions, but may have relatively short-range time perspectives because they involve elements that can be altered if initial decisions about the commitment of resources prove incorrect.

On the other hand, problems involving fixed capital investments have relatively long-term time perspectives, and decisions associated with their resolution can be modified only at considerable public expense. Capital investments yield their benefits over time, while costs frequently accrue in different patterns over the life cycle of the project—research and development costs, investment costs, and operation and maintenance costs. Benefits and costs must be aggregated over time and discounted to present values. A major problem is to determine an appropriate *time horizon* within which to evaluate project alternatives. A reasonable time horizon might be the economic or service life of the project's fixed assets. On the other hand, functional obsolescence may prevail before physical obsolescence takes its toll. Thus, the question of how long a particular good or service will be needed must also be considered.

The problems of municipal solid-waste disposal provide examples of these various time perspectives. So-called sanitary landfill areas represent a satisficing solution to a problem with significant long-term implications. Many municipalities are running out of satisfactory landfill sites, and inadequate controls often permit environmental pollution due to leaching. Longer-range solutions are required, and exploratory studies have been initiated by a number of municipalities.

A community may find its present trash collection schedule inadequate to handle the expectations of its citizens, and as a short-term solution may increase the frequency of collection, using the same equipment but expanding the number of crews. But the new schedule may be unacceptable to residents because of earlier pickup hours that require trash to be placed at the curb the night before and result in a scattering of debris by the wind and by stray animals. Since the expansion of trash collection crews was an incremental decision, the next step might be to purchase additional equipment to provide increased coverage at more suitable hours.

The analysis surrounding a decision to build an incinerator that will meet current standards of the Environmental Protection Administration (EPA) serves to illustrate the capital-investment time perspective. Questions about location, financing methods, cash flow to cover operational costs and debt service (if bonds are issued to fund capital construction), adequate maintenance standards (including possible upgrading of EPA requirements), capacity to meet future needs, and so forth all require a longer-range time perspective than is commonly adopted by local officials and administrators.

In general, the use of resources has a time dimension, and resources that are underutilized during any time period are simply wasted for the most part.[11] This is especially true of human resources; labor services that are used at less than their productive capabilities in any time period are gone forever. Thus, both the time dimension and the distinction between real and money costs strongly suggest the need to find ways to utilize underemployed resources whenever possible. Postponing the initiation of a project may defer money costs, but it may result in real costs if available resources cannot be applied to other uses. In other words, idle resources do not constitute a cost savings.

Discounting to Present Value

The concept of present value must be understood in relation to the costs and benefits generated over time by public programs and projects. Benefits that accrue in the present are "worth" more to their recipients than benefits that occur some time in the future. Similarly, funds that must be expended today "cost" more than funds that must be spent in the future, since presumably one alternative use of such funds would be to invest them at some rate of return that would increase their value over time. Therefore, it is necessary to calculate the present value of both costs and benefits associated with alternative problem solutions by multiplying each stream by an appropriate *discount factor*.

If the alternative is to invest available funds at some interest rate, then an appropriate discount factor can be expressed as:

$$\frac{1}{(1 + i)^n}$$

where i is the relevant interest rate per period and n is the number of periods into the future that the costs or benefits will accrue. If, as is the usual case, 1 is positive, then the further the event is in the future, the smaller its present value. A high discount rate means that the present is valued considerably more than the future. Two reasons exist for discounting public projects: (1) to reflect a social preference for earlier over later benefits; and (2) to reflect the opportunity costs for public investments, that is, the cost of investing in project A over investing in project B at some future time.

In *The Economics of Welfare,* first published in 1912, A.C. Pigou asserts that most people have a "defective telescopic facility" when it comes to benefits; that is, they tend to prefer the present over the future more than they should. This preference leads to too much consumption and not enough investment or saving for the future. Eckstein and Baumol conclude that at least two time preferences exist: one for individuals acting on their own and one for individuals acting collectively.[12] Both agree with Pigou that most public officials give too little weight to the benefits to future generations.[13]

Except in formal applications of cost-benefit or cost-effectiveness analysis, to be discussed in chapter 8, public officials seldom give adequate attention to the concept of discounting. Costs and benefits associated with a particular problem may be considered only in the short run. If a longer time perspective is adopted, a distorted picture may be presented in which benefits are considered at full value, while costs are partially discounted, or vice versa. Such approaches should be avoided, and an adequate time perspective should be adopted to permit a full and complete articulation of costs and benefits over the expected life cycle of the project or program.

The relationship between the discount rate and various intangible benefits and costs is also important. For example, environmental amenities are often destroyed because society places a relatively high discount rate on the future. It may well be however, that certain environmental values should be inflated in the future because they are often irreproducible, increasingly scarce, and increasingly in demand as a function of income elasticities. Over the years, environmental groups have advocated higher discount rates as a way of opposing tenuous projects; for example, a flood control project with a high start-up cost and a lengthy stream of benefits would yield a less attractive benefit-cost ratio if a high discount rate were used. If environmental benefits are eventually rolled into cost-benefit assessments, however, a high discount rate would be dysfunctional. In general, environmental impacts are still considered as *externalities*—costs and benefits not included in the market-pricing mechanism.

Other Time Considerations

The old adage "time is money" often seems to have few adherents in the public sector. Staff resources may be underutilized for a variety of reasons; minor problems are often handled at inappropriate levels within the organization; meetings are held where little is decided other than the time of the next meeting; staff efficiency is reduced by "penny wise, pound foolish" budget cuts that eliminate appropriations for materials, supplies, and other essential support resources. Since most public agencies deal in services, a common argument is that techniques developed to improve private-sector performance are not directly applicable to public activities, particularly non–product-oriented functions. This argument is inherently fallacious. It may be true that many government activities are process-oriented and do not result in an "end product." Nevertheless, these processes do have some objectives that are analogous to a project completion. Furthermore, a range of cost and time constraints clearly can be associated with most government activities. Through effective programming, these activities, in turn, can be organized in an optimal manner so as to minimize activity costs and utilize time constraints more effectively. If such a program is followed, the time saved through the minimization of inefficiencies will enable the staff to undertake new and varied activities without a significant increase in size.

Another aspect of the time-perspective issue is knowing when and where to start—the so-called sequencing problem. Problems often exist in a hierarchical relationship to one another, and the solution of one problem may depend on the solution of another, either higher or lower in the hierarchy. In short, problems are seldom mutually exclusive. A single set of variables may be common to a number of problems; the primary variables of a relatively low-order problem may be secondary variables of a higher-order problem. Therefore, problems must be placed in a queue reflecting their hierarchical relationships. Timing, in a sequential sense, is a critical factor in the successful resolution of these problem sets.

The readiness of the system to accept innovation and to implement change is another important aspect of the time dimension. The urgency surrounding some problems dictates that prompt and dramatic action be taken. However, solutions to such problems should not be advanced without first answering two questions: (1) Are the means (dollar resources) available to achieve these ends? and (2) Are the people (personnel resources) available to carry out the proposed programs? No solution can be better than the individuals or agencies responsible for carrying it out. A commitment to action is doubly important when people must change their behavior, habits, or attitudes to make a solution effective. Responsibility for the action must be clearly assigned, and the measurements, standards of accomplishment, and incentives associated with the proposed action must be changed simultaneously with the introduction of the problem solution.

In many situations, an organization may not be ready for dramatic changes in operations or procedures, and therefore the optimal solution may have to be introduced incrementally. The staging and timing of these incremental changes cannot be arbitrary, however, but must be carefully planned and implemented. While the first step may be most critical, and the final goal temporarily shrouded in obscurity, it is important that the administrator not lose sight of this final objective.

Thus, the performance administrator must develop a balanced time perspective to ensure systems readiness in the short-, medium-, and long-range future. Sufficient flexibility must be maintained to meet a wide range of possible competitive actions and opportunities, while keeping broader systemic concerns in focus.

Policy Typologies and Decision Patterns

Much of the present research by political scientists into the realm of public policy stems from a few simple typologies of decision interaction. Work in this area began in the early 1960s with the studies of welfare policy by Dawson and Robinson.[14] In spite of the impact of this work on empirical research in policy analysis, it has several shortcomings, particularly its failure to explicate the boundaries around categories of policy issues and problems. Considering all policy issues to be in the same category masks important relationships within the policy process; policy making is treated as a unidimensional generic activity. As a consequence, the impacts of some types of policy on other sectors is not clearly identifiable. For example, lumping together measures of spending and of service makes it impossible to discern the interdependencies of factors that actually influence each type of policy decision.

Lewis Froman was among the first to break with the framework established by Dawson and Robinson by suggesting that consideration be given to policies that are *areal* (more universally applied) and those that are *segmental* (applicable to specific districts, groups, or corporate entities within a larger jurisdiction).[15] Eulau and Eyestone offer the categories of *adaptive* and *control* as a basis for distinguishing various policy categories.[16] Theodore Lowi envisioned policy categories in terms of legislative arenas. His typology includes:

1. *distributive policies* that expand the benefits of public programs without creating intergroup conflicts; or those policies that extend existing programs for short terms—one to three years—so as to maintain the status quo, often in the face of impending redistribution of previously authorized resources;
2. *redistributive policies* that result in significant changes in the groups affected when changes are controversial among those groups (for example, the establishment of a price support program for certain agricultural commodities);
3. *regulative policies* that vest discretionary authority in some administrative agency or establish groups to make recommendations on future policies.[17]

To this list Salisbury has added:

4. *self-regulative policies* that vest discretionary authority with the group (for example, self-policing of price levels in the oil industry).

Salisbury also extended Lowi's approach by suggesting that different policy types were likely to emerge as outputs of various types of interaction between two key variables: the *pattern of demands* and the *structure of the decisional system.*[18] Salisbury places these two variables on axes representing the degree of fragmentation-integration in each (figure 7–1).

A highly fragmented demand pattern, such as several counties seeking subsidies for their roads, interacting with a fragmented decisional system such as a state legislature might produce a distributive policy of the classic pork-barrel variety. A highly integrated decisional system, such as one character-ized by a strong executive office, facing a relatively integrated set of demands arising from two conflicting groups, might be forced to choose sides in what would be seen as a zero-sum game—one where there is a winner and a loser. The result is likely to be a redistributive policy. Self-regulatory policy might be expected when an integrated group makes demands of a fragmented decisional system; that is, the decision is likely to be to delegate authority to the demand group through, for example, some form of self-administered licensing proce-dure. The fourth type—regulatory policy—is interpreted by Salisbury as resulting from the interaction of fragmented demands and an integrated decision system, and is characterized by continuing government control over unorganized demand groups.

Decision Costs and Policy Choices

Salisbury and Heinz, in a follow-up paper, added a second typology to this analytical framework, reflecting the relationship between *demand patterns* and the *cost of reaching decisions.* This latter dimension, they suggest, includes information costs, negotiation costs, and exchange values.[19] In short, the cost of reaching a decision is analogous to the cost of problem solving.

Salisbury and Heinz advance the following hypothesis as the most fundamental link between the elements of the cost-benefit calculus and the likely policy outcomes:

The more costly it is to organize the requisite coalition on an issue, the more likely it is that the policy outcome will be structural rather than allocative.

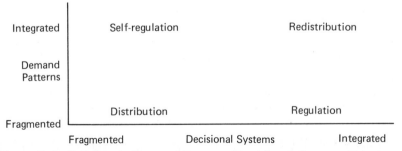

Figure 7–1. Salisbury's Demand-Patterns/Decisional-Systems Typology

This conceptualization results in the typology shown in figure 7–2, which they proposed as a substitute for or an augmentation of the initial diagrammatic relationships.

The implications of these formulations for problem identification should be evident. The dimensions of demand patterns, costs associated with reaching a decision, and the level of integration or fragmentation within the decision system must be considered in formulating the problem, exploring alternatives, and resolving the problem. Figure 7–3 represents a summary of the various elements discussed in connection with the problem dimension of demand patterns.

Redistributive decisions tend to be allocative, adaptive, and focused on segmental issues; they are likely to arise when an integrated decision system is faced with integrated demands. *Distributive decisions,* although they are also allocative and adaptive, tend to have more of an areal focus and are the consequence of an interface between a fragmented decision system and fragmented demand patterns. The cost of reaching a decision in both cases is relatively low.

Increased decision costs lead to regulatory or self-regulatory decisions. *Regulatory decisions* tend to deal with issues of structure and control and to focus on broader areal concerns that arise out of an interface between fragmented demands and an integrated decision system. On the other hand, when a fragmented decision system is faced with an integrated set of demand patterns (which are also likely to come from a particular segment of the broader society) and a high cost of reaching a decision, it is likely to grant *self-regulatory authority* to the demanding group.

Decision costs have rarely, if ever, been carefully examined as a constraint on problem solving. However, the literature on public policy suggests that these costs may predetermine the scope of policy alternatives and, along with other constraints, largely dictate the decision. The discussion now turns to these other constraints.

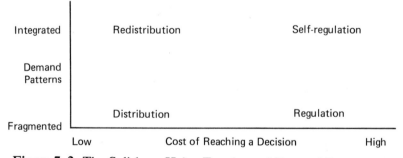
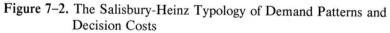

Figure 7–2. The Salisbury-Heinz Typology of Demand Patterns and Decision Costs

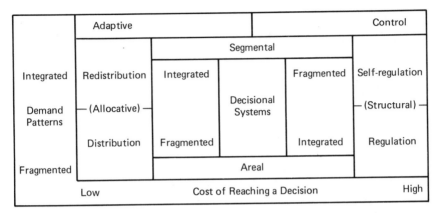

Figure 7–3. Summary of Elements in Demand-Pattern Typologies

Constraints and Boundary Conditions

To be effective, the solution to any problem must satisfy a clearly identified set of boundary conditions. The concept of boundary conditions is derived from the field of operations research and refers to that set of parameters or constraints that determine the range of feasible solutions to a given problem. In more general applications, boundary conditions represent the specifications of what a problem solution must accomplish.

In identifying boundary conditions, six basic questions must be answered:

1. What are the minimum goals (organizational and/or societal) to be attained?
2. What objectives must be met by the solution of the particular problem?
3. What measure(s) of efficiency can be used with respect to each of the objectives?
4. What are the existing or potential constraints on an effective solution to the problem set?
5. What standard(s) can be applied for evaluating possible courses of action in terms of their effectiveness?
6. What definition of "most effective" is applicable in judging the possible solutions to any given problem set?

In many problem situations, the identification of these boundary conditions may be the most difficult phase of the undertaking.

In operations research, boundary conditions are applied in seeking optimal solutions. An optimum can be defined mathematically as that point on some well-defined surface where all the partial derivatives are equal to zero and the appropriate second-order conditions prevail. The point at which the partial derivatives are equal to zero is known as a *saddle point,* a term borrowed from mountain climbing, where it refers to a ridgeline from which the mountain slopes away in several different directions.

In less technical terms, most mathematical applications of operations research and systems analysis involve some set of conditions that can be expressed as functions of two or more sets of variables: (1) *decision variables,* which are assumed to depend on the free choice of the decision maker; (2) a set of "outside" or *exogenous variables,* the values of which are determined outside the particular analysis and must be taken as givens by the decision maker; and (3) a set of *parameters,* the values of which are also assumed to be noncontrollable and externally determined by the "state of nature."[20]

In many current public-decision problems of any consequence, a hard-core optimization is rarely possible. Most likely, the analyst will be lucky if he can get some idea of the signs of the partial derivatives—whether he is moving "up the mountain," so to speak, toward a saddle point, or down the mountain away from the saddle point. In many cases it is difficult to determine even what "mountain" the analyst is on.

If the analytical task is approached in an inflexible manner in dealing with major problems of public choice, the analyst is likely to have trouble. He may soon give up in complete frustration; he may produce such a simplified model that the resulting calculations have little value; or he may present his conclusions long after the critical time for the decision, rendering them of little use to the decision maker.

Most major public-decision problems may ultimately be resolved primarily on the basis of experience and judgment. The points raised in this chapter about problem definition should help to sharpen this experience and judgment. There are also some "hard" analytical tools that can contribute to this process. These analytical methods, approaches, and strategies will be discussed in chapters 8 and 9.

Notes

1. E.B. Raybould and A.L. Minter, *Problem Solving for Management* (London: Management Publications Limited, British Institute of Management, 1971), p. 32.

2. F. Gerald Brown has labeled this human-relations style of management the "Good Shepherd" approach, whereby the manager supervises rather than controls. See "Management Styles and Working with People," in *Developing the Municipal Organization,* ed. Stanley P. Powers et al. (Washington, D.C.: International City Management Association, 1974), pp. 69–83. W.J. Reddin, in his "Tri-Dimensional Grid," labels such a manager as

a Developer, that is, one who is primarily concerned with developing the talents of others in a conducive work atmosphere (*Training Directors Journal* 18(July 1964):9–18).

3. Raybould and Minter, *Problem Solving for Management,* p. 36.

4. Ibid., p. 21.

5. Alex Bavelas and Dermot Barrett, "An Experimental Approach to Organization Communication," *Personnel* 27(1951):368.

6. Victor A. Thompson, *Modern Organization* (New York: Alfred A. Knopf, 1963), pp. 105–110.

7. Richard M. Cyert and James G. March, *A Behavioral Theory of the Firm* (Englewood Cliffs, N.J.: Prentice-Hall, 1963), pp. 124–125.

8. D.T. Campbell, in "Systemic Error on the Part of Human Links in Communication Systems," *Information and Control* 1(1958):334–369, suggests a number of categories of distortion that arise from the coding of messages.

9. Gordon W. Allport and L. Postman, "The Basic Psychology of Rumor," in *The Process and Effects of Mass Communication,* ed. W. Schramm (Urbana: University of Illinois Press, 1954), pp. 146–148.

10. For a further discussion of communication processes in public decision-making, see Alan Walter Steiss, *Public Budgeting and Management* (Lexington, Mass.: Lexington Books, D.C. Heath and Company, 1972), chap. 5.

11. Dick Netzer, *Economics and Urban Problems* (New York: Basic Books, 1974), p. 24.

12. Similarly, Buchanan and others have suggested that the individual in a group situation is more conscious of the potential influence of his selection or vote in determining the final collective action. This awareness often results in a somewhat different "scale of preference" than in the market situation, where the individual will strive to satisfy his own tastes. See James M. Buchanan and Gordon Tullock, *The Calculus of Consent* (Ann Arbor: University of Michigan Press, 1962).

13. Otto Eckstein, *Water Resource Development* (Cambridge, Mass.: Harvard University Press, 1958), pp. 99; William J. Baumol, *Welfare Economics and the Theory of the State* (Cambridge, Mass.: Harvard University Press, 1952), pp. 91–93.

14. Richard E. Dawson and James A. Robinson, "Interparty Competition, Economic Variables, and Welfare Policies in the American States," *Journal of Politics* 25(May 1963):265–289.

15. Lewis A. Froman, Jr., "An Analysis of Public Policies in Cities," *Journal of Politics* 29(February 1967):94–108.

16. Heinz Eulau and Robert Eyestone, "Policy Maps of City Councils and Policy Outcomes: A Developmental Analysis," *American Political Science Review* 62(March 1968):124–143.

17. Theodore Lowi, "American Business, Public Policy Case-Studies, and Political Theory," *World Politics* 17(July 1964):677–715.

18. Robert H. Salisbury, "The Analysis of Public Policy: A Search for Theories and Rules," in *Political Sciences and Public Policy,* ed. Austin Ranney (Chicago, Ill.: Markham Publishing Company, 1968).

19. Robert H. Salisbury and John Heinz, "A Theory of Policy Analysis and Some Preliminary Applications," in *Policy Analysis in Political Science,* ed. Ira Sharkansky (Chicago, Ill.: Markham Publishing Company, 1970).

20. Charles R. Carr and Charles W. Howe, *Quantitative Decision Procedures in Management and Economics* (New York: McGraw-Hill Book Company, 1964), p. 9.

Decision-Analysis Techniques

A variety of techniques have been developed by economists and operations researchers to facilitate decision making under uncertainty, a condition often confronted by public officials and managers. Several of these methods are complex and technical and thus will be discussed here in only a cursory fashion. Fortunately, the techniques of cost-benefit analysis can be applied to specific decision problems without complete mastery of the subtle nuances of welfare economics from which this analytical approach derives its theoretical foundations.[1] Furthermore, it is not difficult to glean a basic understanding of probability and utility functions that can enable most administrators to make more effective use of the information provided by decision analyses.

Economic Decision Theory and Problem Solving

Given its emphasis on rational decisions and utilitarian results ("the greatest good for the greatest number"), economic decision theory has provided the underpinnings of most approaches to decision analysis. To appreciate the relationship of economic decision theory to the objectives of performance administration, it is first necessary to have a nodding acquaintance with the underlying conceptual basis of much of this theory.

Economic Man versus Administrative Man

Nearly all economic decision theory is based on the theory of *riskless choice,* or decision making under certainty. The most important set of assumptions made in this theory is that a person faced with a decision situation will act as an *Economic Man,* defined as someone who is: (1) completely informed, (2) infinitely sensitive, and (3) rational. In most older works on economic choice, it is assumed that the alternatives available to an individual are continuous and infinitely divisible, and that economic man is infinitely sensitive to these conditions. The only purpose of these assumptions is to make the functions that they lead to continuous and differentiable. This requirement is basic to many applications of operations research, particularly to linear programming.

Economic man is assumed to know not only what courses of action are open to him, but also what the outcomes of any action will be. The assumption that Economic Man is rational has two corollaries: (1) Economic Man can weakly order all the states or choices open to him; and (2) he can make his choices so as to maximize or minimize something. These conditions assume a complete utility-ordering or preference hierarchy that can rank all sets of consequences from the most preferred to the least preferred, so that the decision maker only has to select the most preferred consequence in terms of that which he seeks to maximize or minimize.

In the field of economic decision theory, there has been almost no discussion of the possibility that the two essential components of rationality might be in conflict. It is conceivable, for example, that it might be very costly in time and effort to maintain continuously a weakly ordered preference field in order to have sufficient knowledge about all available choices to put them in rank order. Such conditions would therefore result in a negative utility. And under such circumstances, would it be "rational" for the decision maker to have such a preference field?

While Herbert Simon was not the first to be struck by the unreality of the concept of Economic or Maximizing Man, with its attributes of complete information and rationality, he took the lead in offering an alternative model of decision making—the concept of *Administrative or Satisficing Man.* Whereas Economic Man is assumed to make decisions as an owner in an environment of predominantly small firms in a perfectly competitive market, present-day Administrative Man tends to be a professional manager in an environment fraught with imperfectly competitive market conditions. Economic Man theory is normative (what should be done); Administrative Man theory tends to be descriptive (what is done).

Satisficing Man has various motivations in his search for alternatives. When he finds an alternative that is good enough—one that suffices or that resolves his dilemma for the moment—he refrains from further search (that is, he is satisfied), thereby conserving his time, energy, and resources. Satisficing Man is not necessarily concerned with the best or optimal solution, only with moving toward a better position or more satisfactory state. Therefore, the path through which Satisficing Man moves with each incremental feedback of information is characteristic of a stochastic or trial-and-error process. Unfortunately, in some quarters Simon's model has become a normative defense of the status quo, since many political decisions to which it is applied rarely exhibit the use of feedback and periodic adjustments.

Using the satisficing model, however, requires considerable knowledge of such variables as the values of the individual actors, the cost of the search, the obstacles to the implementation of particular proposals, and so forth. Unless such knowledge is available, the satisficing model reveals relatively little about why any particular actor considers any particular alternative solution as good enough.

Uncertainty and Risk

One administrator's uncertainty may be another's acceptable risk; what one public manager may interpret as an uncertain situation to be avoided, another may see as an opportunity, albeit involving some risk. While these two terms often are mistakenly treated as interchangeable, the distinction between uncertainty and risk is an important concept of rational decision theory, and by extension, of performance administration.

Certainty may be defined as a state of knowledge in which the specific and invariable outcomes of each alternative course of action are known in advance. The key to certainty is the presence of only one state of nature (although under some circumstances there may be numerous strategies to achieve that state). This condition enables the administrator to predict the outcome of a decision with one-hundred percent probability.

Uncertainty may be defined as a state of knowledge in which one or more courses of action *may* result in a set of possible specific outcomes, but where the probabilities of the outcomes are neither known nor meaningful. As Archer has observed, uncertainty technically involves a range of conditions in which probability distributions vary from a condition of considerable confidence, based on objective probabilities, to one at the other extreme, a condition of uncertainty with little or no information as to the probable relative frequency of particular events.[2]

If an administrator or public official is willing to assign objective or subjective probabilities to the outcome of uncertain events, such events may be said to involve risk. Thus, *risk* is a state of knowledge in which each alternative leads to one of a set of specific outcomes, each outcome occurring with a probability that is known to the administrator. More succinctly, risk is reassurable uncertainty. Risk is measurable when decision expectations or outcomes can be based on statistical probabilities. The event of drawing a red card from a well-shuffled deck is an example of a risky outcome with a probability of 50 percent; the event of the election of a Republican president in 1984 is an uncertain outcome.

The relationship between Economic Man, Administrative Man, and the problems of risk and uncertainty are summarized in figure 8–1. The range of risk between Economic Man, who operates under complete certainty, and Administrative Man frequently can be defined in terms of objective probabilities, and the conventional methods of probability theory can be applied to reduce uncertainty. The range of risk between Administrative Man and the "ignoramus" (the individual who operates in the realm of complete uncertainty, often out of an unwillingness to accept risk) can be defined in terms of subjective probabilities. The methods of statistical inference and the Bayesian approach to probability provide a basis for dealing with such uncertainty. The effective administrator willingly accepts both the notion of risk and the application of objective and subjective probabilities.

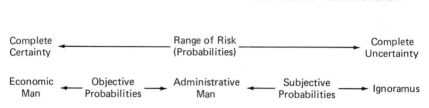

Figure 8–1. The Certainty-Uncertainty Spectrum of Decision Conditions

Probability Functions

The nexus of decisions under uncertainty is the identification of risk, and the key to understanding risk is the calculation of *probability functions.* Establishing a probability function can bring problems within more manageable bounds by reducing uncertainty to some level of risk that may be tolerated by the administrator, depending on his risk threshold. Probabilities can be established either a posteriori (by induction or empirical measurement) or a priori (by deduction or statistical inference).

The basic conditions necessary to establish a posteriori probability are: (1) the number of cases or observations must be large enough to exhibit statistical stability; (2) the observations must be repeated in the appropriate population or universe; and (3) the observations must be made on a random basis. The a posteriori approach offers the maximum opportunity for applied decision theory, because the number of situations in which such objective probabilities can be used is increasing significantly.

Under the a priori approach, probability statements are not intended to predict a particular outcome for a given event but merely assert that in a large number of situations with certain common characteristics a particular outcome is likely to occur. In short, a statistical inference is made regarding the probable outcomes arising from a somewhat uncertain event or series of events. Thomas Bayes (1702–1761), an English mathematician, first expressed in precise, quantitative form the mode of statistical inference. The Bayesian approach to decision making tends to treat uncertainty problems as if they were problems of risk by relying on personal, subjective probabilities, rather than the relative frequency, or objective, probabilities. In effect, the Bayesian approach bases probabilities on the administrator's confidence in the validity of specific propositions, which depend, in turn, how well prepared he is.

Expected Value and Expected Utility

The uncertainty and risk that administrators face come from two primary sources: the environment and the organization itself. Consequently, the broader environment must be considered in terms of the sources and types of influences that can affect the problem-identification and problem-solving process. When the environment is uncertain, the *expected value* approach often can be applied. Expected value is determined by multiplying the value products across all possible outcomes. In mathematical terms, expected value (*EV*) can be expressed as follows:

$$EV = p_1\$_1 + p_2\$_2 + \cdots p_n\$_n,$$

where *p* stands for probability, $ stands for the value of an outcome, and

$$p_1 + p_2 + \cdots p_n = 1.$$

Thus, in order to make a decision, the administrator must review the information available on various payoffs arising from choice elements in the decision environment. This review often is facilitated by the construction of a *probability payoff matrix* or *decision tree* that represents combinations of the feasible strategies, the states of nature (with their probabilities of occurrence), and the strategies used.

A decision tree is a device used to enumerate all the possible outcomes of a sequence of events where each event can occur in a finite number of ways. The construction of a tree diagram is illustrated in the figure 8–2. Three machines—A, B, and C—produce respectively 50 percent, 30 percent, and 20 percent of the total number of items manufactured by a particular factory. For each machine there is a definable level of defective output—3, 4, and 5 percent, respectively. If an item is selected at random from the factory's daily output, what is the probability that it will be defective?

The decision tree illustrates the various "paths" that influence the problem outcome. A fundamental theorem in probability theory states that sequential or conditional probabilities (that is, where the probability of one event occurring is conditioned by the occurrence of a previous event) can be calculated by multiplying the probabilities associated with each event. In other words, the probability of a defective item coming from machine A is .50 times .03 or .015. A second basic theorem is that all probability paths leading to the same outcome are additive. Therefore, the probability of a defective item being selected from all items produced by these machines is $(.50)(.03) + (.30)(.04) + (.20)(.05)$ or .037. With these data it is also possible to determine the probability that the defective item was produced by a particular machine, for example, machine A, by dividing the probability of a defective item from that machine (.015) by the total probability of a defective item being produced (.037).

The assumption that people actually behave rationally in the manner suggested by the mathematical notion of expected value is often contradicted by observable behavior in risky situations. People are willing to buy insurance,

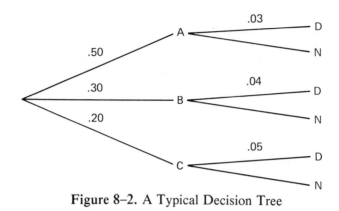

Figure 8–2. A Typical Decision Tree

even when they recognize that the insurance company makes a profit. People are willing to buy lottery tickets even though the lottery makes a profit. Consideration of the problem of insurance and the so-called "St. Petersburg paradox" led Daniel Bernoulli, an eighteenth-century mathematician, to propose that these apparent contradictions could be resolved by assuming that people act so as to maximize their *expected utility* rather than expected value.[3] Thus, people buy insurance because the consequences against which they are insured are significant in view of the costs, including the profit made by the insurance company. People are willing to invest a small amount of money in a lottery ticket, even though the probability outcome is highly uncertain insofar as any individual is concerned, because the payoff is quite high relative to their expected utility.

Social Preference and Risk Aversion

Extensive research has been performed in the area of risk and uncertainty because the behavior of decision makers so often appears to violate commonly accepted axioms of rational behavior. While no exact probabilities may exist for the success or failure of a particular event, Kassouf has observed that an individual with "... clear-cut, consistent preferences over a specified set of strategies ... will act as if he has assigned probabilities to various outcomes."[4] The values for the probabilities will be unique for each individual and not unlike the values of utility that might be assigned to an individual through a study of his social preferences. The obverse of social preferences, of course, is social risk aversion, a subject on which there are various opinions.[5]

As most economists will now admit, utility theory alone will not resolve the disputes over social preferences and/or aversion to risk. There are numerous situations in which policy analysts and managers will have to obtain a more careful reading of the various utility functions or preferences of their clientele and the community as a whole. As Stokey and Zeckhauser explain, policy choice under uncertainty is a threefold process.[6]

1. Alternatives must be assessed to determine what lotteries (probabilities and payoffs) are implied for individual members of the population.
2. Attitudes toward risk of these individuals must be evaluated to determine the certainty equivalents of these lotteries.
3. Having estimated the equivalent benefits that each alternative offers to different members of the population, the decision maker must select the preferred outcome.

While this process may sound simple, it is often very complex in application. Fortunately, some basic tools and strategies have been developed to aid the analyst and program manager in unraveling these complexities. These tools include: (1) dynamic equilibrium analysis, designed to identify policy makers' relative aversion to risk; (2) Markov chains, a highly instrumental modeling technique which traces probabilities for various states of the system over time; and (3) distribution analysis, which provides for the calculation of the level of divergence from an equal distribution of policy payoffs.[7]

These relatively mechanical techniques come into play only after one has a fairly good understanding of organizational and/or community preferences. To gain these insights, the analyst must develop a fairly rigorous set of strategic planning and public interaction procedures. These will be discussed in chapter 9. Once the groundwork for approximating utility has been laid, the analyst is prepared to address uncertainties in a systematic fashion.

A basic objective of performance administration is to reduce uncertainty by bringing to light information that will clarify relationships among elements or variables in the public decision-making process. This reduction of uncertainty may cause the risk associated with a particular choice to remain unchanged; to decrease (as in the case where a reduction in uncertainty permits assessment of more definitive probabilities); or even to increase (as happens when the additional information reveals risk factors previously unknown). Thus, although risk and uncertainty are interrelated, they must be treated independently in many situations.

Externalities and Intersystem Transfers

For decades, economists have analyzed a closely related set of considerations that arise from the misallocation of resources and are known as external economies and diseconomies, or simply as *externalities*. Despite important recent progress in clarifying the concept, considerable disagreement still exists among economists as to the causes and effects of externalities. As a consequence, the term may be somewhat loosely used in applied studies and is often overused and abused.

The fundamental notion behind the concept of externalities is that the actions of one individual or institution may affect the welfare of another in ways that are difficult to regulate by private agreement among the affected parties.[8] When the effects of these actions extend to a large enough group, their impacts may become a matter of public concern, and efforts may be made to limit such externalities by law. By the same token, however, public policies may produce both positive and negative externalities. The classic example of negative externalities arising from public action is cited by Burkhead and Miner:

> ... any public policy (for example, taxation) not unanimously approved by those legally bound by it produces an external cost of its own which must be compared with the external costs generated by the private market solution to the same problem. ... The external costs of nonunanimously approved public policies are the costs imposed on the citizen by tax and/or expenditure decisions to which he is legally bound despite the absence of his consent. ... [T]he implication follows that only policies approved by all members of a community are acceptable under the Pareto criterion.[9]

The public administrator foraging into the literature of economics and public finance in search of an answer to the problem of externalities is soon likely to be frustrated by the complexities of jargon that he or she will encounter. If one can get past the basic concepts of welfare economics, such as "Pareto optimality" and the "Kaldor-Hicks criterion," he must then try to comprehend: (1) the notion of a public or social good ("defined so that one person's consumption does not reduce another's"[10]), (2) the application of private-good joint-supply solutions to public goods,[11] and (3) the theory of market failure ("the fundamental factors which account for the inability of decentralized private markets to attain economic efficiency"[12]). At this point, the public servant is likely to find that, although practically all economists concur that private agreements cannot allocate resources to abate external diseconomies, considerable controversy still exists among leading theorists as to exactly why private agreements do not work.

Two distinct approaches characterize the examination of sources of market failure. One attempts to reduce all instances of market imperfections to a single concept.[13] The other approach segregates the determinants of market failures into a few distinct categories.[14] Buchanan has suggested the elimination of the distinction between externalities and public-good joint supply—a distinction fundamental to these other categorizations.[15]

Thus, although the concept of externalities has an important bearing on public problem solving and decision making, the theoretical complexity of this concept and the controversy surrounding it have limited its application and understanding by most public officials and administrators. In layman's terms, then, what are externalities and intersystem transfers?

In the private marketplace, transactions between buyers and sellers (producers and consumers) are presumed to be based on their respective interpretations of the costs and benefits that will accrue to them, that is, internal costs and benefits. For example, market prices and profit maximization induce a firm to operate efficiently from the point of view of the broader society in terms of the input-output relations of production. Consumers, in turn, are assumed to purchase goods and services in accordance with some principle of utility maximization.

Many economic transactions, however, have some effects on third parties, and in some cases, those impacts on people's welfare may be dysfunctional. The classic example is that of smoke emission. If an industry creates smoke that spreads over the community, the residents' welfare is reduced. If, however, the fuel that produces the smoke is an important input to the firm's manufacturing process, and if the smoke is not too harmful to the public, a certain amount of smoke may be worth its cost to the firm and to the public. These considerations, however, are seldom taken into account in the normal calculations of the marketplace. If "too much" smoke is produced, it is said to be an external diseconomy, and efforts may be initiated to limit this externality through public regulations such as EPA smoke-abatement and air-pollution-control regulations. Public intervention is necessary in such situations because a private agreement on such an issue would be extremely difficult and costly to specify and negotiate, that is, the "transaction cost" of such an agreement would be high.[16]

As our society becomes more complex, interdependent, and urbanized, the occurrence of significant externalities has sharply increased. "We are growing increasingly concerned about the external effects of individuals' decisions on waste disposal, or on land use, or on modes of transportation, or about the lack of educational attainment by some children."[17]

Given the increase in social and environmental externalities, new schools of economic thinking have arisen to seek alternatives to direct regulation. Resource Economists, for example, attempt to internalize externalities back in the marketplace by assigning "effluent fees" to such things as water pollution. In this way the classical pricing mechanism still functions. However, it is noteworthy that the government must still act as the pricing agent.

Governmental Intervention as an Externality

Once an important externality is identified, the next question is what to do about it. The usual answer is that government should tax or regulate the private activity in an approximation of the missing market mechanism. Such taxation regulation, however, creates additional costs to the firm which may be transferred to other parts of the system. *Intersystem transfers* create further externalities which also must be considered in the decision to invoke governmental controls. These intersystem transfers often affect individuals and groups beyond the initially affected population, resulting in secondary and even tertiary externalities. Unfortunately, these costs seldom are fully identified. As Mills has observed: "Sometimes government programs become cumbersome because the government must bear exactly the transaction costs that prevented the private sector from undertaking the transactions in the first place."[18]

Although the discussion so far has emphasized external diseconomies, it must be acknowledged that private transactions may also produce external benefits. A major concern in public policy making, therefore, is to seek means to minimize external costs arising from decisions in both the private and public sectors, and to maximize potential external benefits. In other words, the marginal costs and benefits arising from government intervention should be equal. Policy selection should depend on the transaction costs of the policies and on the extent to which they approximate efficient resource allocations.

Not all decisions in contemporary society give rise to significant externalities. Netzer has observed that, "In a society that prizes freedom of choice and action by individuals, groups, and local governments, it is important to pinpoint those decisions that do not involve major externalities, those decisions that can be made on the basis of internal costs and benefits. Such freedom has the major economic advantages of being consistent with the more effective allocation of resources."[19]

Decision Costs

The fact that public decisions produce external costs has led some economic theorists to abandon the criterion of Pareto optimality for some other, less strict criteria for welfare judgments. The alternative is to accept inefficiencies in public decisions because of an inability to make impersonal comparisons with respect to the relative burdens arising from the incidence of externalities under alternative policies.[20]

Buchanan and Tullock attempt to resolve this dilemma through the development of a rationale for political decisions that neither violates Pareto optimality nor requires the veto power. In so doing, they invoke the concept of *decision cost*—the sharply increasing cost of reaching agreement as the size of the group increases so that a particular individual "cannot predict with any degree of certainty whether he is more likely to be in a winning or losing coalition on any specific issue."[21] Therefore, the individual chooses a decision rule that most generally will maximize his utility in the face of uncertainty regarding particular outcomes. That is, he is willing to accept a rule of less than unanimity with regard to collective action without the need for inter-personal comparisons. In place of unanimity, therefore, Buchanan and Tullock propose that decisions be made by that portion of the public for which decision costs (the cost of reducing uncertainty) are minimized.

Criticisms of these formulations have centered on the issue of the proposed decision rule. Under the suggested approach, a relatively small minority could block a policy that would remove existing costs borne by a large segment of the population, and could prevent the imposition of external costs by the majority on the minority.[22] Thus, Baumol has argued for majority rule by suggesting that it is:

> ... the rule which may be said to minimize the tyranny of a conservative minority while not at the same time offering any minority the unilateral power to institute change. ... Power resides both in the group which can impose and the one which can prevent. Majority rule is the one arrangement which makes the smaller of these groups as large as possible.[23]

Regardless of the propriety of majority rule, studies of *demand patterns* (or the policy arenas through which problems are addressed) suggest that solutions to problems are significantly affected by the *decision demands* (the political costs involved in developing and maintaining a particular policy). Minority groups can thus affect decisions by raising the decision costs. Helen Ingram contends that environmental groups, for example, have effectively shifted the arena through which policies flow by raising the decision costs for influential legislators.[24] This notion of decision demands and decision costs brings the discussion full circle, back to the points raised in chapter 7 regarding demand patterns as an important component in problem identification.

Cost-Benefit and Cost-Effectiveness Analysis

In terms of evaluative scope, the techniques of cost-benefit and cost-effectiveness analysis are more ambitious than most other methodologies of management science, and are therefore more vulnerable to criticism at certain well-recognized points. As Prest and Turvey have observed: "One can view cost-benefit analysis as anything from an infallible means of reaching the new Utopia to a waste of resources in attempting to measure the unmeasurable."[25] Although some of these criticisms are based on misconceptions, others are perfectly valid. Many of these valid criticisms, however, are applicable a fortiori to other analytical techniques. All too often, the argument for replacing relatively poor analysis with better approaches degenerates to assertions that, since analysis is difficult, costly, and troublesome, it should be abandoned in favor of more intuitive approaches.

Unfortunately, the techniques of cost-benefit and cost-effectiveness analysis often are misunderstood by public officials and misapplied by unscrupulous analysts. The objective of these analytical techniques is not to make decisions, nor to justify previous decisions, nor to delay matters so that some prior course of action or commitment of resources has a greater chance of acceptance or continuance.

Objective Function, Constraints, and Externalities

Cost-benefit analysis seeks to rank alternative uses of fiscal resources. In the usual situation, several projects are competing for the same scarce resources, and each project can be pursued at one or more levels of effort. The problem may be to choose which alternative to adopt and then to choose its optimal scale from the several that may be available. In the traditional formulation of the cost-benefit approach, as first outlined by Otto Eckstein, the allocation problem is clarified through the identification of: (1) an objective function, (2) constraints, (3) externalities, (4) time dimensions, and (5) risk and uncertainty.[26]

An *objective function* is a measure of the benefits and/or costs associated with each alternative under consideration (quantified in dollar terms as much as possible). In theory, an objective function should represent an indicator of success—a benefit measure—that is to be maximized. In practice, however, public managers are often instructed to minimize costs in carrying out their programmatic responsibilities. As a consequence, cost-benefit analysis often is reduced to cost-efficiency analysis—an attempt to obtain the maximum possible level of output or performance at some fixed level of cost (often inadequate for true program effectiveness).

Constraints specify the "rules of the game," that is, the limitations within which solutions must be sought. Solutions that are otherwise optimal often must be discarded because they violate these imposed rules. Constraints often can be incorporated into mathematical models as parameters or boundary conditions. *Externalities* are those factors—inputs (costs), outputs (benefits), and constraints—that initially are excluded from the statement of the problem in order to make it more manageable. The long-range effects of these externalities should be examined, however, after the objective function or model has been carefully tested and the range of feasible and acceptable alternatives has been narrowed.

In examining the *time dimensions* of various alternatives, it is necessary to delineate *life-cycle costs and benefits*. Life-cycle costs can be grouped as follows: (1) research and development costs associated primarily with the development of new programs or capabilities up to the point at which they are ready for operational use; (2) investment costs incurred beyond the start-up development phase, frequently in the form of capital construction and equipment costs; and (3) recurring operational costs needed to support and maintain a program or capability. The initial funding required to undertake a program or project should not be the primary consideration, nor should the funding requirements of any particular time period dominate the decision. Rather, the decision to undertake a particular course of action should take into account the total life-cycle cost impacts.

Benefits also may vary widely over the life of a program or project. There may be a time lag between the initiation of a project and the realization of the first increment of benefits. Benefits may build up gradually or may accumulate rapidly; they may reach a peak and decline rapidly or may taper off slowly. In short, the timing of costs and benefits cannot be ignored. It is not sufficient merely to add the total benefits and subtract the total costs estimated for a given alternative. Rather, it is necessary to consider a measure that reflects the impacts of deferred benefits and future costs.

Benefit/Cost Ratio

First developed in the implementation of the Flood Control Act of 1936, the benefit/cost ratio has remained one of the principal criteria of program analysis. This ratio can be expressed mathematically as follows:

$$R = \frac{\displaystyle\sum_{n=0}^{N} B_n (1 + i)^{-n}}{\displaystyle\sum_{n=0}^{N} C_n (1 = i)^{-n}} = \frac{B}{C}$$

Thus, if the discounted stream of benefits over the life of the project equals $1,000,000 and the discounted stream of costs equals $800,000, the benefit/cost ratio is 1.25.

A variation on the basic benefit/cost ratio tends to emphasize the return on invested capital by segregating operational costs and subtracting them from both sides of the ratio. In the previous example, assume that the present value of operational costs represents $200,000 of the total stream of costs; subtracting operational costs from both benefits and total costs results in the following net benefit/cost ratio:

$$\frac{\$1,000,000 - \$200,000}{\$800,000 - \$200,000} = 1.333$$

As operational costs account for an increasingly large portion of total costs, the net benefit/cost ratio becomes larger. In the above example, for instance, if operational costs account for half of the discounted total costs (or $400,000), the net benefit/cost ratio becomes 1.5. Net benefit/cost ratios may be preferable for private enterprises in which capital is more constraining than operational expenses, especially when taxes are considered. A number of economists argue for the use of gross ratios in the public sector, however, on the basis that legislative bodies should consider operational costs as well as capital costs, giving agencies credit for savings on operational costs by permitting them to spend more on capital costs.

Internal Rate of Return

Since the costs associated with any investment decision usually accrue first, the undiscounted sum of benefits must be considerably larger in order to yield a favorable project. This characteristic of long-term investments is implicit in the analytical technique of internal rate of return, a well-established concept in the business world and a legacy of such prominent economists as John Maynard Keynes and Kenneth Boulding. The internal rate of return (r) is defined by the following equation:

$$ r = \sum_{n=0}^{N} \frac{B_n}{(1 + r)^n} \; :: \; \sum_{n=0}^{N} \frac{C_n}{(1 + r)^n} $$

It should be noted that the internal rate of return is not set equal to anything. The right-hand side of the equation is the present value of costs; the left-hand side is the present value of benefits. The internal rate of return is that interest rate r that brings the two sides of the equation into equilibrium, that is, the return on investment (discounted benefits) that equals the cost of capital.

The internal rate of return provides a reasonably good measure of investment potential when all alternatives are of the same order of magnitude. When the alternatives are of different scales, however, it has less practical value, since it reveals little about the absolute size of the net benefits. Although it is applied with some success to private-investment decisions, the internal rate of return has only limited application in the public sector.

Net Benefits

Net benefits is the criterion recommended, if not used, most frequently in contemporary cost-benefit analysis. The formula for calculating the present value of net benefits is:

$$N = -C_0 + \frac{(B_1 - C_1)}{(1 + i)} + \frac{(B_2 - C_2)}{(1 + i)^2} + \ldots + \frac{(B_n - C_n)}{(1 + i)^n}.$$

Two projects with equal net benefits might not be regarded indifferently, however. Suppose that two projects each offered net benefits of $10,000, but one involved a present value of benefits of $2 million and a present value of costs of $1.99 million, while the other project had a present value of benefits of $100,000 and a present value of costs of $90,000. Suppose that something goes wrong, so that the calculations of costs and benefits were off by ten percent. The first project might have negative benefits of as much as $200,000, whereas the second would do no worse than break even.

Net benefits measure *difference,* whereas benefit/cost calculations produce a *ratio;* the results of these two techniques are not always interchangeable. The fact that the net benefits of alternative A are greater than those of alternative B does not imply that the benefit/cost ratio of A is greater than that of B. For example, suppose the benefits in alternative A have a present value of $300,000, while the costs have a present value of $100,000. The net benefits of this alternative would be $200,000 and the benefit/cost ratio would be 3.0. If the present value of benefits in alternative B were $200,000 and that of costs $40,000, alternative B would have lower net benefits ($160,000), but a higher benefit/cost ratio ($200,000/$40,000 or 5.0). In addition to knowing the benefit/cost ratio for a given project, it is also necessary to know the size of the project before as much information is available as is given in the present value of net benefits.

Cost Savings as Benefits

Certain items may be treated in cost-benefit analysis either as benefits or as cost savings. In this respect the net-benefits criterion is superior to the benefit/cost ratio method. For example, suppose that the construction of an expanded sewage treatment facility is estimated to cost $1,000,000 and to have measurable benefits of $1,250,000 in present value terms. In addition, it is estimated that this project will increase land values in some parts of the community by an aggregate of $500,000 (as a consequence of the increased service), while decreasing other land values (those of properties in proximity to the project) by $250,000. It would be appropriate to include these land-value changes in the cost-benefit study if it can be determined that they are not simply capitalization of otherwise measured benefits and costs, the inclusion of which would result in double counting. How to treat these additional factors, however, remains the problem. Land-value increases could be included as benefits, while decreases in land values could be considered as a cost, resulting in a benefit/cost ratio of $1,750,000/$1,250,000, or 1.4. Or the net change in land values ($500,000 minus $250,000) could be included as benefits ($1,250,000 plus $250,000 divided by $1,000,000), resulting in a ratio of 1.5, or as "cost savings" ($1,250,000 divided by $750,000), yielding a ratio of 1.67.

In considering several alternative investments, elaborate accounting rules and procedures must be devised to keep the analysis comparable. Such ambiguity does not exist, however, in the application of the net-benefits criterion, as long as the algebraic sign and the time period in which benefits and costs accrue are known.

Monetary Surrogates

The "ideal" cost-benefit analysis is one in which all inputs and outputs are evaluated in monetary terms. In principle, however, any other common unit will serve equally well. It is unlikely that in the foreseeable future public-sector applications will succeed in evaluating all inputs and outputs in commensurable terms. It may be difficult to identify precisely the outputs of such public activities as hospitals, libraries, recreational facilities, and so forth in direct dollar terms. Such outputs often must be approximated through the use of crude surrogates—indirect measures that purport to guage benefits in monetary terms. Further refinements may be possible through the development of information indicating how participants view the mission of a program. These referents or "proximate criteria," which should be empirically measurable, can then be used to describe different levels of output (performance) in terms of participants' expectations.

The problem of direct measurement of benefits in monetary terms has led some analysts to return to the more fundamental criterion of *average cost.* An average-cost calculation is similar to the reciprocal of a benefit/cost ratio, with costs in the numerator and output in physical terms in the denominator. For example, assume a comparison of two programs designed to encourage students to remain in high school and to stimulate their interests in vocational opportunities. Alternative A is estimated to cost $800,000 and is designed to reach 160 students who are potential dropouts, whereas alternative B costs $1,200,000 and is designed to reach 200 students. The average cost figure for alternative A is "$5000 per dropout prevented," whereas the average cost for B is "$6000 per dropout prevented." If it is assumed that the completion of vocational training will add about $10,000 to the life-earning capacity of each student (a rough surrogate of benefits), then the benefit/cost ratio of alternative A is 2.0, whereas the benefit/cost ratio of B is 1.67. The "net benefits" of A would equal $800,000, but so would the "net benefits" of alternative B. Some other criterion is needed to judge which program is more effective relative to its costs.

Cost-Effectiveness Analysis

The perfect analogue of average cost is the cost-effectiveness ratio. Under this criterion, the effectiveness of an alternative is measured by the extent to which that alternative, if implemented, will attain some desired goal or set of final objectives. There is usually more than one way of achieving a set of objectives. The purpose of cost-effectiveness analysis, therefore, is to determine the most effective program from among several alternatives at each level of goal achievement or output. The preferred alternative usually is the one that produces the desired level of effectiveness for the minimum cost, or the maximum level of effectiveness for a given level of cost. Although costs can ordinarily be represented in monetary terms, levels of achievement usually are expressed by nonmonetary indexes or effectiveness measures. Such indexes measure the direct and indirect impacts of public resource allocations.

Effectiveness measures involve a basic scoring technique for determining the status of a given program at any point in time with respect to the achievement of a goal. Such measures often are expressed in relative terms, for example, the percentage of reduction in unemployment; the percentage of reduction in the incidence of a disease; or the percentage of increase in some measure of educational attainment. In the evaluation of alternatives, it is desirable to array effectiveness measures along an *effectiveness scale* to indicate the degree of goal achievement evidenced by each alternative.[27]

In cost-effectiveness analysis, a cost curve is developed for each alternative, representing the sensitivity of costs (inputs) to changes in the desired level of effectiveness (outputs). Costs may change in approximate proportion to the level of achievement, that is, each additional increment of desired effectiveness may require approximately the same increase in units of expenditure. However, if effectiveness increases more rapidly than costs, then the particular alternative is operating at a level of increasing returns; this is represented by a positively sloped curve that accelerates at an accelerating rate, as illustrated by the initial segment of cost curve A in figure 8–3. If costs increase more rapidly than effectiveness, the alternative is operating in an area of diminishing returns. Increasing returns do not mean that an alternative should be automatically adopted (or expanded, if it is an ongoing program). Conversely, diminishing returns should not automatically disqualify a program alternative. It is useful to know, however, that an additional commitment of, for example, $200,000 to one alternative will carry it 20 percent closer to an established goal, whereas the same resources added to another alternative will carry it only 5 percent closer.

Cost-effectiveness analysis requires the construction of a model that can relate incremental costs to increments of effectiveness. For some types of problems, practical models can be developed with relative ease; for other problems, cost curves can be approximated from historical data. Construction

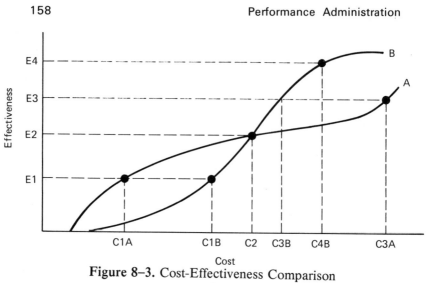

Figure 8–3. Cost-Effectiveness Comparison

of cost curves and effectiveness scales should become increasingly more sophisticated as the input-output relationships associated with the various alternatives are better understood.

Given that the cost and effectiveness of each alternative can be determined separately and for different levels of input-output relationships, the problem remains of how to choose among these alternatives. In principle, the criterion or rule of choice should be to select the alternative that yields the greatest excess of positive impacts (attainment of objectives) over negative impacts (resources used, or costs and externalities or spillovers that reduce effectiveness). In practice, however, this ideal criterion is seldom applied, since there is no practical way to subtract dollars spent from the nonmonetary measures used to identify effectiveness.

The Optimum Envelope

Therefore, a *cost-effectiveness comparison* of alternatives must be undertaken, as shown graphically in figure 8–3. Alternative A achieves the first level of effectiveness (E1) with a relatively modest level of cost (CA), whereas twice the level of resources (C1B) would be required to achieve the same level of effectiveness using alternative B. Both alternatives achieve the second level of effectiveness (E2) at the same level of cost (C2). Alternative B requires a lower level of resources (C3B) to achieve the third level of effectiveness. And only alternative B achieves the fourth level of effectiveness; the program cost curve of alternative A is not projected to reach this level of effectiveness.

Which of these two alternatives is more desirable? To answer this question, it is necessary to define the *optimum envelope* formed by these two cost curves. If resources in excess of C2 are available, alternative B clearly provides the better choice; however, if resources less than C2 are available, alternative A provides greater effectiveness for the dollars expended. In general, it is not possible to choose between two alternatives just on the basis of cost and effectiveness unless one alternative dominates at all levels of effectiveness. Usually, either a desired level of effectiveness must be specified and then costs minimized for that effectiveness level, or a cost limit must be specified and effectiveness maximized for that level of resource allocation.

At times, the government programs that are implemented do not represent the most effective programs technically available. Among the more obvious reasons for such suboptimization are political and legislative constraints, intergovernmental expectations, community attitudes, employer rights, intergovernmental expectations, community attitudes, employer rights, union rules, and so forth. *Cost-constraint analysis* examines the impacts of these factors by comparing the cost of the program that could be adopted if no constraints were present with the cost of the constrained program. Once this cost differential is identified, decisions as to the feasibility of attempting to remove the constraints can be made. On the basis of this analysis, public managers can provide decision makers with an estimate of how much would be saved through the relaxation of a given constraint. The cost of the constraint also is indicative of the amount of resources that might be committed to overcome a constraint, if such an effort were acceptable. In some cases, maintaining a constraint may be more valuable for social or political reasons than implementing a more effective program.

Incremental Costing

Cost-effectiveness analysis can be viewed as an application of the economic concept of *marginal analysis.* The analysis must always move from some base that represents existing capabilities and existing resource commitments. The problem is to determine the level of additional resources required to achieve some specified additional performance capability (the program objective) or, conversely, how much additional performance capability would result from some specified additional expenditure. Therefore, *incremental costs* are the most relevant factors in cost analysis. The economic concept of marginal analysis must be distinguished from the accounting concept of associating total costs, including an allocated share of indirect expense, to an end product or activity. Ideally, incremental cost is the difference between two programs, one with some desired improvement and one without this improvement.

In measuring incremental costs, it is important to exclude *sunk costs* (although such costs should form a part of the total program analysis in program budgeting). Sunk costs or costs that have been incurred in the past are not relevant to the question, "What will it cost in the future to acquire a future performance capability?" No matter how unfair it may seem, past costs should be excluded from the analysis regardless of how much money is involved. Even if sunk costs result in an *inheritable asset* or a resource capability that will become available to the program under analysis, the sunk costs of that asset should be excluded even though the asset itself is included in the analysis.

Output Orientation of Cost-Effectiveness Analysis

The techniques of cost-effectiveness analysis are relatively new, having originated in the early 1960s. Consequently, they have not yet reached full maturity. Cost-effectiveness analysis was initially developed for application when benefits could not be measured in units commensurable with costs. In these early applications, the output or level of effectiveness was usually taken as a given, and several methods of achieving this level were examined in the hope that one would have lower costs than the others. These initial applications revealed many important aspects of public decision making with respect to the allocation of scarce resources.

In contemporary applications, cost-effectiveness analysis provides an explicit output orientation for the evaluation of program alternatives. It places particular emphasis on goals and objectives and on the use of effectiveness measures to monitor progress toward these goals. The extended time horizon adopted in cost-effectiveness analysis leads to a fuller recognition of the need for life-cycle costing and marginal analysis and of the importance of incremental costs.

As with the other analytical techniques discussed in this chapter, the cost-effectiveness model need not be adopted "whole cloth." A number of subroutines of this approach may be introduced into ongoing program-analysis procedures. Particularly important are considerations developed through the technique of cost-effectiveness curve analysis. As the complexity of the resource-allocation problem becomes more evident, other subroutines may be adopted, depending on the availability of data and the needs and capabilities of the analysts.

The successful application of all the techniques discussed in this chapter depends on the full articulation of appropriate decision alternatives. The best decision analysis is of limited value if the most effective alternative courses of action are not considered. The formulation and evaluation of such alternatives, therefore, will be the subject of the next chapter.

Notes

1. E.J. Mishan, *Cost-Benefit Analysis* (New York: Praeger, 1976), p. 382.

2. Stephen H. Archer, "The Structure of Management Decision Theory," *Academy of Management Journal* 8(December 1964):283.

3. L. Somner, trans., "Specimen Theoriae Novae de Mensura Sortis," *Comentari Academiae Scientiarum Imperiales Petropolitanae* 5(1738): in *Econometrica* 22(1954):175–192.

4. Sheen Kassouf, *Normative Decision-Making* (Englewood Cliffs, N.J. Prentice-Hall, 1970), p. 46.

5. For a broader discussion of this point, see Jack Hirshleifer and David L. Shapiro, "The Treatment of Risk and Uncertainty," *Public Expenditures and Policy Analysis,* 2nd ed., Robert H. Haveman and Julius Margolis (Chicago: Rand McNally, 1977), pp. 180–203.

6. Edith Stokey and Richard Zeckhauser, *A Primer for Policy Analysis* (New York: W.W. Norton, 1978), p. 252.

7. For a more detailed discussion of decisions under uncertainty, see Howard Raiffa, *Decision Analysis* (Reading, Mass.: Addison-Wesley, 1968). For more about dynamic equilibrium, see Stuart Nagel and Marian Neef, *Operations Research Methods* (Beverly Hills, Calif.: Sage Publications, 1976). For an introductory discussion of Markov chains, see Stokey and Zeckhauser, *A Primer for Policy Analysis,* chap. 7.

8. Edwin S. Mills, *Urban Economics* (Glenview, Ill.: Scott, Foresman and Company, 1972), p. 131.

9. Jesse Burkhead and Jerry Miner, *Public Expenditure* (Chicago: Aldine Atherton, 1971), p. 122.

10. Ibid., p. 27.

11. Burkhead and Minor *(Public Expenditure,* p. 27), suggests that, "The resulting equilibrium solution, however, is not one which would ensue from any feasible market arrangement. It is argued that for goods which are essentially similar to polar public goods a solution approximating the equilibrium position requires public intervention."

12. Ibid., p. 102.

13. Kenneth J. Arrow, "The Organization of Economic Activity: Issues Pertinent to the Choice of Market versus Nonmarket Allocations," in *Public Expenditures and Policy Analysis,* eds. Robert H. Haveman and Julius Margolis (Chicago, Ill.: Markham Publishing Co., 1970), pp. 59–73; John G. Head, "Public Goods and Public Policy," *Public Finance* (1962):197–221.

14. Francis M. Bator, "The Anatomy of Market Failure," *Quarterly Journal of Economics* (August 1958):351–379; Tibor Scitovsky, "Two Concepts of External Economics," *Journal of Political Economy* (April 1954): 143–1251; J.E. Meade, "External Economics and Diseconomics in a Competitive Situation, *Economic Journal* (March 1952):54–67.

15. James M. Buchanan, "Joint Supply, Externality, and Optimality," *Journal of Political Economy* (November 1966):404–415.

16. Mills, *Urban Economics,* p. 132.

17. Dick Netzer, *Economics and Urban Problems* (New York: Basic Books, 1974), p. 25.

18. Mills, *Urban Economics,* p. 132.

19. Netzer, *Economics and Urban Problems,* p. 25.

20. Burkhead and Miner, *Public Expenditure,* p. 122.

21. James M. Buchanan and Gordon Tullock, The *Calculus of Consent* (Ann Arbor: University of Michigan Press, 1962), pp. 94–95.

22. Burkhead and Miner, *Public Expenditure,* p. 125.

23. William Baumol, *Welfare Economics and the Theory of the State* (Cambridge, Mass.: Harvard University Press, 1965), p. 44.

24. Helen Ingram, "The Changing Decision Rules in the Politics of Water Development," *Water Resources Bulletin* (December 1972):1177–1189.

25. A.R. Prest and R. Turvey, "Cost Benefit Analysis: A Survey," *The Economic Journal* (1965):583.

26. Otto Eckstein, *Water Resource Development* (Cambridge, Mass.: Harvard University Press, 1958).

27. E.S. Quade, *Analysis for Public Decisions* (New York: American Elsevier Publishing Company, 1975), p. 92.

9

Formulation and Evaluation of Alternative Solutions

A principal function of performance administration, as herein defined, is to assist public officials in determining appropriate courses of action, implementing these decisions, and thereby achieving some broader set of goals and objectives. The performance administrator, therefore, must devote considerable time and effort to the identification, explication, and assessment of alternatives. Only particularly perceptive or specially trained decision makers are likely to conduct systematic and exhaustive screenings of the entire set of possible alternatives. The constraints of limited resources and/or time often force decision makers to satisfice—to be satisfied with some alternative that suffices for the moment. This process, of course, is also known as "muddling through." Consequently, public officials tend to operate in a relatively narrow problem-solving mode, where the objective is to resolve the most obvious disparities between desired performance and actual accomplishments. Even when more systematic analysis is applied to this search process, certain alternatives may be dismissed out of hand for no better reason than: "We simply don't do things that way." However, as Quade has observed:

> ... no process of evaluation will designate the best alternative if it is not even considered in the analysis. Thus a strong effort should be made to search out and discover further alternatives, or to invent and design them, before a decision to select a particular one if finally made.[1]

Improving the Probability of Rational Decisions

In truly effective decision making, choices are made from a fully articulated set of alternatives. Alternative solutions are the only means of bringing the basic assumptions about a given situation up to an appropriate level of consciousness. At this level, it is possible to examine and test the validity and reliability of these assumptions. (Validity reflects the degree to which information contributes to resolving the problem. Reliability is the extent to which consistent results are achieved through the data or the methods for generating the data.) Alternative solutions are no guarantee of wisdom or of making the right decision, but they are helpful in avoiding what would have been identified as wrong decisions had the problems been thought through more carefully.

Rational and Nonrational Decisions

Decisions—the consequence of a search for and screening of alternatives—
often are judged to be "rational" or "irrational" depending on the particular
perspective of individuals involved in the decision-making situation. Public
decisions frequently do not appear rational in the sense that economic
decisions generally are. Therefore, many writers have concluded that the
criteria of rational decision processes often are inapplicable to public-decision
situations.

A decision generally is defined as rational or nonrational according to
some set of rules that delineates what actions are reasonable and consistent
with a given set of premises. It is possible to identify four basic categories of
nonrational decisions: (1) illogical decisions, (2) blind decisions, (3) rash
decisions, and (4) ignorant action. Illustrative of each of these categories are
the following "decisions" made by a hypothetical local governing body in an
effort to expand the economic base of the community.

1. *Our community needs more industry to provide jobs. Therefore, we
have decided to zone that large tract of vacant land out by the bypass for
industrial use. In this way, we will attract all the industry we need.*

This is clearly an *illogical* decision since it confuses a possible outcome
(the location of new industry) with a necessary consequence of the decision to
zone for industrial use. The mere availability of land for development
represents no guarantee that industry will select the designated location. In
many parts of the United States, localities are significantly "overzoned" for
industry, so that the aggregate supply of land may exceed the potential demand
by as much as 400 to 500 percent, even when this demand is projected far into
the future.

2. *The planning director has suggested that site development and
market feasibility studies be undertaken before capital construction funds
are invested in the improvement of our new industrial park. Such studies will
take time; and while we are waiting for the results, we could be reaping the
benefits of new industry. Therefore, we have decided to go ahead with the
extension of sewer and water improvements to the site.*

This is an example of a *blind* decision, one that operates in the absence of
complete information regarding the consequences of certain actions. The
carrying capacity and configuration of the sewer system installed prior to the
development of these proposed studies may prove to be inadequate or
inappropriate to serve the needs of the future occupants of the industrial park.
In the meantime, a considerable amount of public funds will be tied up in the
construction project.

3. *Since industry A has announced its intentions to locate in this part of
the state, we have decided to put up a shell building in the industrial park and
offer them rent-free space. We are sure to get our initial investment back
several times over in increased tax receipts.*

This *rash* decision is made after an incomplete or hasty review of the discernible alternatives. Industry A may or may not be interested in a shell building (it may have its own space needs) and may or may not find the offer of rent-free space attractive. There is also no assurance that the community's investment in such a facility will be recouped in increased taxes.

4. *Since we have limited funds for capital improvements, we have decided to put the money where the town is likely to get the best results. Forget about buying land for public recreation, extending street lighting in residential areas, or adding the wing to the public library. We're going to improve the facilities in the industrial park now and worry about those other things later, after we get the industry that can pay the taxes.*

The proposed action ignores the fact that many of these community improvements are among the very features that attract industry by making the community a more desirable place to live and thereby improving the competitive position of the community vis-a-vis other possible locations. Thus, it is *ignorant* action based on either mistakes about the facts or omission of relevant facts.

Accepting the distinctions outlined above, however, it may be suggested that nonrational decisions are not completely devoid of consistency. Indeed, such decisions are perfectly consistent with their premises—it is the premises that are in error. Therefore, what may be judged as a nonrational or irrational action by an observer may seem totally rational to the actor, based on his or her set of premises. A principal objective of performance administration, therefore, should be to assist in making public decisions more rational, that is, to circumvent the shortcomings brought about by the previously enumerated forms of nonrational action.

Transrationality

In the highly convoluted nomenclature of policy studies and management science, another distinction is often made which bears mention here—the notion of *transrationality*. The transrational aspects of policy and management are those which ". . . are not easily reconstructed into a logical, orderly presentation, such as political values, tactical judgments, and conflicting objectives."[2] If transrationality is considered to be the political and/or professional elements of or influences on policy, it is well to note that most policy making is substantially transrational. These influences, however, are neither illogical or irrational; they merely imply the existence of special or disproportionately influential ingredients of policy. Failure to account for these influences may well render the planner or policy analyst prostrate.

Anthony Catanese, in his treatise on the role of politics in planning, sets forth the basic premise that ". . . the political process usually will overrule long-range and comprehensive plans based solely upon rational principles of planning."[3] For rational planning and analysis to survive in a highly transrational world, they must be made more sensitive to political factors, with a shorter range and time perspective and with the development of their own bases of support in a thorough understanding of social goals and objectives. In short, they must rely on what we have called "strategic planning," the basic concepts and techniques of which will be discussed further in subsequent sections of this chapter.

Toward a More Systematic Approach

A basic objective of science is to construct, from fundamental bases, new and creative approaches to the discovery of additional relationships among phenomena that will facilitate greater degrees of predictability. To accomplish this objective, a systematic approach should be adopted, including the following elements: (1) clarification of goals and objectives; (2) identification and classification of problems; (3) formulation and testing of hypotheses; (4) explication of assumptions; (5) gathering and evaluation of data; (6) identification and assessment of alternative solutions; (7) selection and implementation of the "optimal" or best alternative; and (8) evaluation and renegotiation, as necessary, of decisions regarding the problem solution. These elements parallel the states of scientific thinking as defined by John Dewey.[4] Dewey hastens to add, however, that these states do not necessarily follow one another in an orderly fashion.

Goal Clarification and Problem Classification

Goals represent the broadest aims of government, implicitly or explicitly suggesting guidelines for more specific action. Goals are relatively long-term in perspective and normally are not quantifiable; they set forth the broad purposes and desired conditions to be reached by public policies and programs. They specify the "why" of program activities. Objectives, on the other hand, provide more specific standards of desired performance by which to measure the success or failure of component programs and activities. They require a greater degree of quantification in order to provide a basis for the measurement of achievement. Objectives should specify a single key result to be accomplished within a specific target period.

Problems can be classified into three major categories, each having a somewhat different relationship to goals and objectives:

1. *Tactical problems*—where both the conditions of the situation and the requirements that must be satisfied are known in advance and the

available courses of action are completely specified. The solution to such problems consists primarily in selecting a "best" alternative from those available, where the criterion of choice is usually one of economy (for example, least cost or most efficient).

2. *Adaptive problems*—where the search is for the means that will yield a course of action that is better than any other course known and available at the time. Adaptive solutions seek to alleviate built-up pressures by eliminating the more immediate manifestations of the problem.

3. *Strategic problems*—where a search must be conducted to determine the ends (goals and objectives) to be achieved, as well as the means that will yield an appropriate solution. Such problems arise either when unfamiliar demands result in a lack of general agreement as to the appropriate responses to achieve a particular goal, or when there is disagreement as to the goals themselves.

The second and third of these problem categories—problems requiring adaptive or strategic solutions—derive the principal benefits from the scientific approach.

Adaptive solutions provide a means of modifying established patterns of response and thereby of reestablishing a more or less stable flow of productive activity. Since accommodation is relatively less painful and less disruptive to the status quo, many dysfunctional situations confronting an organization are dealt with through the adaptive approach. Adaptive solutions lead to only minor revisions in the participants' expectations—the indigenous criteria by which affected persons gauge a solution's efficacy. However, since such adaptations may not eliminate the root causes of the problem, they are often only temporary solutions. As pressures of displacement continue to mount, adaptive solutions may no longer suffice; in some instances they may even contribute to the total stress on the systems.

In one sense, a more innovative *strategic solution* differs from an adaptive one principally in terms of the rate at which change comes about. A series of adaptive solutions eventually may introduce as substantial a change in the system as would result from a strategic solution. The two modes differ in intent, however, for the strategic approach is a deliberate attempt to deal with a problem through a direct frontal attack, rather than through a series of oblique, incremental operations. This is not to deny the value of incremental decisions. The highest art of decision making is the ability to know when to induce change in genuine increments and when to use the bold stroke of innovation. However, problems requiring strategic solutions usually involve issues that are at the root of the system—issues so central and compelling that they cannot be disposed of either obliquely or incrementally.

An overt appraisal of goals and objectives often brings to the surface conflicting motives distributed among several otherwise discontinuous roles within the organization. Since any organization consists of an aggregate of people collaborating through some imposed system inherited and continually remade by them, individual goals and objectives frequently diverge and become inconsistent with the overall goals of the system. As long as conflicting goals and objectives remain unstated, these inconsistencies may go unnoticed even when they are dysfunctional to the organization. When innovation is introduced, however, these goals must be made more explicit; at this point conflict becomes evident and must be dealt with if the organization is to remain stable.

Hypothesis Formulation and Model Building

The formulation of testable hypotheses is essential to the scientific approach, particularly as it relates to the solution of strategic problems. Hypotheses are the necessary link between theory and any investigation that may lead to the discovery of additional knowledge. They are leading ideas or tentative guidelines to be used in initiating and directing the collection of problem-related information. No pretense of predictability should be made in hypothesis formulation, however. The primary function of a hypothesis is to direct the search for order among facts.

Hypotheses can be stated in different ways according to their level of abstraction:

1. Hypotheses may state the existence of *empirical uniformities,* observable facts leading to assertions about simple similarities and differences. These hypotheses frequently, although not always, represent the scientific examination of common-sense propositions. For example, an analysis of expenditure patterns among public agencies may lead to certain conclusions regarding the "cost multipliers" that apply when an agency's workload is increased.

2. Hypotheses may be concerned with more complex *ideal types.* Such hypotheses test the existence of logically derived relationships between empirical uniformities, leading to specific coincidences of observations. To refer to the previous example, certain "standard costs" might be derived that can be used to measure the marginal operating efficiency of an agency under various workload levels.

3. Hypotheses may be concerned with the relationship of *analytical variables,* requiring the formulation of a relationship between changes in one property and changes in another. For example, it might be hypothesized that an increase in the level of professional training among staff members would result in an increase in the marginal operating efficiency of the agency.

Hypotheses must be specific and conceptually clear, and should have empirical referents. Often hypotheses are expressed in such general terms, and with so grandiose a scope, that they simply are not testable. Such grand ideas are tempting, however, because they seem impressive and important. The analyst should never be satisfied with a general proposition if it can be broken into more precise subhypotheses. Forming subhypotheses clarifies the relationship between the data sought and the conclusions, enhances the linkages to empirical referents, and makes the specific problem-solving task more manageable.

Hypotheses should be related both to a body of theory and to available techniques. The theorist who does not know what techniques are available to test his hypotheses may have difficulty in formulating usable questions. Similarly, the mechanical application of available techniques without a thorough grounding in the underlying theory that should guide these applications can lead to the common analytical shortcoming of "a solution in search of a problem."

While the term *model building* often engenders images of complex mathematical formula, models can take a number of different forms, each of which is valid. A well-drawn hypothesis, in fact, is a *verbal model* that states in words a set of measurable or observable characteristics, as well as a set of controllable and uncontrollable factors that are considered to be causally linked to these variables. The ultimate purpose of a model is to predict outcomes from choices made in specific situations.[5] However, more basic and attainable purposes include the discovery of relevant components (that is, variables and constants) in a problem situation and their relationships to one another. These depictions enable administrators to observe phenomena (receive information) that can then be measured. These measurements, in turn, provide bases for determining whether the model confirms or rejects the theory, hypotheses, or other concepts underlying the model's construction.

Control variables must be selected carefully so as to permit experimentation with various alternatives in seeking possible resolution of the problem in the context of the real world. Exogenous variables also must be carefully considered, for they indicate conditions that cannot be changed and side effects that might arise. Determining the functions that relate these variables is often the most difficult task in analysis. If the function is based on incomplete knowledge of the problem, the model will be inadequate to the task.

As Krueckeberg and Silvers observe, models must be closely linked to the statements of goals and objectives: ". . . if properly done, systems models are no more and no less than more detailed and elaborate restatements of goals and needs."[6] Models can provide a focus for discussion in an effort to generate awareness and concern for the problem, information about the problem, or support for the proposed action. A model can also serve as the basis for a decision, once adequate analysis of alternatives has been carried out.

The Search for Alternatives

The formulation of hypotheses or the development of assumptions is often the first step in the search for alternatives. The generation of alternatives is a creative act, however, and must involve much more than an examination of the possible combinations and permutations of existing information. The need to seek out and evaluate a wide range of alternatives in order to maintain a competitive advantage is generally recognized in the private sector, as evidenced by the departments in industry and business devoted to research and product development, investment planning, market analysis, and so forth.

Examples of opportunistic analysis and planning are rare in the public sector. As E.S. Quade suggests, in public management ". . . the normal processes of planning and budgeting tend to obscure rather than display alternatives as explicit options for consideration by either managers or bodies with control over funding allocations."[7] Although the more systematic approach discussed here does not guarantee a totally synoptic vision, it may relieve some of the myopia that characterizes public-sector analysis.

Incrementalism, Efficiency, and Risk

Obstacles to the search for effective alternatives in the public sector tend to stem from three basic factors: (1) the incremental nature of public decisions, (2) the emphasis on efficiency rather than effectiveness in most government operations, and (3) the relatively low risk threshold of most public officials.

Public agencies tend to operate in fairly traditional ways, relying on established practices or "standard operating procedures." As a consequence, their budget and personnel requirements for the next fiscal year are based on their programs for the current year. Seldom are the problems that gave rise to these programs reexamined, or are other methods and programs considered that might contribute to the more effective resolution of these problems. Incrementalism and tradition combine to limit the search for alternatives and to reinforce the status quo.

Incrementalism may also have an impact on the initial evaluation of alternatives. Alternatives that build incrementally on what was found acceptable in the past, rather than on estimates of actual effectiveness, are most likely to survive this initial evaluation. In many situations, however, little is gained by beginning the evaluation of alternatives by asking what is acceptable, since in the process of answering this question, important aspects of the problem may be overlooked and thus any chance of coming up with an effective solution—let alone the right answer—may be lost.

When asked to describe their accomplishments, many agency heads cite workload data—number of cases handled per case worker, tons of trash collected per work crew, number of citations per traffic officer, and so forth. These data may provide some indication of the overall efficiency of the activities described, especially if comparisons over time are available. However, they seldom give any direct indication of how effective the agency has been in carrying out its programmatic responsibilities. It is possible to be very efficient *in doing the wrong things.* Any evaluation of effectiveness requires the establishment of clear program objectives and the development of measures to determine the level of accomplishment in pursuit of these objectives. It also requires periodic and systematic analyses of alternative ways of achieving these objectives, as well as frequent reexamination and refinement of the objectives themselves.

Public officials who must stand for election every two or four years soon develop a relatively low tolerance for risk. They may take action to remedy the more obvious shortcomings in the delivery of public services, but they are often reluctant to innovate or to seek new program opportunities except when the chances of success are almost certain. Administrators and other appointed officials often reflect similar attitudes; as one county administrator put it: "In this business, it is a whole lot easier to fail than to succeed, so why take any unnecessary chances."

Truly innovative alternatives, as opposed to trivial modifications of existing approaches, are often difficult to formulate. In part, this difficulty stems from the way we are taught to think; much of our public education system is based on an inductive approach to learning. In the inductive approach, general assertions are developed from a number of observed particulars; conclusions about the observed particulars seldom go beyond the facts observed. For example, children learn mathematics—the most deductive of the academic disciplines—through exposure to particular examples from which they must derive general applications. The formulation of alternatives, however, often must begin with a deductive process, that is, with analytical reasoning from the general to the particular or the less general. Although deduction and induction may interact in a creative problem-solving situation, the inability to take the first deductive step often results in an incomplete or ineffective process.

On the other hand, it is seldom feasible—nor would it be reasonable—to consider all the possible courses of action that might be generated in a given problem situation. Except for narrow problems that permit completely closed mathematical formulations (and that are seldom found except in textbook examples), the search for alternatives must be limited by the practical constraints of time and available resources. The techniques of operations research, such as linear programming, may be applicable to the solution of subproblems or components of larger, more complex problems. However, these techniques have only limited application in the formulation of alternatives. As noted previously, it is for this reason that management science has tended to concentrate on particular classes of problems where the promise of success if quite high.

The concept of *satisficing,* as originally formulated by Herbert Simon, provides a strategy for narrowing the search and screening process without necessarily reverting to incrementalism. Although Simon, in his discussion of satisficing, tends to be relatively indifferent to high-level goal-determination processes, he makes it clear that one can call an alternative "satisfactory" only if it meets some set of standards established prior to its selection.[8] Such standards, however, must be equated with goals and objectives. If they themselves are not ultimate goals, they must be evaluated on the basis of their relation to some set of ultimate goals. This notion of formulating standards of adequacy at the outset of the search process is closely related to the concept of "means-ends chains" introduced by Simon in his examination of administrative behavior. The process involved in balancing ideals, estimates of feasibility, and probable costs of further search is generally far more subtle than many of the interpretations of Simon's conceptual framework would suggest; the phrase *successive approximations* seems appropriate in this respect.

In the use of this approach, the standards established at the outset of the search and screening process would serve as the mechanisms for evaluation of alternatives, and although certain alternatives in the initial set might be set aside temporarily, they would not be totally discarded. Subsequently, in the development of successive approximations, some of these alternatives or elements of them might be reconsidered and combined with other alternatives to form a new, more effective alternative. Such an alternative would more closely approximate the expectations established by these standards or objectives.

Search and Screening: A Two-Stage Process

Alternatives may follow different paths (means) to the same objective (ends). Therefore, the search for alternatives should be guided by a two-stage process:

1. identification of broad categories of possible solutions
2. investigation of more specific solutions within a given broad category of alternatives.[9]

Although the broad categories of alternatives may be mutually exclusive, the more specific courses of action may represent subtle variations on a basic theme.

Ineffective analysis can often be traced to an unwillingness to go far beyond the initial problem definition in the search for alternatives. A conscious effort must be made to combat the tendency to assume that solutions are confined to the functional areas or organizational units in which the problems were first identified. Problems often do not conform to existing patterns of administrative responsibilities, and more effective solutions may lie outside established procedures for policy development. The underlying problems or root causes may require highly innovative solutions that go beyond the scope of existing organizational capabilities.

As John Dewey has observed, the search for alternatives is a "progressive" process:

> The more facts of the case come to light in consequence of being subjected to observation, the clearer and more pertinent become the conceptions of the way the problem constituted by these facts is dealt with. On the other side, the clearer the idea, the more definite . . . become the operations of observation and of execution that must be performed in order to resolve the situation.[10]

Changing the way a problem is stated or looking at the issue from different points of view often leads to the consideration of fresh alternatives. Traditional, conventional, or "most plausible" ways of carrying out programmatic tasks are not the only ways of accomplishing objectives. Parochialism, the belief that the established ways of doing things are the best and/or the only appropriate means of achieving stated objectives, is, according to Kahn and Mann, ". . . the single, most important reason for the tremendous miscalculations made in forecasting and preparing for technical advances or changes in the strategic situation."[11]

Even for relatively small-scale problems, the set of alternatives that can be considered in any detail must be reduced to a manageable number. Fortunately, the vast majority of the attributes that define the basic categories of alternatives will be incompatible with other attributes, and consequently the number of possible alternatives will be reduced. No alternative should be completely discarded, however, and all alternatives should be reviewed periodically at critical stages in the subsequent evaluation as additional information is revealed and uncertainties are reduced. The correction of weaknesses in particular alternatives through the adjustment of parameters may lead to the creation of new alternatives. In short, the finding and screening alternatives should be viewed not as a one-shot process but as an iterative one, with greater clarity emerging as further information comes to light.

Assessing Alternatives

If such procedures are assumed to be in place, the analysis can proceed to an assessment of the possible consequences, byproducts, and side effects associated with each of the suggested alternatives. This examination should

include identifiable direct and indirect costs and benefits; the distribution of
positive and negative impacts; the issues of feasibility (political, economic,
social, legal, technological, and so forth, as appropriate); and any other factors
pertinent to the decision being contemplated. One question often overlooked at
this stage of the analysis—frequently with dire consequences in later stages—
is: "What will it take to implement this alternative?" Preliminary estimates of
the organizational resources and programmatic strategies required for implementation must accompany this evaluation and comparison.

If the process has been adequate up to this point, either there will be
several alternatives to choose from, each of which would solve the problem, or
there will be half a dozen or so that fall short of perfection in different ways.
Whenever analysis leads to the comfortable conclusion of one and only one
solution, such a "solution" may be little more than a plausible argument for a
preconceived idea. The "eureka phenomenon," or what Quade calls the
"intraocular traumatic test" whereby the best alternative hits everyone right
between the eyes, seldom operates in complex problem-solving situations.[12]
As Gene Fisher has observed, the analyst can rarely come up with a preferred
or optimal solution, in the sense that one mix of alternatives completely
dominates all others.[13] However, decision makers should be better off with the
results of such analytical efforts than if they operated in the absence of such
information. They are likely to make more informed and hence more rational
decisions, and this is the basic objective of analysis.

Even when the alternatives have been compared and one of the available
courses of action has been chosen for implementation, the selected alternative
may need further development or fine tuning. Thus the work of the analyst does
not stop with the identification of a "best" alternative. Further modification
may be necessary to gain acceptance of the recommended course of action, to
accommodate the expectations of the system and its readiness for change, and
to convert the decision into action commitments.

Strategic Planning

The concept of *strategic planning,* previously mentioned only in passing, can
provide a useful framework within which to address more fully various
techniques for the formulation of alternatives. Strategic planning is a fairly
straightforward notion. It refers to those procedures and processes designed to:
(1) clarify goals and objectives, (2) select policies for the acquisition and
distribution of resources, and (3) establish a basis for translating policies and
decisions into specific action commitments.[14] Thus strategic planning embodies procedures for the identification and evaluation of relevant alternatives.

The primary objective of strategic planning is to broaden the base on
which to make decisions. Expedient decisions frequently have important long-

range implications which, if overlooked or ignored, may have serious repercussions. Strategic planners must attempt to identify the long-range needs of the organization or community, to explore the ramifications and implications of policies and programs designed to meet these needs, and to formulate strategies that maximize the positive aspects and minimize the negative aspects of the foreseeable future.

Strategic Planning in the Private Sector

Strategic planning has long been a vital ingredient of corporate decision making. As King and Cleland explain, private-sector strategic planning:

> . . . involves the development of objectives and the linking of these objectives with the resources which will be employed to attain them. Since these objectives and resource deployments will have impact in the future, strategic planning is inherently future oriented. Strategic planning, therefore, deals primarily with the contrivance of organizational effort directed to *the development of organizational purpose, direction, and future generation of products and services,* and the design of implementation policies by which the goals and objectives of the organization can be accomplished.[15]

Robert Anthony has set forth the principal characteristics and distinctions between strategic planning and management control.[16] He describes strategic planning as the process of deciding on organizational objectives, determining needed changes in recognized objectives, and developing related resource policies. The importance Anthony ascribes to strategic planning is in the long-term as well as the cumulative effects that strategic decisions may have on the organization. Strategic planning, therefore, is not merely a synonym for long-range planning, since short-range decisions may also produce long-term consequences. Management control is described as a process by which management finds the means to use resources effectively and efficiently. Effectiveness, as defined by Anthony, is related to the attainment of a desired result; efficiency is defined as an optimal relationship beween resource input and output.

The distinction between strategic planning and management control is one of degree, which varies according to the size of the organization. In small organizations, both responsibilities may have to be carried out by the same personnel. As the size of the organization increases, however, strategic planning is likely to take place at a separate administrative level, while management control will most likely be delegated to supervisory personnel at operating levels. Administrators will be involved in setting both short- and long-range objectives and in making strategic decisions to deal with unanticipated events, while management control will be expected to operate within the established objectives.

Strategic Planning in the Public Sector

It is common practice in public planning to formulate a plan for some specific target date twenty-five to forty years in the future. Using this approach, population is projected and future growth is assigned to a defined period of time, with considerable attention to the identification of more immediate problems of growth or lack thereof and to suggested solutions of those problems. With this approach, planning frequently becomes a *cumulative process;* that is, all the component parts are added up to determine what the whole will look like. By definition, this cumulative process amounts to short-range planning over a long period of time. The results, benefits, and profits to be gained from such plans will not be guaranteed in the long run and may, in fact, be lost in the crises of problem solving.

A plan has limited value if it does not look far enough ahead to anticipate change rationally and logically. The more dynamic methods of strategic planning involve the systematic combination and extension of facts and possibilities to come up with policy alternatives for long-range development. This evaluation should be undertaken in a manner that subjects deliberations to constant correction and refinement in establishing a desirable range within which public choice can and should be made.[17]

A conceptual basis for this approach is expressed schematically in figure 9-1. Fundamental to this model is the concept that theoretical constructs—which are derived from a concentration of data concerning the jurisdiction under study and from the formulation of preliminary goals and objectives concerning the desired future state of the system—must be completed as a pivotal step in the strategic-planning process. These theoretical constructs, in turn, serve as a basis for policies and decisions. The process of plan formulation, then, consists of a fusion of the ideal with practical information from various inventory studies and technical analyses. The goal-formulation process is a vehicle for avoiding the common tendency to posit future plans based on existing conditions. *Policies*—factual premises representing what *can* be done—are tested against *goals*—value premises representing what *should* be done. The outcome of this interface should be an amalgamation of ideal and practical elements in the public-policy-formulation process.

As in corporate strategic planning, the establishment of a *planning horizon*—the farthest point in the future that can be extrapolated from existing data trends—is basic to the application of strategic planning in the public sector. Just as with the natural horizon, the planning horizon recedes as short-term objectives are approached, necessitating, and facilitating adjustments in long-range goals. The planning horizon can be changed, revised, or even dismissed as the body of knowledge on which it is based is enlarged and clarified. The planning horizon establishes the parameters of goal attainment and thereby closes the gap between esoteric "futurology" and myopic "fire fighting." In using the horizon concept, strategic planning deviates from the traditional cumulative approach by offering a basis for a *thesis* rather than a *synthesis*.

Discovering Social Goals

Discovering and distilling social goals is perhaps the most difficult task facing the policy analyst. While most economic theories merely posit public-preference functions on an "armchair" basis, recent legislative requirements that the public be included in decision processes give rise to a need to further clarify these functions through direct public interaction. Analysts must now get out of their armchairs and "mingle with the masses," an assignment with which many are not particularly comfortable.

Public hearings or *meetings* are by far the most common devices for interacting with the public. Unfortunately, they have also been the least effective mechanism of public access. This general lack of efficacy stems from the following factors:

1. There has been little consensus among the promoters of increased public involvement as to whether participation is a means to improving policy or an end in itself.[18]
2. Hearings have tended to emphasize the "education" of the public rather than to facilitate two-way communications.[19]
3. Hearings are usually attended by middle-class whites who have the time and the communication skills to dominate the proceedings.[20]
4. Hearings, because of their highly selective nature, often promote a stalemate between bipolar community elites (for example, environmentalists versus developmentalists).[21]

Despite these drawbacks, public hearings can be useful devices for gaining more detailed information on the preferences of selected publics. However, a more concerted effort must be made to identify those publics most affected by a given set of alternatives and to underwrite the organizational costs of these affected publics. As Sherry Arnstein suggests, a system of paid involvement akin to jury duty might be used to increase the turnout of lower-income persons.[22] At the public hearing itself, workshops on meaningful involvement can be conducted prior to the introduction of more substantive issues.

It is also useful to apply certain democratizing techniques to enhance the involvement of timid or less skilled citizens. One such technique, the *nominal group method,* involves small-group brainstorming; issues are first discussed in small groups and then brought to the main body by group delegates. In the small groups, everyone has an equal opportunity to express his or her views,

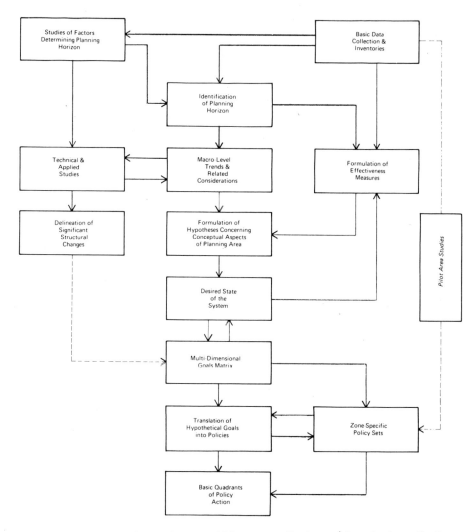

Alan Walter Steiss, *Public Budgeting and Management* (Lexington, Mass.: Lexington Books, D.C. Heath and Company, 1972), p. 205.

Figure 9–1. Schematic Diagram of the Strategic Planning Process

and duplication of viewpoints is acceptable as each member takes a turn.[23]

An increasingly popular means of augmenting the inputs from public meetings is the *citizen survey.* Surveys can provide a highly representative appraisal of interests if the sample is carefully drawn and the survey instrument appropriately structured and administered. Thomas Heberlein, in his comparison of involvement techniques, suggests that:

One strategy to eliminate the unrepresentativeness of participation at the public hearing is the public opinion poll; whatever its other limitations, a carefully conducted survey can insure a representative sample of a given population within statistical estimates of probable error.[24]

Hatry and Webb have found that such surveys are highly instrumental in developing the following "products": (1) citizen perceptions of the effectiveness of public services, including reasons for disliking or not using such services; (2) pretests of demands for new services; (3) determination of broader citizen awareness and opinions of local government programs; (4) increased citizen participation in planning and policy formulation; and (5) reduced isolation and alienation from government.[25]

If survey data are to provide an effective input to policy formulation, it is important that instrument design, sampling techniques, survey execution, and the tabulation of results be carried out with a certain degree of precision.[26] The analyst or program manager with little or no experience in survey techniques would do well to rely on public-opinion professionals and/or university research teams. The cost of bringing in outside assistance can often be compensated by using community volunteers or students as interviewers.

Closely related to the citizen survey in both design and format is the *citizen delphi,* which uses a selected set of community opinion leaders and/or interest group representatives as a "panel of experts." In the first round, participants respond anonymously to a battery of carefully designed questions. Responses are tabulated in the aggregate and presented to the respondents prior to the second and third rounds (usually three iterations are sufficient). The key assumption of the delphi is that each successive round will bring the group closer to a consensus and thereby reduce the conflict associated with diverse policy viewpoints.

Similar to the citizen delphi, the so-called *fishbowl planning* technique involves a more broadly defined audience (although community elites still tend to dominate), an elaborate feedback mechanism, and abandonment of the anonymity of the delphi. A series of public meetings are held to prepare and refine a public brochure describing the pros and cons of various policy alternatives. The main drawback of the fishbowl technique is the time and expense involved.

Although carefully designed public-interaction strategies are important, ultimately they are no substitute for the skillful application of professional judgment. Judgment, however, is both episodic and despotic, and therefore it is essential to invoke systematic procedures for generating a full range of policy alternatives whenever possible.

Narrowing the Field of Alternatives

If program analysts and managers are judicious in the pursuit of alternative solutions, they will succeed in making a good deal more work for themselves.

However, the exercise of narrowing the field of alternatives is the stuff of which good analysis is made, and can involve a variety of techniques of varying degrees of sophistication. The narrowing process might employ any or all of the following: (1) issue papers, (2) optimization analysis, (3) cost-benefit analysis, and (4) life-quality accounting systems. Fundamentally, these techniques are cumulative; used in concert, they can provide a broad-based assessment of the potential impacts of a variety of alternative solutions.

The Issue-Paper Technique

As previously suggested, there is no way to avoid altogether the imposition of professional judgment. Policy analysts are often hired for their intuitive skills as well as their analytical capabilities. After all, policy analysis—whether judgmental or mechanical—is really only a continuum of orderly and systematic thinking. The issue-paper technique is one example of an attempt to move the judgmental or intuitive elements of policy a little further along this continuum.

The issue-paper technique was developed during the heyday of PPBS to augment program-analysis and budgeting procedures. As originally conceived, the purpose of an issue paper was to explore a problem in sufficient depth to provide decision makers with a fairly complete idea of its dimensions and the possible scope of its solution. On the basis of this initial exploration, decision makers could determine further courses of action and commitments, including the development of more definitive policy and program recommendations.

In practice, however, the issue paper has evolved as a formal, systematic assessment of what is currently known about a particular problem or issue, based on readily available data but not involving additional in-depth analyses or extensive data-gathering efforts. Thus, an issue paper serves as a first-phase study; its objective is to isolate program priorities and to explore problems in sufficient depth to avoid the "iceberg syndrome"—the tendency to treat symptoms rather than root causes—of traditional program and project development.

An issue paper is an attempt to identify the real problem or problem set, to isolate the fundamental objectives involved, to suggest appropriate measures of effectiveness and alternative courses of action, and to identify the population subgroups currently affected or likely to be affected by the problem. Government agencies and private-sector organizations concerned with various aspects of the issue are identified, and resources are listed that are currently available and that can be readily applied to the problem. However, an issue paper stops short of the actual investigation and evaluation of the impacts of various alternatives.

The specific procedural steps in the development of an issue paper include:

1. articulation of the *sources and background* of the problem—a clear, concise description of the problem situation, its origins, manifest symptoms, and root causes.
2. identification of *reasons for attention*—why the situation warrants the assignment of analytic resources and possible consequences if the problem is permitted to continue unabated
3. identification of *groups or institutions* toward which corrective activities are directed—general characteristics of target population, such as age group, race, income, special needs, and geographic location.
4. delineation of *beneficiaries* of program efforts—clientele groups that may not be the same as the target group
5. identification of *related programs* currently underway—to the greatest possible extent estimation of related program costs and their impacts on the target and beneficiary groups.
6. definition of *goals and objectives* in sufficient detail to guide the formulation of appropriate *effectiveness measures*
7. exploration of *analytical framework*—tentative investigation of methodological approaches, including a determination of data requirements and major assumptions
8. preliminary identification of *alternatives*—a brainstorming of possible options, including the possibility of mixed solutions or combinations and permutations arising from the "pure" or distinct alternatives.

Possible *recommendations* that might arise from this preliminary analysis are: (1) to undertake a full-scale study; (2) to continue the analysis, but on a low-priority basis; or (3) to terminate any further analysis, since the problem is below some threshold of concern. The issue paper is primarily an agenda for further analysis, but it may be appropriate, especially if either of the latter two recommendations is made, to conclude with an identification of a few "most likely" alternatives, based on the preliminary assessment of the problem. Occasionally, sufficient information may come to light during the development of the issue paper to provide the basis for decisive conclusions regarding one of the alternatives, thereby warranting an immediate action recommendation. In such cases, the preliminary design has, in fact, become the study.

An issue paper should be concise and clear enough to be read in its entirety in a relatively short period of time. Therefore, technical materials should be relegated to an appendix, including any extensive authoritative references, backup tables, charts, special exhibits, computer printouts, and any other items that might be helpful to others in verifying the information contained in the issue paper.

Optimization Techniques

Taking the selection of alternatives one step further, it is often advantageous to develop optimal mixes of competing or multiple alternatives. Such optimization analyses are most useful, however, when it is clear what goals and objectives are to be achieved or optimized. As Nay et al. have noted, a manageable program must begin with:

1. *measurable objectives* agreed to by those in charge of the program and including any necessary measures of program costs, program activities, intended outcomes, and intended impact on the problem addressed
2. *plausible, testable assumptions* linking the application of resources to program activities, activities to intended outcomes, and outcomes to program objectives
3. *motivation, ability, and authority* to manage on the part of those in charge of the program.[27]

Programs can be considered more or less manageable according to the extent to which these three criteria are satisfied.

Government programs, of course, seldom fulfill all of these criteria. More often than not, the purpose of analysis is to alert program managers and policy makers to existing deficiencies. However, some analytical techniques, especially those borrowed from operations research, can proceed only marginally in situations of policy uncertainty. *Linear programming,* for example, builds on deterministic assumptions of complete certainty, that is, that goals and objectives, as well as constraints, are known. If issue papers and subsequent professional brainstorming have failed to reduce uncertainty, optimization analysis will be tenuous at best.

Several specific methods can be applied in these situations to reduce some of the uncertainty. These include:

1. *sensitivity analysis*—designed to measure (often crudely) the possible effects on alternatives under analysis that would result from variations in uncertain elements by assigning various levels of "expected values" to these elements
2. *contingency analysis*—designed to examine the effects on alternatives under consideration when a relevant change is postulated in the criteria for evaluating the alternatives; a form of "with and without" analysis
3. *a fortiori analysis*—from the Latin expression meaning "with stronger reason," this method deliberately "stacks the deck" in favor of one alternative to determine how it might stand up compared with other alternatives.

In most problems, considerable uncertainty surrounds a few key parameters. Analysts faced with this situation must first attempt to determine a set of expected values for these parameters, as well as for all other parameters. Recognizing that these expected values, at best, may be "guesstimations," the analysts should use several values (optimistic, most likely, and pessimistic) in an attempt to ascertain the relative sensitivities of the alternatives under consideration to potential variations in the uncertain parameters.

Contingency analysis can be used to determine the effects of a major change in the general environment within which a problem situation exists. In the field of public health, for example, various alternative approaches to a state's responsibility for environmental health programs might be evaluated with and without a major new program of health-code enforcement. In the context of a local community, various possible park sites might first be evaluated under conditions of existing population distribution and configuration of access routes, then reevaluated assuming different population distributions and various new route configurations.

Suppose that in a particular decision situation, the generally accepted judgment prior to analysis strongly favors alternative C. In performing the analysis of C, the analyst may deliberately choose to resolve the major uncertainties in favor of C and then determine how each of the other alternatives compares under more adverse conditions. If some alternative other than C looks good, the analysts may have a strong case for dismissing the initial intuitive judgment concerning alternative C. Such a fortiori analysis might be carried out in a series of trials, with each alternative in turn being favored in terms of the major uncertainties.

Once a reasonable approximation of basic goals and objectives has been reached, techniques such as *linear programming* can be introduced to determine the optimal mix of alternatives. Linear programming is the most widely used and therefore the most powerful method of operations research. Simply stated, linear programming is an algebraic or geometric modeling device for allocating resources under conditions of scarcity. Mathematicians have known for some time how to design and solve linear programming equations. However, the solutions were so difficult to calculate that few practical applications arose. Since the advent of computers and of a geometric routine known as the Simplex method, linear programming has become widely used in policy and program analysis. The key to such applications is in the design of the problem. While this is not a minor task, it can be carried out by nonmathematical program managers and policy makers who have a basic familiarity with the concepts involved.

The problem design must begin with an identification of those activities or alternatives that have a linear relationship to the program goals. Here the concept of linearity implies that an increase in the activity will yield a proportional increase in goal achievement. Nonlinear programming can be used in situations where there are diminishing returns at certain levels of effort, resulting in a curvilinear relationship; logarithms are computed for the basic functions and the explanatory power of the curved line is then tested.[28]

The *objective function* defines what is to be accomplished through the selection of the "best" alternative. The classic example of a linear programming problem has as its objective function the maximization of nutritional value at the minimum cost. A myriad of other so-called "max/min problems" have been built on this basic formulation.[29] The objective function is expressed as an equation in which the goal is related to the levels of activity and their resource requirements. The capacity functions and other constraints are then expressed in similar equations.

Although linear programming is the most widely used optimization-analysis technique, its application to more complex policy problems has been relatively limited. The relationships between goals and objectives and program activities in such problems seldom are linear, and the constraints, if identifiable, rarely provide a closed feasible set. Nevertheless, linear programming techniques can often be applied successfully to solve subelements of more complex problems. The analytical task then becomes one of integrating these subelement solutions.

Comparisons of Alternatives Based on Costs and Benefits

Cost-benefit analysis or something similar to it has been around for many years; this technique has been traced back to the Rivers and Harbors Act of 1902. It was first formalized, however, in 1936 with the National Flood Control Act, in which the federal government accepted responsibility for the construction of flood-control structures whenever it could be demonstrated that the "benefits to whomsoever that they might accrue, are in excess of the cost." Benefit guidelines for water projects have gone through a number of incarnations since the 1930s, culminating with the New Principles and Standards for Water Resource Planning in 1973.

Meanwhile, cost-benefit analysis became a full partner in the movement toward systems analysis that began in the 1960s. Defense analysts such as Roland McKean redefined cost-benefit analysis in the nomenclature of systems analysis. According to McKean, cost-benefit assessments entail the following procedures:

1. definition of program objectives—what must be achieved to yield the desired benefits
2. identification of alternative courses of action (policies and programs) to achieve stated objectives
3. estimation of costs associated with each alternative

4. construction of mathematical models to assist in the estimation of benefits and costs and in the subsequent choice between alternative policies, programs, or systems
5. development of a *criterion of preferredness* or *social discount rate* to assist in the selection of the "best" alternative.[30]

The final item—the social discount rate—has been the subject of considerable debate over the years. As Kenneth Arrow's famed "impossibility theorem" demonstrates, it is difficult to design a system that accurately reflects social preferences.[31] Generally, economists have held that the appropriate discount rate for public expenditures is one equal to the *opportunity costs*, that is, the lost return (expressed in percentage terms) that the same resources would have yielded in the private sector.[32]

Cost-benefit analysis may be particularly useful when applied in conjunction with new budgetary processes, such as Zero Base Budgeting (ZBB). ZBB explicitly assumes that a marginal comparison of program alternatives is being applied in the reassessment of program activities below last year's expenditure levels (the base). Therefore, cost-benefit analysis could be used to illustrate the level of benefits possible at various funding levels for similar program alternatives.

Life-Quality Accounting Systems

As has been suggested, the techniques of alternative selection are somewhat cumulative. Cost-benefit analysis, for example, is actually the "first cut" at a thorough social-impact assessment of program alternatives. While the full range of life-quality effects, both social and environmental, associated with a given project may not always be considered, cost-benefit analysis at least demonstrates how much those impacts would have to total in dollars and cents for citizens to suffer a measurable loss when the project or program is enacted.

For example, a particular project may destroy wildlife habitat, the exact value of which is unknown. However, the economic benefits of the project may be known, and therefore a public discussion can be generated as to whether maintenance of the habitat justifies foregoing those benefits. Of course, if endangered species or other forms of irreproducible environmental resources are involved, a dollar value is a very poor indicator indeed. Moreover, the true costs that accrue to the public at large from such activities as nuclear-waste disposal may be very difficult to determine, and most citizens as well as many decision makers are likely to ignore various invisible costs.

For these reasons, many policy analysts have become increasingly concerned with an expansion of the alternative-selection process to include various life-quality accounting systems. Life-quality accounting implies an overarching set of policy-impact indicators, involving both environmental and social systems and including both subjective and objective measures. In this respect, the concept of life-quality accounting encompasses traditional concepts such as social well-being and quality of life, as well as the more current enterprise of social-impact assessment.

Research on social indicators has been going on for many years, but it has not been primarily focused on policy. As Judith Innes de Nuefville suggests: "The authors of these compendia did not know precisely how data might be used, but they felt they would somehow help to improve society."[33] It was not until 1969, with the introduction of social-accounting systems in the Department of Health, Education, and Welfare, that the notion of policy-relevant indicators began to gather momentum. Formal requirements for broad-based social and environmental considerations were set forth in the National Environmental Policy Act of 1970 (Public Law 91-190). Comprehensive social accounts were mandated under the *Principles and Standards of Water Resources Planning,* passed by Congress in 1973 and subsequently reinforced by the Water Resources Council.[34] Social-accounting systems have become increasingly important to policy development, and the future is likely to witness more and more formal requirements.

Life-quality accounting is a fairly laborious process entailing a vast array of indices, grouped into broad categories and usually developed along the following lines:

1. *Economic opportunities* can be measured by aggregating such factors as personal income, poverty levels, financial concentrations and mobile capital, productivity rates, employment rates, and individuals' perceptions of their relative financial security and economic well-being.
2. *Environmental security* is associated with pollution levels, noise levels, congestion (for example, population per square mile), as well as natural amenities such as climate, inversion factors, recreational and aesthetic opportunities, and so forth.
3. *Health and safety factors* usually include morbidity rates, medical-care facilities per population served, risks associated with employment opportunities, crime rates, level of police and fire services, and so forth.
4. *Sociopolitical security and opportunities* often include such factors as individual feelings of personal efficacy, level of community involvement, level of professionalism in government, and general satisfaction with service delivery systems.

Individual indices entail a complex set of factors that attempt to isolate and clarify the full range of quality dimensions. Consider, for example, the indices of aesthetic opportunities developed by the TECHCOM Group of the Thirteen Western States Water Resources Research Centers, as shown in figure 9–2. Generally speaking, physical indicators of life-quality, such as levels of particulate matter in the atmosphere, are scaled through some type of *standardized additive method* and/or *factor analysis* to create viable composite measures. A standardized additive method normalizes the scores to a common unit of measure through the use of standard deviations or by assigning fixed gradations. Factor analysis, on the other hand, is aimed at verifying relationships between sets of variables, usually involving a max/min calculation (that is, maximum amount of variance explained with the minimum number of linear combinations).[35]

The real challenge in the development of indicators seems to be the integration of objective or physical indices (for example, number of sunny days) with more subjective or attitudinal indices (for example, the value that

Air Aesthetics	Landscape Aesthetics	Visitor Day Use per Acre	Biota Aesthetics
Odor (Elimination of)	Urban Dominated	Agriculture Dominated	Population
Concentration of SO₂	Acres of Parks per Capita	Percentage Time Land Fallow	Biomass (tons per acre)
Concentration of Hydrocarbons from Sewage Chemicals (ppm)	Percent of Area Covered by Below-ground Transmission Lines	Miles Above-ground Transmission Lines per Section	Population (number of animals/acre)
Visibility	Percent Industrial Area	Visitor Day Use per Acre	Location
Miles of Visibility Irritants	Percent High Density Residential Area	Forest Dominated	Percentage of Area Where Species are Located
Concentration of SO₂ (ppm)	Percent of Area with Medium Density Residential Development	Method of Harvest (percent clear cut)	Variety
Concentration of Ozone (O₃) and PAN (ppm)		Miles Above-ground Transmission Lines per Section	Number of Species (percent of species in natural ecosystem of the area)
Particulates (ppm)	Percent Freeway Area	Visitor Day Use per Acre	
	Mountain Dominated	Water Dominated	Equality of Aesthetic Opportunity
Water Aesthetics	Miles of Above-ground Transmission Lines per Section	Percent of Area of Bosque Developed (industrial for residential)	Intermittent Sound
Clarity			Maximum dB Level
Suspended Silt Load (ppm)	Visitor Day Use per Acre	Percent of Area Covered by Water	Average dB Level
Biochemical Oxygen Demand (ppm)	Desert Dominated	Average Flow (millions of acre feet per year)	Background Sound
Floaters	Miles of Above-ground Transmission Lines per Section		Average Natural dB Level
Percentage of Total Sewage Effluent which is Untreated		Miles Above-ground Transmission Lines per Section	Sound Aesthetics:
Odors (Elimination of)		Visitor Day Use per Acre	Gini Coefficient* of Income Distribution
Biochemical Oxygen Demand (ppm)			Distribution of Neighborhood Parks per Capita by Income (gini coefficient)
Phenols (ppm)			

*The Gini Coefficient represents the extent to which the actual distribution diverges from an equal distribution.

Figure 9–2. Aesthetic Opportunity

individuals place on a sunny day). As several researchers have discovered, subjective indicators—how persons perceive the quality of their lives—are often more important than the actual physical and social attributes of their milieu.[36] Obviously these aspects are interrelated, yet individual perceptions are highly idiosyncratic. Nevertheless, in a free society, individual perceptions should have some impact on public policies. Since perceptions are difficult to measure, analysts often simply assume that most individuals value various aspects of the system in roughly the same way that they do.

One way to overcome this elitist bias is to interject life-quality accounting mechanisms along with other procedures for public access such as hearings, workshops, and surveys. This would permit citizen weightings of social indicators to be systematically polled. Kenneth Hornback and his associates have suggested a method for integrating subjective and objective measures once attitudinal data have been gathered to develop a general life-quality index.[37]

Beyond computing the weighted average of objective and subjective rankings, some life-quality accounting systems develop *trade-off functions* by having a panel of experts establish plausible relationships between subgoals and social indicators; regression calculations are then performed on these relationships. These full-scale life-quality accounting models are often described as *multiattribute models* and therefore have been lumped together with various techniques of systems dynamics and input-output modeling.[38]

Although most of these systems models may seem esoteric with respect to the more practical policy concerns of most public administrators, the notion of life-quality accounting is not. Moreover, life-quality accounting does not necessarily require elaborate multiattribute computer modeling. Assuming that the prudent administrator or program analyst is already integrally involved in some form of public monitoring, life-quality accounting merely becomes a logical extension of that process. In short, life-quality accounts are a means of translating public inputs into meaningful policy indicators. Furthermore, life-quality accounts may afford administrators an opportunity to develop programs that may not be justifiable through standard cost-benefit criteria. Examples of these types of programs can be found in the areas of water resource development and alternative energy systems.[39] With proper application, life-quality accounts can become the hydraulic fluid of the strategic-planning machinery.

Notes

1. E.S. Quade, *Analysis for Public Decisions* (New York: American Elsevier Publishing Company, 1975), p. 116.

2. Michael J. White et al., "Problems and Prospects for Management Science and Policy Science," in *Management and Policy Science in American Government*, ed. Michael J. White, Michael Radnor, and David A. Tansik (Lexington, Mass.: Lexington Books, D.C. Heath and Company, 1975), p. 7.

3. Anthony J. Catanese, *Planners and Local Politics* (Beverly Hills, Calif.: Sage Publications, 1974), p. 24.

4. John Dewey, *Logic, The Theory of Inquiry* (New York; Henry Holt, 1938).

5. Anthony J. Catanese, *Scientific Methods of Urban Analysis* (Urbana, Ill.: University of Illinois Press, 1972), p. 6.

6. Donald A. Krueckeberg and Arthur L. Silvers, *Urban Planning Analysis: Methods and Models* (New York: John Wiley and Sons, 1974), p. 18.

7. Quade, *Analysis for Public Decisions*, p. 116.

8. Note the discussion of Simon's formulations in Robert T. Golembiewski et al., *A Methodological Primer for Political Scientists* (Chicago: Rand McNally Company, 1969), p. 208; also note Herbert A. Simon, *Administrative Behavior*, 2nd ed. (New York: The Macmillan Company, 1957).

9. Quade, *Analysis for Public Decisions*, p. 118.

10. Dewey, *Logic, The Theory of Inquiry*, p. 109.

11. Herman Kahn and I. Mann, *Ten Common Pitfalls*, RM-1937 (Santa Monica, Calif.: The Rand Corporation, 1957).

12. Quade, *Analysis for Public Decisions*, p. 123.

13. Gene H. Fisher, *The Analytical Basis of Systems Analysis*, P-3363 (Santa Monica, Calif.: The Rand Corporation, 1966), pp. 11–12.

14. For a comprehensive discussion of these procedures in the private sector, see Robert N. Anthony, *Planning and Control Systems: A Framework for Analysis* (Cambridge, Mass.: Harvard University Press, 1965).

15. William R. King and David I. Cleland, *Strategic Planning and Policy* (New York: Van Nostrand, Reinhold, 1978), p. 6.

16. Anthony, *Planning and Control Systems*, pp. 24–68.

17. For a further discussion of these points, see Alan Walter Steiss, *Public Budgeting and Management* (Lexington, Mass.: Lexington Books, D.C. Heath and Company, 1972), chap. 9.

18. Note Daniel Moynihan, *Maximum Feasible Misunderstanding* (New York: The Free Press, 1970).

19. For a further discussion of this point, see John H. Strange, "The Impact of Citizen Participation on Public Administration," in *The Dimensions of Administration*, ed. Joseph A. Uveges, Jr. (Boston: Holbrook Press, 1975), pp. 554–579; for a more optimistic view, see Gary English, "The

Trouble with Community Action," in Uveges, *The Dimensions of Administration,* pp. 580–593.

20. Sherry Arnstein, "Maximum Feasible Manipulation," *Public Administration Review* 42(October 1972):337–408.

21. This phenomenon is discussed in Gregory A. Daneke, "Public Involvement in Natural Resource Development," *Environmental Affairs* 6, no.1(Summer 1977):11–31.

22. Sherry Arnstein, "A Working Model of Participation," *Public Administration Review* 45(January–February 1975):70–73.

23. For further discussion of this method, see Michael Appleby, "Nuts and Bolts of Participatory Decision-Making," paper presented at the National Conference of the Council of University Institutes of Urban Affairs (New Orleans, March 1977).

24. Thomas Heberlein, "Some Observations on Alternative Mechanisms for Public Involvement," *Natural Resources Journal* 16, 1(January 1976):204.

25. Harry Hatry and Kenneth Webb, *Obtaining Citizen Feedback* (Washington, D.C.: The Urban Institute, 1973), pp. 15–27.

26. For a general discussion of these items, see Gregory A. Daneke and Patricia Klobus-Edwards, "Survey Research for Public Administrators," *Public Administration Review* 39(Fall 1979).

27. John N. Nay, et al., "If You Don't Care Where You Get To, Then It Doesn't Matter Which Way You Go," in *The Evaluation of Social Programs,* ed. C.C. Abt (Beverly Hills, Calif.: Sage Publications, 1976), p. 97.

28. For more on nonlinear programming, see William J. Baumol, *Economic Theory and Operations Analysis,* 4th ed. (Englewood Cliffs, N.J.: Prentice-Hall, 1977).

29. For several excellent examples from politics and the law, see Stuart S. Nagel and Marion Neef, *Operations Research Methods* (Beverly Hills, Calif.: Sage Publications, 1976).

30. Roland N. McKean, *Public Spending* (New York: McGraw-Hill Book Company, 1968), pp. 136–138.

31. Kenneth J. Arrow, *Social Choice and Individual Values,* 2nd ed. (New Haven, Conn.: Yale University Press, 1963).

32. See William J. Baumol, "On the Discount Rate for Public Projects," in *Public Expenditure and Policy Analysis,* 2nd ed., ed. Julius Margolis and Robert H. Havemann (Chicago; Ill.: Rand-McNally, 1977), pp. 161–179.

33. Judith Innes de Nuefville, *Social Indicators and Public Policy* (New York: American Elsevier Publishing Company, 1975), p. 41.

34. Water Resources Council, "Establishment of Principles and Standards," *The Federal Register* 37, no. 1–74(September 1973).

35. Ben-Chieh Liu, *Quality of Life Indicators in U.S. Metropolitan Areas* (New York: Praeger, 1976), pp. 90–93.

36. See Mark Schneider, "The Quality of Life and Social Indicators Research," *Public Administration Review* 46(May-June 1976):297–305.

37. Kenneth E. Hornback et al., *Studies in Environment,* volume 2: *Quality of Life* (Washington, D.C.: Environmental Protection Agency, 1974).

38. See John P. van Gigch, *Applied General Systems Theory,* 2nd ed. (New York: Harper and Row, 1978), pp. 293–336.

39. See Gregory A. Daneke, "Life Quality Accounting and Organizational Change," *The Bureaucrat,* (Summer 1978):27–35; Gregory A. Daneke and Andrew Lawrence, "Life Quality Accounting and Alternative Energy Systems," paper presented at the International Conference on Energy Use Management (Los Angeles, October 1979).

10 Policy Implementation and Maintenance

Tasks associated with the implementation of policy often are regarded as purely management functions that are beyond the purview of the policy analyst. However, policy and administration are so tightly interwoven that any sharp demarcation between policy determination and execution is, at best, highly artificial. As students of public policy well know, much of the substance of policy is developed in the implementation process. The principal task of policy maintenance is to ensure that the fleshing out of policy is in keeping with original goals and objectives.

Analysis of Implementation Procedures

The vast realm known as implementation is much like the weather—everyone talks about it, but no one does anything about it.[1] The literature of implementation has been largely an elaborate cataloging of ineffective accomplishments and bureaucratic foul-ups.[2] These taxonomies of managerial and bureaucratic pathologies are helpful, but they rarely provide any explicit specification of what successful implementation would entail. Admittedly, complete programmatic success in the public sector is rare; however, it is not impossible. Furthermore, as public pressure mounts for more effective as, well as efficient, public policies and programs, skillful program management will certainly have to become a high art. While the strategies discussed here may not qualify as high art, they can provide a point of departure for the development of a more thoroughgoing analysis of implementation procedures.

Considering Implementation Feasibility

Ideally, implementation feasibility should be assessed prior to the affirmation of a policy decision, since a highly cost-effective program alternative may be extremely difficult to implement. All too often, however, policy makers assume that if they can design it, someone can implement and manage it. This fallacy is particularly rampant among legislative policy makers, who more often than not give scant attention to the specifics of program management. Many public policies are adopted with absolutely no knowledge of the particular actions that will be necessary to implement them.

These blanket investments in "bureaucratic discretion" merely shift the responsibility for authentic policy making to the administrative apparatus. And if the bureaucratic manager has any choice among alternatives, relative management difficulty is likely to be a major deciding factor. Therefore, programs chosen to implement broad public policy often take the path of least resistance rather than the most appropriate course to an effective problem solution. To the extent that policy analysis is becoming more closely aligned with functional management, responsibility for *implementation feasibility* must be close to the heart of the performance administration process.

Even if an implementation assessment is not performed until after a specific policy decision has been made, useful knowledge can be gained that will increase the likelihood of successful implementation. Since such an analysis can be costly in terms of both financial and other resources, a quick and direct method has been devised for determining the need for such an assessment. This approach involves an analysis of each alternative in terms of: (1) the *degree of consensus* among the individuals or groups involved in or affected by the program and (2) the *magnitude of change* that the program alternative represents, as measured against existing policies. In general, programs having high consensus/low change present few problems in implementation; whereas those with low consensus/high change present many difficulties. Alternatives evidencing high consensus/high change or low consensus/low change may require further assessment of implementation feasibility, at the discretion of the manager or analyst.

The nature of government policy is the most important factor in determining the magnitude of change. Incremental policy changes, in which new programs depart only slightly from present programs, require the least change. New nonincremental programs, designed to foster sweeping developmental and social changes, require a much higher degree of change and are therefore more difficult to implement. The degree of consensus should be based on an evaluation of the attitudes of at least five groups of actors: (1) the target group; (2) political leaders; (3) administrative and operating bureaucracies charged with program implementation; (4) elites in active constituencies, such as interest groups and community leaders; and (5) "oversight" groups, such as consultants, program evaluators, and internal analysts.

Political, Social, and Organizational Constraints

Assessing implementation feasibility involves a projection of the political, social, and organizational constraints associated with the set of program options under consideration. Specifically, the following issues must be raised:

1. Whose ox is likely to be gored (political and economical climate)?
2. What qualitative and quantitative resources are required for successful implementation (resource climate)?
3. How well does the program option fit with existing agency missions (organizational climate)?
4. What factors of community or client disposition may affect implementation (social climate)?
5. How have the proposed implementation agencies or similar agencies performed in the past, and what difficulties are they likely to encounter in the future (climate of agency competency)?
6. What are the innovative aspects of the program option that may require major attitudinal shifts among the participants (climate of innovation)?[3]

The *ox-goring* issue may seem obvious, but trade-offs between conflicting interest groups are seldom clear cut. Someone is helped and someone else is hurt by even a fairly innocuous policy of systems maintenance. Even when it appears that there are no losers, "relative deprivation" may produce the impression of a loss among certain groups. In essence, if a policy makes one group better off, another group may feel worse off.

The *political environment* surrounding the implementation of a program may harbor potential problems which should not be overlooked. Therefore, it is important to examine some specific questions, such as:

1. To what extent are private interest groups mobilized in support of or opposition to the program? What is the degree of cohesion or articulateness of opposing groups?
2. Are there existing client groups (support groups) whose interests will be affected adversely by the proposed program?
3. What is the partisan character of the implementing organization (or jurisdiction)?
4. To what extent does the alternative threaten important officials with a reduction of power, prestige, or privilege?
5. Are there complicated legal questions, and if so, to what extent is new legislation required for successful implementation? Does existing legislation or legal precedent hinder implementation?
6. Has a recent crisis lent support to the program? Could the program be more successful if implemented at a different time?

Future economic conditions are often difficult to predict, especially when dealing with a policy that requires a long implementation period. Several questions must be asked about the economic implications of a policy proposal:

1. To what extent will prevailing economic conditions be affected by the implementation of the program?

2. Will future economic resources be sufficient to support successful program implementation?
3. To what extent can future political developments affect resource availability?

It is incumbent on the skillful manager-analyst to examine these questions before implementation and to assess potential disruptive effects on various interest groups. Standard forms of public involvement such as public hearings may not provide all the necessary clues. Citizen surveys and informal contacts with decision leaders may prove more useful in making this assessment. In either case, the analyst should strive to reduce the level of uncertainty regarding project or program impacts, and to identify the program option that will require a lower level of entrepreneurship, in terms of adjusting for competing claims, on the part of the program managers.

Qualitative resources required for successful implementation often are implicit in the cost-benefit or other analyses of alternatives. The cautious analyst, however, will attempt to make these resource issues more explicit. Qualitative resources might include highly specialized personnel, technological uncertainties (such as the availability of a particular computerized information system), or merely a certain level of required coordination between agencies. All these resources have intangible costs, and the manager-analyst should try to calculate these costs, albeit crudely, and to identify the program option with the lowest qualitative costs.

All programs require *quantitative resources,* such as money, personnel, and time, for successful implementation. The following questions might be useful in analyzing these constraints:

1. What sources of funds are definitely available and how flexible are they in terms of allocations to different aspects of the program? Does the program require additional funds in the face of tight revenue constraints?
2. Will the program require space, facilities, and support services that may be difficult to obtain?
3. Does the program involve significant technological or procedural uncertainties?
4. To what extent are special personnel capabilities and/or training required?
5. Are significant organizational adjustments required to achieve effective program implementation?

The *organizational climate* is a critical variable in the assessment of implementation feasibility. Program options which go against the grain of existing missions and/or organizational behavior patterns are likely to encounter difficulties in implementation. Ashley Schiff demonstrated this point well in his now famous case study of forest rangers asked to conduct controlled burning of underbrush. The rangers had a difficult time adjusting to the idea of starting fires.[4] If the options of the agency are limited, the choice exercised should be well grounded in a thorough knowledge of organizational ethos.

The *degree of influence* exerted by a bureaucracy is dependent on: (1) political support, (2) organizational vitality, (3) organizational leadership, (4) the nature of the organization's task, and (5) the skills and expertise of the organization. Several characteristics of the *bureaucratic structure* that should also be of interest to the manager-analyst include organizational history, traditional and legal bases, agency incentive systems, degree of decision-making autonomy, agency norms, and operating procedures.

Effective implementation requires that the standards and objectives of the program be known and understood by those individuals responsible for their achievement. The existence of performance indicators tied to identifiable goals and objectives is also important. Public officials often must rely on institutional mechanisms and procedures to increase the likelihood that agency staffs will act in a manner consistent with program standards and objectives. In addition to the standard mechanisms of personnel control—recruitment and selection, assignment, advancement, and promotion—a wide variety of sanctions and symbolic or material rewards may be applied. Effective use of these mechanisms requires open and distinct lines of communication, both horizontally and vertically.

Community climate or client ethos is equally important to the choice of program options. While reflected to some degree in the assessment of interest groups described above, community climate is a broader and often more nebulous concept than interest-group attitudes. Consideration of community climate involves a general assessment of recent events and trends that may impinge on the range of program options. Unlike trends used for forecasting in the strategic planning or policy formulation stages of analysis, elements of the community climate have more immediate effects. For example, a recent crisis may lead to support for one of the program choices, and this support in turn can be used by the program manager to aid in the mobilization of resources. The fifty-five-mile-per-hour speed limit might have eventually been legislated in the United States for reasons of highway safety, but the 1973 gasoline shortage resulting from the oil embargoes accelerated the process. Exploring the horizon for catalytic social and economic events may thus aid the program-implementation process.

The success of any new program rests ultimately on its acceptance by that portion of the community or society which it serves. Public opinion can be extremely influential in determining whether and how a policy change is implemented. It is important to know the extent to which public opinion has been mobilized for or against the program and the degree to which community elites, such as business and social leaders, favor or oppose implementation.

More broadly, how much and in what ways prevailing social conditions will be
affected by program implementation should be determined.

Past performance of the designated agency is an obvious factor in
implementation feasibility. Regular and systematic evaluation of performance
are rare, however, and choice of the implementing agency or agencies may be
predetermined. Consequently, analysts may fail to consider fully the difficulties that particular agencies are likely to encounter with certain policy or
program options. In the absence of clear data about one's own agency,
information about similar agencies in other communities may prove useful.

Since the various policy components must be filtered through the
perceptions of those who implement the policy, several elements of the
implementors' response must be examined: their cognition or comprehensive
understanding of the policy; the direction of their response toward it
(acceptance, neutrality, rejection); and the intensity of that response. The
following questions may be helpful in perceiving these potential barriers to
implementation:

1. Does the new program conflict with employees' values?
2. To what extent does the program require changes in the attitudes or
    behavior of government employees?
3. What will be the reaction of organized labor to this new program? To what
    extent does the program threaten jobs?
4. What will be the difficulties associated with overcoming the natural
    resistance to change?

When research indicates that certain characteristics of the new program
might affect its successful implementation, these characteristics that might
either hinder or help a program become operational can be identified by asking
the following questions:

1. Can the *relative advantage* be observed (that is, the degree to which the
    new program is perceived as better than the idea it supersedes)?
2. Is the innovation *compatible* with existing values, past experiences, and
    the needs of the client group or groups?
3. Is the innovation perceived as being *complex* to understand and to use?
4. Is the innovation *trialable* (for example, can it be experimented with on a
    limited basis)?
5. Are the results of the innovation *observable* to others?

Although the relative advantage of a new program may be measured in
economic terms, factors of social prestige, convenience, and satisfaction are
often of equal importance. An idea that is not compatible with the prevailing
values and norms of the community may experience considerable difficulty in

achieving acceptance. Some innovations are readily understood by most members of the client group; others are not, and consequently, will be adopted more slowly. New ideas that can be tried on an installment basis will generally be adopted more quickly than those which must be accepted all at once. The easier it is for an individual to see the positive results of an innovation, the more likely he or she is to adopt it.

It must be realized that these dimensions of program implementation are not always of equal importance. In some cases, one or more of these factors may have little significance for successful implementation. In other instances, one aspect, such as political support or technological uncertainty, may be so vital that an indication of difficulties in this dimension would be sufficient to eliminate an otherwise attractive program alternative. To be successful, the manager-analyst must diagnose the situation and assign appropriate relative weights to each factor.

In summary, these various aspects of implementation feasibility should affect decisions at the onset of policy development. As policy analysts become more involved in both the formulation and implementation of policy, these types of feasibility analyses may become more frequent and more significant. At present, however, the analyst—to the extent that he participates in the implementation process—is usually involved in carrying out certain analytical tasks for the program manager. These tasks, while more mechanical and rudimentary, are nonetheless essential to the success of the program.

Improving the Possibilities for Successful Implementation

Analyses for successful implementation provide many formidable challenges. They can be used to enhance coordination and, occasionally, adjustment or realignment of political, physical, fiscal, and human resources. Such concerns require that attention be given to multiple actions over an extended period of time. In this respect, the manager-analyst must have timely answers to questions that arise during the implementation process. Failure on the part of the manager to have these answers can be costly or even disastrous to the organization. In order to maintain control, the manager-analyst must develop a dynamic system for planning, scheduling, delivering, monitoring, and evaluating program operations—a system that will produce the best possible initial operations plan while simultaneously allowing for reaction and adjustment to changing conditions.

There are several arenas in which analysis can enhance the possibility of successful implementation. These include: (1) goal clarification and task delineation; (2) task optimization and coordination; (3) delegation and motivation; and (4) evaluation and renegotiation.

Goal Clarification and Task Delineation

Goal statements are often too vague to be of any practical use in defining the specific tasks to be undertaken. The War on Poverty in the 1960s, for example, set forth a goal that was little more than: "Eliminate poverty in America." Poverty is obviously a complex set of relationships and cycles, including opportunities for education and mobility. The failure to provide large amounts of carefully guided strategic planning at the outset led to inadequate problem definition and, in turn, to policies and programs that at best treated the symptoms rather than the causes of poverty.[5] *Without clear goals and concise objectives, effective implementation is virtually impossible.* In the implementation process, systemic goals and objectives must be reassessed and disaggregated. Conflicts between goals must be identified and optimal mixes worked out.[6] Once a congruent set of goals has been established, the associated objectives must be delineated into manageable tasks.

While several managerial media are well suited to task delineation, those procedures that involve "structured brainstorming," such as MBO, are perhaps most useful. In these encounter sessions, the views of various program managers and their analytical staffs can be merged into a more comprehensive picture of the entire set of administrative and technical interactions necessary to carry out the defined goals and objectives. Moreover, a semidemocratic approach to task selection affords added opportunities for motivation. In essence, if a particular staff member sets forth the tasks that his unit can perform, the commitment to those tasks is more substantial than if they were merely assigned from above.

Task Optimization and Coordination

After the subdivision of goals and objectives into their constituent elements or tasks, the next analytical challenge is to reassemble these elements into coherent packages. Reassembly involves not only decisions about ordering and scheduling, but also possible decisions about the appropriate level of activities associated with various tasks. Resources always are scarce, and analysts must often work out optimal mixes of resource allocations.

Various techniques from systems engineering and operations research may prove indispensable in achieving these mixes and in coordinating program activities. If the problem or issue has been clearly defined and goals and objectives are fully articulated, then techniques such as *linear programming* may be useful in achieving an optimal distribution of resources. As Stokey and Zeckhauser describe this process: "Programming is a means of optimizing; that is, programming is concerned with choosing the best level for various activities in situations where these activities compete for scarce resources, or with choosing the minimum-cost method of producing required outputs." [7] It is well to note, however, that programming is merely a guide to thinking. It seldom provides an outright solution to problems. It is especially important that analysts in the public sector realize that the values to be optimized must be fully clarified before a particular mathematical model is applied.

Building the optimization model involves formalizing the results of strategic planning and budgetary processes. Values to be maximized are set forth as *control* or *decision variables*. In this context, goals may be defined as codifications of desirable patterns of performance, as exhibited by individuals and institutions or by physical, social, economic, and political variables. [8] The policy-making process must facilitate the manipulation and control of these variables if the goals—the desired state of the system—are to be achieved. Goals are not mutually exclusive, however. A single set of variables may be common to a number of goals; the primary variables of a low-priority goal may be secondary variables of a high-priority goal.

Resource limitations and other constraints represent *effectiveness parameters*—the "boundary conditions" within which the search for an effective solution must be conducted. *Effectiveness measures,* in turn must be developed and applied to determine the level of goal achievement. Effectiveness measures can be defined as indicators that measure the direct and indirect impacts of resource allocations. They involve basic scoring techniques for determining the state of a given system (policy or program). Careful selection and application of effectiveness measures can go a long way toward overcoming some of the difficulties and ambiguities of public decision making.

More specific *program objectives* are defined by: (1) establishing current levels and types of performance for each discrete program category or activity: (2) estimating the current impacts of agency resources on that performance; and (3) defining desired levels and types of performance. The development of positive statements of performance provides a basis from which to define and evaluate change—an approach predicated on the concept of marginal change from the current state. [9] A fundamental assumption of this approach is that performance can be defined in goal-oriented terminology based on program and policy (control) variables. Current operations and their effects must be under continuous surveillance. Continuous program evaluation is the most effective means available for initiating a goal-oriented decision-making system in an existing government structure. [10]

For example, assume that a police chief wants to develop a work assignment schedule that uses his officers most efficiently and that, it is hoped, will increase the effectiveness of public protection (control variables). However, he is constrained by manpower resources—number, grade, and expertise of staff—and union agreements, such as a prohibition on split shifts. With the help of his analytical staff, work assignments can be broken down into component activities, the impact (performance effectiveness) of current resource allocations can be determined, and a simple linear equation can be designed that spells out the maximum possible utilization of available personnel under resource constraints.[11]

A more widespread application of operations research techniques for the improvement of implementation has come with the further development of *queuing and network analyses.* These analytical techniques provide a road map of the sequence in which activities should be undertaken and assist in the coordination of the schedule of events so as to meet predetermined deadlines. The best known of these devices are the Program Evaluation and Review Technique (PERT) and the Critical Path Method (CPM), both of which will be discussed at greater length in subsequent sections.

Delegation and Motivation

Ultimately, implementation analysis is useless if people cannot or will not perform the assigned tasks. Delegation is a relatively informal but crucial resource-allocation problem. The program manager must decide who should, who can, and who will carry out the specific tasks of the program. The analyst can merely provide information about past performance based on standardized effectiveness criteria, but the crucial decisions of task assignment are a mixture of these performance guides and the manager's intuition. Nevertheless, a carefully designed program *monitoring and control apparatus* can be a substantial aid to intuition.

Motivation is also highly intuitive. Different employees respond to different types of stimuli, although coercive measures are rarely effective. To a large extent, the amount of cooperation a manager receives from the staff depends on the degree to which he or she is willing to let them program their own specific tasks. The manager must avoid the hazards of "over-programming" the tasks of others and must be willing to use the technique of program control known as *management by exception.*

Exceptions are the deviations or differences between what is anticipated and what actually does happen. *Dynamic control,* then, means responding with corrective action within an appropriate time period to make such action useful and meaningful. The timeliness of corrective action can be increased if staff members are involved in programming their specific tasks and are given responsibility for monitoring the effectiveness of their own activities.

Thus, using the concept of management by exception, the program manager does not have to wade through a sea of data about every facet of the program's operations only to discover that things are going smoothly. Rather, a series of critical *milestones* or schedule checkpoints are established at the outset of the program (with the assistance of the implementing staff), and progress toward these milestones is monitored. Each staff member responsible for a series of tasks within the larger program might identify his or her own, task-specific milestones. The pace of accomplishment, and therefore the motivation to achieve an effective output, is determined through cooperative interaction.

Evaluation and Renegotiation

The final stages will be discussed in chapter 11, on *policy feedback,* and are mentioned here only briefly. As suggested earlier, many policies are made in the process of implementation, and therefore strategic renegotiations are often more important to the product than initial formulations. To ensure that these adjustments are not merely elaborate admissions of defeat, the program manager and the analytical staff must design a set of systematic feedback or follow-up procedures at the onset of implementation.

Feedback procedures should be designed to keep the program moving along predetermined lines, they should also indicate where fine tuning is necessary to salvage a poorly designed program or policy. In addition to monitoring activities, the evaluation attempts to project the overall impact of the program while the program is unfolding. In cases where public goals and preferences have shifted somewhat, projected results may no longer be completely desirable. In these cases, evaluation is tantamount to a reinitiation of the policy formulation process.

Program-Maintenance Techniques

Program maintenance in the public sector is often more of an art than a science. Since profit motives do not determine program performance, effectiveness frequently is associated with clever leadership or with readily attainable goals and objectives. By setting program targets relatively low, an agency can demonstrate "performance effectiveness" without making a significant contribution to the resolution of the problems that the policy was intended to address.

Although it is true that skillful manipulation of resources and personnel is essential to successful program maintenance, some of these skills are readily communicable and thus not necessarily associated with personal charisma. In general, a basic set of techniques has proved useful to program managers. Most of these techniques have been borrowed from the private sector; however, they acquire a unique character when applied to the maintenance of public programs and policies.

Operational Control

In the private sector, these techniques and strategies fall generally within the rubric of operational control. Jerry Dermer describes the control process in business and industry as follows:

1. determining if a problem exists by collecting information about ex-
    pectations and actual performance and then comparing these data
2. generating alternative courses of action that will eliminate or minimize the
    deviation between actual and expected
3. evaluating alternative courses of remedial action available and selecting
    the appropriate solution
4. ensuring that the appropriate action does actually close the deviation
    between actual and expected.[12]

These procedures may seem relatively simple, but in application many
complex steps are needed to manage, manipulate, and motivate men,
machinery, and money in the pursuit of a predetermined end. The following
techniques represent some of the generic control devices used in this process:

Value analysis: Techniques used to ensure most cost-effective operations.

Gantt and bar charts and time-line diagrams: Work scheduling techniques that graphically display the relationships between tasks and time.

Line of Balance (LOB): A technique that measures and compares operational outputs with forecasted completion time and quantities.

Network analysis: Techniques, including PERT and CPM, which schedule, coordinate, and plot the course of operations to ensure that activities
will occur in the proper sequence and with minimum slack time.[13]

These techniques are quite modest in their application and involve the less
difficult aspects of operational control. The more troublesome tasks of control
entail the regulation and modification of human behavior. Here too the private
sector has done much to advance the art of successful implementation. Several
techniques designed to clarify and engender commitment to organizational
goals find their origins in business administration.

Management by Objectives (MBO) foregoes the rigidity and formal
processes of traditional administration for a more open, fluid, and democratic
approach. Employees at each level of the organization are called on to participate in the formulation of programmatic objectives that are then integrated
with broader organizational objectives. In MBO, it is assumed that the results
of this identification and integration process will be a commitment to both individual organizational objectives. The committed employee—one who is aware
of his own role and subsequent progress—can be expected to display a high
level of performance and productivity.

Based on Drucker's concept of self-control, this approach gives the employee responsibility for the evaluation of his own performance in meeting the objectives that he previously established.[14] The employee also has the corresponding responsibility to make the necessary adjustments suggested by this evaluation. Thus, management must delegate the authority as well as the responsibility to achieve individual objectives. A common complaint in the public sector is that authority is not commensurate with responsibility, and although MBO does not address this complaint explicitly, its assumptions involve an attempt to correct this situation. This issue is pursued further in Management by Responsibility (MBR), a basic variation on MBO. A number of public organizations are experimenting with MBO and MBR.

Control Systems in the Public Sector

Public sector employees have been less than enthusiastic about accepting rigorous control systems, in spite of many attempts to soften the character of private-sector applications.[15] There seems to be a fear that control systems will precipitate an ever-increasing need for greater control. As Roethlisberger explains: ". . . breakdown of rules begot more rules to take care of their breakdown or the breakdown of close supervision and as a result, the continuous search and invention of new control systems to correct the limitations of the previous ones."[16]

Whether or not such fears are justified, the problems of applying systematic implementation strategies wholecloth to the public enterprise are manifold. Basically, these techniques tend to ignore, or at least to underestimate, the sociopolitical constraints illustrated by the proponents of implementation feasibility analysis. Moreover, as the literature on public-sector productivity suggests, improving performance in labor-intensive public service organizations is very different from improving outputs in capital-intensive industries.[17] Monitoring and motivation both pose several unique problems:

1. Public goods and services, by definition, are nonexclusionary.
2. The lack of a pricing mechanism makes the calculation of dollars-worth-of-production per man-hour very difficult.
3. Benefits produced by public programs are often intangible.
4. Workload measures, such as number of police patrols, may have little relationship to productivity.
5. Result measures, such as crime rates, may or may not be causally linked to productivity.
6. Such measures also may be subject to manipulation and misrepresentation.

The existence of these problems does not imply that public policies are doomed to aimless meanderings or limited achievements. Something analogous to control is possible if program managers are willing to apply some basic organizational techniques in the areas where they are most appropriate. These areas might include: (1) coordination of tasks; (2) distribution of personnel and other resources, (3) establishment and attainment of deadlines, and (4) designation of points of evaluation. In short, the techniques are not substitutes for critical management decisions. Rather, they are merely tools for structuring tasks once decisions have been made and mechanisms for alerting management to future decision junctures.

Network Analysis

The most straightforward way to map the process of implementation is through application of the techniques of network analysis. In its simplest forms, networking is merely a visual display—an outline—of the tasks to be performed. More detailed networks are not that much more difficult to construct than simple ones, and thus most businesses and many public enterprises rely on comprehensive network approaches. Networks are particularly crucial to projects in which several operations must be carried out in proper sequence. The Army Corps of Engineers, for example, requires that all subcontractors utilize extensive network analyses for even the most rudimentary construction projects.

The Origins of Network Analysis

Managers of industrial processes have used many of the terms and concepts of network analysis in their production planning since the turn of the century. Before World War II, industrial engineers developed process-flow charts and programming techniques, such as line-of-balance charts, that are quite similar in concept to the network theory that forms the basis for PERT. Business analysts have long utilized a topological approach in work programming that is parallel to the network algorithms of PERT and CPM.

The evolution of network analysis can be traced back to the work of pioneers in scientific management. The time-and-motion studies of Frederick Taylor are familiar to every student of industrial engineering and administration. Bar charts developed by Henry Laurence Gantt form the basis for many modern production scheduling systems. The relative conceptual simplicity of the Gantt chart is one reason why this technique continues to be widely applied. A common form of Gantt chart used in contemporary program management is the so-called *time-line diagram.*

A fundamental weakness of the original Gantt bar chart, however, is its inability to deal effectively with the problems of "concurrency" in large-scale projects, that is, the interdependencies of overlapping or interrelated activities. *Milestone charts* represent one relatively successful attempt to modify the Gantt approach to increase management awareness, if not the effective display, of the interdependencies among tasks. Milestones are key elements or points in time that can be identified as a program or project progresses. The milestone chart provides a sequential list of the various critical tasks to be accomplished. Although a milestone system does not provide explicit mechanisms to measure the effects of changes or slippages in a program schedule, it does improve on the reporting of these problems.

The Emergence of CPM and PERT

In 1956 a DuPont engineer, Morgan R. Walker, and a Remington-Rand computer expert, James E. Kelley, Jr., headed a comprehensive study of the extent to which a computer might be used to improve the planning, scheduling, and progress reporting of DuPont engineering programs. Late in 1957, they ran a test system using a unique arrow-diagram or network method which subsequently came to be known as the Critical Path Method (CPM). Concurrently, the U.S. Navy Special Projects Office established a project called Program Evaluation Research Task (PERT), aimed at formulating techniques for the efficient management of huge, complicated weapons-development programs (in this case, the POLARIS submarine). PERT provided an approach to the fast-multiplying problems of large-scale projects in which technical innovations, complex logistics, and concurrent activities must be integrated.

By 1961, numerous articles, reports, and papers had been published on CPM, PERT, and PERT-like systems, making them perhaps the most widely publicized, highly praised, sharply criticized, and widely discussed management techniques ever devised. Enthusiastic proponents—eager to identify with progress—spawned a multitude of acronyms. As these spin-offs multiplied, responsible managers in industry and the military became increasingly concerned about standardization. Although many of these systems had minor differences, they all were network-based. Various high-level efforts were mounted to minimize the differences and to develop a standard nomenclature and more uniform application. The result was general acceptance of the techniques of PERT and CPM.

As both methods were subsequently revised and improved, attractive features of one were incorporated into the other. The "arrow diagram" or network is common to both methods. It is necessary to identify a "critical path" in the development of a PERT network, and the "three time estimates" approach of PERT can be applied in CPM. PERT remains an *event-oriented* form of network analysis, whereas CPM is more *job-* or *activity-oriented.* However, this is more a difference in the format of application (and the resulting diagrams) than one in the underlying conceptual framework.

PERT is the more sophisticated of the two techniques, designed to deal with: (1) large-scale projects or programs, with (2) unclear objectives, (3) multiple and/or overlapping management responsibilities, (4) high levels of time and cost uncertainty, (5) complex problems of logistics, and (6) problems with sufficient operational complexity to justify the use of the computer. CPM, on the other hand, has been described as a "back-of-an-envelope" or "in-the-field" technique, with much less dependence on data-processing and computer-programming experience. CPM techniques are particularly applicable to well-defined projects that are under the management direction of a single organization and that have relatively low levels of uncertainty. Because of its relative ease of understanding and application as a tool of program management, it is CPM which draws further attention in this discussion.

Application of the Critical Path Method

A CPM network is essentially a "graphic plan of action"; CPM facilitates the selection of a "best route" to be followed to reach program objectives as well as the identification of potential obstacles and delays that might be encountered. Under CPM, management functions are divided into two distinct phases: (1) *planning*—deciding what should be done; and (2) *scheduling*—determining when activities should be initiated. This separation of functions makes it possible to determine what operations or activities actually control significant completion times. Thus, supervision of the program can be based on the concept of management by exception; principal attention can be directed to controlling activities that are most critical to the achievement of program objectives.

In applying CPM, all the identifiable activities or events in the program should first be listed and the immediately apparent linkages among them should be noted. An *event* may be defined as the completion of an activity (that is, a milestone). Often at the outset of an operations plan, the linkages among activities or events may be only partially perceived. CPM helps expand these perceptions. Informal brainstorming sessions with the program staff may aid in the identification of these activities and their relationships. Often in such brainstorming sessions the ideas will flow in a somewhat unstructured fashion, and this approach should be encouraged to ensure that all ideas are brought out in the open.

To establish the links between various events or activities, three basic questions must be asked about each activity: (1) What must be done before this

Table 10–1

**Linkages and Predecessor-Successor Relationships for a
Thirteen-Event Project**

Activity or Event	Linked to:	Preceded by:	Followed by:
A	C,D,M	C,D	M
B	G,J,L	J	G,L
C	A,I	I	A
D	A,I	I	A
E	M,K,F	M,K,F	None
F	E,H	H	E
G	B,K	B	K
H	F,J,K	J	F,K
I	C,D	None	C,D
J	B,H	None	B,H
K	E,G,H	G,H	F.
L	B,M	B	M
M	A,E,L	A,L	E

activity can begin? (2) What must immediately follow this activity? (3) What activities can be undertaken concurrently? The answers to these three questions identify the *predecessor-successor relationships* among activities and events. Table 10–1 illustrates these relationships for a project with thirteen activities or events.

The information presented in table 10–1 is more ordered than that available from the initial perceptions of these relationships. This information can easily be converted into an arrow diagram, the initial portrayal of a CPM network. If an activity is denoted as a direct link between two nodes (events) in a network, an arrow (symbolizing the activity) indicates the direction of time flow from one event to another. Table 10–1 is translated into an arrow diagram in figure 10–1.

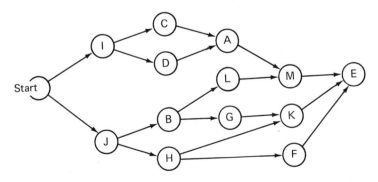

Figure 10–1. Arrow Diagram for Thirteen-Activity Project

Since the nodes represent the completion of an activity (an event), the term *start* is used to anchor the initiation of the arrow diagram. Each arrow represents a linkage between events, and more than one arrow can designate the same activity; for example, the two arrows that terminate at node A represent activity A. This approach has certain advantages in determining time durations and in delimiting the critical path, as will be illustrated.

The arrow diagram is composed of a series of sequential *paths*. Each path must be completed in the indicated sequence in order for the various activities to be carried out in the proper relationships to one another and for the overall program to be successfully implemented. Once these connections have been drawn, a critical route can be determined and progress can be measured against a list of key checkpoints or milestones.

Calculations on the Network

Associated with each arrow in the network is a time estimate called its *duration*. The duration of an arrow is the amount of time required to complete the activity represented by this arrow. The next step in the CPM process, therefore, is to assign time estimates to each of the paths.

Suggested time durations for each of the thirteen activities in the maternal health care clinic project have been loaded on to the arrows in the network (figure 10–2). Note that each arrow (activity) leading to a given node (event or activity completion) is assigned the time duration for the designated activity. In this way, all possible paths to that event can be easily traced. At this point, no effort has been made to draw the diagram to a time scale.

Beginning at *start*, the time duration for each path should be summed to determine:

1. the earliest possible time that an activity (arrow) that terminates at a given node (event) can be completed—known as the *earliest possible occurrence* or EPO

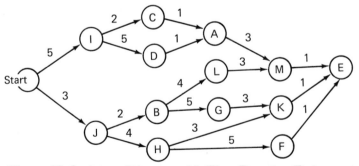

Figure 10–2. Arrow Diagram with Time-Duration Estimates

2. how long it will take to complete the entire project (project duration)
3. which activities establish and control the project duration (the critical path)
4. how much leeway there is in the activities that do not control the project duration (the "float").

In figure 10–2, for example, the path from *start* to I to C to A would take eight time units, whereas the path from *start* to I to D to A would take eleven time units. Therefore, the EPO for event A is eleven time units—activities dependent on the completion of activity A cannot begin until a point eleven time units into the project is reached. The EPO of the final activity node has added significance, since it is the earliest possible completion time for the entire project, that is, it defines the *project duration.*

Operational Leeway—Float

Float is the amount of time that an activity can be delayed or its duration lengthened without affecting the EPO of any other activity. To determine this operational leeway, calculations are made by taking the EPO of the final activity node and subtracting the time duration back to the nodes that lead to this final activity. This process is repeated for each node in turn back to *start.* These calculations determine the *latest possible occurrence* or LPO for each node—the latest possible time that all activities that terminate at a given node can finish without causing the project duration to exceed the originally determined completion time. Whereas the EPO is the longest path (time duration) from *start* to a given node, the LPO is the shortest path from the termination of the project back to a given node. The EPO and LPO for each node is illustrated in figure 10–3. The number above the node indicates the EPO; the number below, the LPO.

The Critical Path

It should be clear that no activity with a positive float can control the duration of the entire project. The durations of these activities can be shortened as much as is physically possible or lengthened by an amount equal to the float they possess without affecting the EPO of any other activity. This means that the EPO of the last activity node will not be affected and hence the project duration will not be altered. This characteristic of float limits the search for "critical" activities to those that have floats of zero.

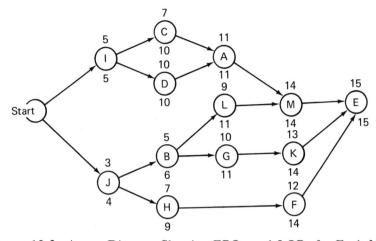

Figure 10-3. Arrow Diagram Showing EPOs and LOPs for Each Node
(Event)

Not all activities with zero floats control the project duration, however. The activities that do control are the ones that have zero float *and* form a continuous path starting at the first activity and ending at the last one. In figure 10–3, this path is made up of the links between I, D, A, M, and E. If any of these activities is delayed, the project completion time will be increased by the amount of that delay. It is this sequence of activities that defines the *critical path.* The arrow network can be redrawn on a time scale that shows the relative positioning of each activity node in terms of the total project duration and the critical path.

The preceding discussion can best be summarized by listing the steps involved in applying the critical path method to a project or program.

1. Define all the activities that make up the project or program.
2. Define the linkages and sequence of performance for each activity.
3. Draw an arrow diagram that defines the sequence of performing the various activities.
4. Estimate the duration of each activity.
5. Calculate the EPO and LPO of each activity node or event.
6. Determine the float for each activity and locate the critical path.

Once the actual program is placed into operation, the critical path can be continuously monitored so that any delays can be determined before they occur. By shifting personnel, materials, or other resource inputs to the critical path from those paths that have float, such delays can be circumvented. Therefore, the identification of the critical path also provides a dynamic control dimension.

In addition, the CPM network offers a convenient form of shorthand for managers, programmers, and decision makers to express a complex set of relations. It offers a medium of communication and prognostication, and it facilitates the subdivision of work so that each person and unit involved in the implementation process may proceed with the more detailed planning of his or her part of the program or project. The CPM approach provides the basis for an analysis of the costs involved when an attempt is made to use float time to reduce overall project costs, or the cost of a *crash program* in instances where the critical-path time is to be reduced. In general, the CPM approach determines the sequential ordering of activities, the maximum time required to complete the job, the costs involved, and the ramifications in terms of time and cost of altering the critical path.

Programming Limited Resources

The Critical Path Method provides an optimal operations plan, assuming the availability of unlimited resources to complete the identified activities. However, the usual problem facing the program manager is the allocation of scarce resources, especially personnel, among the various programmed activities. This allocation must be made in such a way that the program schedule is maintained, while the resource costs are held to a minimum.

Some fundamental guidelines to assist the manager in scheduling limited resources can be derived from the following relatively simple program heuristics:

1. Allocate resources progressively in time; that is, for the first time period, schedule all activities possible given the available staff or other limited resources, then do the same for the second time period, and so forth.
2. When several activities compete for the same resources, give preference to those with the least float or slack time.
3. Reschedule noncritical activities (those not on the critical path) if possible in order to free resources for scheduling critical (nonslack) jobs.

Estimating Time Durations: The Problem of Uncertainty

Often a manager/analyst is unable to predict the exact time duration of any given activity in a program or project. The time estimate chosen may reflect the *most probable value of an unknown distribution function.* If the *variance* of this distribution is relatively small, the most likely time duration may provide a reasonably close approximation of the actual time required to complete the activity. If the variance is large, however, the duration is said to verge on *uncertainty.*

One of the assignments of the original PERT team was to estimate time requirements to achieve any given event, together with a measure of uncertainty. These efforts led to the adoption of the so-called *beta distribution formula,* as shown below:

$$t_e = 1/6(t_a + 4t_b + t_c),$$

where: t_a = the most optimistic time estimate,

t_b = the most likely time estimate, and

t_c = the most pessimistic time estimate.

The application of the beta distribution formula is relatively simple. When doubt exists as to the appropriate duration of any activity, the manager-analysts should ask those who will be responsible for carrying out the activity: "If everything goes right with this job, what is the shortest time you will require to complete this activity?" Then the manager-analyst should ask: "If everything goes wrong—if the absolute worst happens—what is the longest time period required to complete this activity?" Finally, assuming the range established by the answers to the first two questions, the manager-analyst should ask, "What is the most likely time required to complete this activity?"

Expected time and variance, although statistically related, act somewhat independently in real-world situations. *Expected time* is a statistical term that corresponds to "average" or "mean" in common language; there is a 50 percent probability that the estimated time will be exceeded by the actual duration. *Variance,* on the other hand, is a measure of uncertainty; if the variance is large, there is greater uncertainty as to the time in which the activity will be completed. If the variance is small, it follows that the uncertainty will be small.

The concept of variance can be used to evaluate the risk or probability of meeting a specific schedule time. By subtracting the earliest possible occurrence of any given event from some imposed schedule-completion time (S) and dividing the result by the standard deviation for that event, an F value can be determined. This F value can then be interpreted in terms of the probability of meeting the imposed schedule by consulting a table of values for the normal curve.

To illustrate these procedures, assume that the duration of a project is 15 weeks with a standard deviation of 2 weeks. What is the probability of completing this project in 14 weeks? The calculations to determine the F value are as follows:

$$F = \frac{\text{Imposed Schedule Deadline minus Expected Duration}}{\text{Standard Deviation of Expected Duration}}$$

$$= \frac{14 - 15}{2} = -0.5$$

From a table of values for the standard normal distribution function, it can be determined for an entry of -0.5 that the value is 0.3085, that is, there is approximately a 30.85 percent chance of the project being completed in 14 weeks.

This method of assessing risk can be applied in reverse to determine an appropriate duration for any element in a project, or to determine total project duration, given some acceptable level of risk as determined by the project manager or decision maker. Using the expected duration in the previous example, assume that a 20 percent risk level is chosen. What time duration should be allowed for the completion of the project? The appropriate formula is as follows:

$$\text{Imposed Schedule Deadline} = F(\text{Standard Deviation of } t_e) + t_e$$

The F value for a 20 percent level of risk (an 80 percent probability of success) is approximately 0.843. Therefore, the project duration to achieve this projected level of success would be:

$$0.843(2) + 15 = \text{approximately 16.7 weeks}$$

To raise the probability of success to 90 percent would require approximately 2.5 additional weeks, or a total of 17.5 weeks, whereas to approach a success level of 100 percent would require nearly 7.75 weeks beyond the 15-week duration. The F values for various levels of risk (probability of success) are provided in table 10–2.

This brief discussion provides an important insight into the concept of risk based on the normal distribution function. It may be possible to reduce the level of risk (increase the probability of success) from the 50-percent level assumed by the beta distribution by adding a relatively small amount of time to the estimated project duration. However, beyond the 90-percent level of success, the increments of time required become increasingly large, often beyond any realistic expectations. Changes in the standard deviation of the

Table 10–2
F Values for Various Levels of Risk/Probability of Success

Probability of Success (%)	F Value
55	0.1208543
60	0.2516285
65	0.3821697
70	0.5225311
75	0.6727744
80	0.8429417
85	1.0428190
90	1.2825607
95	1.6417270
100	3.8700000

expected duration will have a significant impact on the additional time required to increase the probability of success. Reducing the standard deviation (reducing the uncertainty) will reduce the additional time duration required for any chosen level of success.

The result of using three time estimates is, in most situations, a more pessimistic outlook than would be obtained using only the most likely duration. In many projects, the manager-analyst should use the best time estimate possible and then control the project in a dynamic fashion. In short, regardless of how the time estimate is obtained, a major responsibility of management is to control the project once it is implemented.

Program Monitoring

Any form of operations planning and scheduling is only as good as its actual application. CPM can aid in identifying the tasks that are essential to project completion, but it cannot motivate individuals toward that completion. The concepts of control associated with CPM and PERT, however, imply more than a mere attempt to limit deviations from a mutually determined path.

Dermer contends that effective operations planning must be: (1) participative, (2) continuous, (3) coordinative, (4) integrated, and (5) experimental.[18] On one level, operations planning is an extension of strategic planning into the implementation process. External controls must be interpreted in terms of the interaction among the political structure, the community, and the program's implementors. Internal controls, on the other hand, involve a complex set of management practices and productivity-improvement techniques. The devices of external monitoring will be discussed at length in chapter 11 on *evaluation*. Internal mechanisms of control are the primary focus of the remainder of this chapter.

Internal Control

Managing complex organizations is obviously a monumental task. The history of modern administration has generally been written in terms of leadership, and leadership structure is often a key to organizational control. Reorganization and realignment also continue to be major themes of public reform. Frequent reorganization of public agencies may prove dysfunctional, however, because it tends to interrupt program continuity, to contribute to insecurity and low morale among personnel, and to disrupt agency–client-group relations. Furthermore, increased leadership and/or structural reorganization may have relatively little impact on the problems of effective program implementation if the real impediments are in the processes of *service delivery.* The effective manager must be well-informed about these processes and have overall control of them.

Process information may be generated during the building of the budget (for example, in the formulation of program strategies or decision packages) or through the procedures of policy analysis. In the absence of these more sophisticated approaches, however, a few basic techniques of process identification and measurement may prove useful; these include activity analysis, program analysis, and goal modeling.

Activity analysis involves a number of rudimentary exercises, such as layout identification and activity-flow and -distribution studies, designed to assess the appropriate mix of personnel resources needed to perform a given task. An activity analysis shows *who* does *what, when, where,* and *how.* Such an analysis should not merely provide a time-and-motion study; rather, it should suggest how various units within the organization function or fail to function in relation to organizational goals and policies. It provides a check on the validity of time and resource allotments and a means of identifying where help is most urgently needed should a given subunit or task fall on the critical path.

While *program analysis* is most appropriately part of the budgetary process, even when it is performed correctly there it may have to be reiterated in the implementation phase. There may be divergence from the chosen program path as social and organizational goals evolve. Moreover, what were initially perceived as appropriate program actions may become too difficult or too costly to accomplish. These changes in program status can be caused by various unforeseen fluctuations and interventions by exogenous factors in the previously defined system. For example, a rapid decline in the local economy may change perspectives on community services, or a realization of fixed or declining productivity in a delivery system such as education may lead to a redefinition of boundaries and capabilities. The emergence of conflicting goals, as with Affirmative Action, may cause the organization to redesign its strategies of implementation. All these circumstances and others may lead an agency to recycle some or all of the steps of program analysis, as previously described.

Goal modeling can often be used to explore different goal alignments in situations where goals and objectives have fallen into disarray or where new alternatives present themselves. Although goal modeling in the public sector may be more judgmental than mathematical, the purpose is basically the same as in the private sector—the isolation of basic goals and their association with critical tasks. It may be helpful to describe the rapidly changing demands on and constraints within the organization in order to clarify these processes.

In some cases, subgoals within a public program may conflict with one another or may contradict the goals of other programs. Goal projection and comparison may help to explicate these conflicts. For example, in the case of public welfare programs, some assistance programs may actually detract from the home environment of welfare recipients. The home environment, in turn, may critically affect the educational attainment of the children of the welfare family, and this ultimately may be integral to their economic mobility. Thus, an objective that is viable in the short run may prove disruptive to other programs (in this case, educational programs) and dysfunctional to its own program over time.

Admittedly, these dysfunctions should be explored in the strategic planning stage through such techniques as issue analysis. In some cases, however, they may not become apparent until a program is implemented and specific objectives are associated with manageable tasks and activities. In such situations, a restatement of goals and of the parameters of the system may be the only way to save the program.

Organizational Behavior and Policy Maintenance

Discovering program dysfunctions and organizational drift away from goals is a relatively simple task, particularly when linked to periodic evaluations, which will be discussed in chapter 11. That is to say, discovery is relatively simple *compared to* the task of getting agency personnel to accept their mistakes and of motivating them to do better. One strategy that combines goal-clarification procedures with motivational considerations is known generically as Management by Objectives (MBO). The element of MBO that is of interest here is its tendency toward *managerial democracy.* Based on the observations of organizational theorists, some forms of MBO are attempts to create commitments to improved performance through collective goal assessment. The logic of this approach is that individuals will demonstrate greater attachment to goals that they have helped to develop.

MBO also helps to stimulate increased organizational communications and to link choices to simple performance criteria. As Harry Havens points out, ". . . the major difficulty in evaluating the accomplishment of goals stems from inadequate information and communication for setting program objectives."[19] In dealing with this evaluative problem, MBO establishes goal alignments through a process of open communication in which managers at different levels evaluate individual performance in terms of mutually developed organizational goals.

This information process also provides multiple entry points for external reviewers. Sherwood and Page contend that MBO has the ". . . potential for reassuring legislators and policy makers that government units actually are committed to specifying objectives and reporting progress toward them."[20] Increased visibility and perhaps increased accountability should yield increased credibility of public programs.

Generally speaking, MBO involves the following elements:

1. a clarification of organization or community objectives in reference to broader societal goals
2. an open atmosphere in which administrators are encouraged to make innovative contributions to the realization of the goals of the organization
3. a specification of tasks and responsibilities of individuals with reference to the goals of the organization
4. a set of standards by which individual and programmatic decisions can be evaluated in terms of their goals achievement
5. the provision of systematic reassessment and continued innovation in the pursuit of the goals of the organization.

MBO is not a rigorous methodology, but is more a managerial philosophy. Its success or failure will depend largely on how it is applied and on what type of assessment it fosters in a given situation.

Productivity in the Public Sector

Productivity—the relationship between outputs and inputs, usually expressed as a ratio—has become as important a watchword in the public sector as it is in business and industry. As with so many borrowed concepts, however, its meaning in the public sector is unclear. Briefly stated, productivity in the public sector is "the efficiency with which resources are consumed in the effective delivery of public services."[21] This definition includes elements of quality as well as quantity. However, it is too general to be applied directly in a practical manner.

Public-sector productivity is vastly different from productivity in the private sector. As Charles Wise explains, gains in productivity in the private sector are brought about by the following factors:

1. *process factors*—the use of capital equipment, automation, work simplification, reorganization, revised procedures and workflow, and technical improvements
2. *product factors*—large gains in volume, making possible the use of economy-of-scale techniques, workload stability, and product redesign and diversification
3. *personnel factors*—flexible hours, job enrichment, career development programs, and amenities in the work environment.[22]

Given the capital-intensive nature of industry, substantial gains have resulted in private sector productivity from a focus on the first of these factors. In the public sector, on the other hand, the highly labor-intensive nature of activities makes the third factor (and some elements of the second factor, such as economies of scale) most important. It is unlikely that public agencies will see the massive improvements in productivity experienced in, say, agriculture, when human labor was replaced by machinery and energy. Public-sector productivity is a matter of small but significant incremental gains.

An important distinction must be made between productivity improvement and productivity measurement. *Productivity improvement* implies the actual process of changing the ratio of inputs to outputs. *Productivity measurement* involves an analysis aimed at reducing uncertainty about organizational outputs. Public-sector analysts may measure productivity in order to understand better the constraints on implementation, not necessarily to improve productivity. Obviously, improvements may result from such measurement; however, some ratios may not be amenable to change, yet information about them is equally important to social choices.

Government agencies provide various types of services, often of an intangible nature (for example, welfare programs). The lack of physical outputs is less problematic in the private sector because productivity can be estimated by using the prices associated with services provided. However, since public services generally are provided without direct charge, this method of productivity measurement is not applicable.

This measurement problem has led to the establishment of two distinct categories of outputs in the public sector:

Activity measures involving direct service units or work units, such as the number of police patrols

Result measures involving indirect impacts assumed to be causally linked to activities identified as direct outputs, such as the crime rate.

The simplest form of measurement entails the creation of proxy output measures or surrogates when the actual output is unknown. Improvements in management techniques and money-saving measures taken by government agencies have also been used as indicators of increased productivity. (The latter approach has been used in New York City, where productivity improvement has become vital to continued existence.)

An alternative approach developed by Ross and Burkhead avoids difficult output calculations. This approach utilizes fluctuations in expenditure data, which are divided into three components: cost, workload, and a residual factor reflecting changes in quality.[23] Identifiable changes in the ratio of inputs to outputs are then "measured" in terms of these factors. This technique holds some promise, particularly for local governments, for which expenditure information is readily available and proxies for cost and workload are relatively simple to devise.

Another set of problems confronting the implementation of productivity improvements in the public sector can be summarized as follows:

1. It may be necessary to implement a productivity measurement/ improvement program on a government-wide basis. Focusing on individual agencies may be dysfunctional to agency programs or, alternatively, may create a "halo effect." It may be advisable to establish a separate agency to oversee productivity.
2. The costs to be considered in implementing productivity measures are both the monetary costs and the disruptive effects agencies. In the long run, the tangible and intangible costs.
3. Agencies may not want to be evaluated on this basis and may make conscious efforts to undermine such programs.[24]

The need to discover methods for reducing expenditures without reducing public services is manifested in the growing fiscal difficulties facing many local and state governments. Productivity improvement in the delivery of public services is one way of achieving this goal. As devices of internal management and implementation, productivity accounts present a formidable resource, especially if implementation can be linked to periodic program evaluations.

Conclusions

The implementation process has been a sorely neglected aspect of public policy. However, as the linkages among programming, implementation, and evaluation are more tightly drawn, the mysterious haze surrounding the processes of policy implementation and program maintenance may dissipate. Tools and strategies will undoubtedly be improved in the wake of such integration. Meanwhile, implementation will continue to be a subtle blend of operational analysis and basic management techniques—an amalgamation of both subjective and objective approaches. Forging a systematic framework out of this loosely knit set of techniques may be difficult. Nevertheless, it appears to be a necessary and worthwhile endeavor.

The history of implementation is a chronicle of numerous "slips 'twixt cup and lip." This history must not be allowed to repeat itself, for as resources dwindle each spill becomes more important. James Boren, former president of the National Association of Professional Bureaucrats, has suggested that the real role of bureaucracy is to ensure "dynamic inactivism" in order to avoid implementation failures. The current public mood, however, is not likely to prove sympathetic to this bureaucratic axiom. Careful analysis, implementation, and maintenance of policy obviously is required not only to ensure the continued existence of public agencies, but also to guarantee the continued existence and improvement of our way of life.

Notes

1. See Gregory A. Daneke, "Implementation: The Missing Link Discovered?" *International Journal of Public Administration* 2, no. 1 (Winter 1980).

2. Note, for example, the classic study by Jeffrey Pressman and Aaron Wildavsky, *Implementation—How Great Expectations in Washington Are Dashed in Oakland; Or, Why It's Amazing that Federal Programs Work at All, This Being a Saga of the Economic Development Administration as Told by Two Sympathetic Observers Who Seek to Build Morals on a Foundation of Ruined Hopes* (Berkeley: University of California Press, 1973).

3. This list is similar to the questions developed by Harry Hatry et al. in *Program Analysis for State and Local Government* (Washington, D.C.: The Urban Institute, 1976), pp. 100–101.

4. Ashley Schiff, *Fire and Water: Scientific Heresy in the Forest Service* (Cambridge, Mass.: Harvard University Press, 1962).

5. Much of this confusion, of course, occurred in the implementation process. See Robert Levine, *Public Planning: Failure and Redirection* (New York: Basic Books, 1972), esp. pp. 80–89.

6. For a discussion of conflict-identification procedures through the construction of a multidimensional goal matrix, see Alan Walter Steiss, *Public Budgeting and Management* (Lexington, Mass.: Lexington Books, D.C. Heath and Company, 1972), chap. 9.

7. Edith Stokey and Richard Zeckhauser, *A Primer for Policy Analysis* (New York: W.W. Norton, 1978), p. 177.

8. Steiss, *Public Budgeting and Management,* p. 232.

9. Charles Kepner and Benjamin B. Tregoe, *The Rational Manager* (Princeton, N.J.: Princeton University Press, 1965).

10. Steiss *Public Budgeting and Management,* p. 233.

11. For a more detailed discussion, see Stokey and Zeckhauser, *A Primer for Policy Analysis,* pp. 178–199. For a discussion of more complex mathematical modeling techniques, see Harvey M. Wagner, *Principles of Operations Research,* 2nd ed. (Englewood Cliffs, N.J.: Prentice-Hall, 1975).

12. Jerry Dermer, *Management Planning and Control Systems: Advanced Concepts and Cases* (Homewood, Ill.: Richard D. Irwin, 1977), p. 14.

13. For a more elaborate discussion of these techniques, see William Taylor and Thomas Watling, *Practical Project Management* (London: Business Book, 1973).

14. Peter Drucker, "What Results Should You Expect? A Users' Guide to MBO," *Public Administration Review* 36(January-February 1976).

15. Note Harold F. Cortner, *Administration in the Public Sector* (New York: John Wiley and Sons, 1977), pp. 162–163.

16. Fritz J. Roethlisberger, *Toward A Unified Theory of Management* (New York: McGraw-Hill Book Company, 1964), p. 54.

17. Note Raymond Horton, "Productivity and Productivity Bargaining in Government," *Public Administration Review* 36(July–August 1976); and Nancy Hayward, "The Productivity Challenge," *Public Administration Review* 36(September–October 1976).

18. Dermer, *Management Planning and Control Systems,* pp. 29–30.

19. Harry S. Havens, "MBO and Program Evaluation, Or Whatever Happened to PPBS," *Public Administration Review* 36(January-February 1976):8

20. Frank P. Sherwood and William J. Page, "MBO and Public Management," *Public Administration Review* 36(January-February 1976): 11.

21. Nancy S. Hayward, "The Productivity Challenge," *Public Administration Review* 36(September-October 1976).

22. Charles R. Wise, "Productivity in Public Administration and Public Policy," in *Public Administration and Public Policy,* ed. H. George Frederickson and Charles R. Wise (Lexington, Mass.: Lexington Books, D.C. Heath and Company, 1977), pp. 177–178.

23. John P. Ross and Jesse Burkhead, *Productivity in the Local Government Sector* (Lexington, Mass.: D.C. Heath and Company, 1974).

24. For a discussion of union resistance to productivity measures in New York City, see Raymond D. Horton, "Productivity and Productivity Bargaining in Government: A Critical Analysis," *Public Administration Review* 35 (July-August 1976):407–414.

11 The Feedback Stage: Policy and Program Evaluation

Evaluation has been a watchword for nearly two decades in the pursuit of more effective public policy. Despite considerable fanfare, however, detailed and systematic assessments of public programs remain more a promise than a practice. As mentioned in previous chapters, public goals and objectives are often nebulous and ill defined, and consequently the identification and measurement of program results is even more elusive. Therefore, it is not surprising that the payoffs of public sector evaluations have been something less than sterling.

From Postmortem and Postaudit To Program Improvement

To begin with, the term *evaluation* has been applied to so many different activities that it has all but lost its functional meaning. Perkins, for examples, identifies six basic types of evaluations:

1. *Strategic evaluations* are concerned with underlying causes of social problems, focusing on "implicit theories" that serve as the foundations for ameliorative programs.
2. *Compliance evaluations* examine the consistency of programmatic objectives with broader legislative aims and attempt to ensure that funds are allocated in accordance with program guidelines.
3. *Program design evaluations* test the measurability of program assumptions, the overall logic of the approach, and the assignment of responsibility and accountability for program results.
4. *Management evaluations* focus on the efficiency and effectiveness with which managers deploy available resources to achieve program objectives.
5. *Intervention effect assessments* attempt to establish the relationship between program interventions and outcomes or, in some cases, the processes involved in producing those outcomes.
6. *Program impact evaluations* deal with program delivery systems and with the relationships between the outcomes and legislated goals and program objectives [1]

A common theme of these different types of evaluation is, as Carol Weiss suggests, "the notation of judging merits."[12] *Merit,* in turn, implies that policies and programs are achieving their basic goals.

Evaluation Research

Early efforts at systematic evaluations involved full-blown scholarly efforts, or what has been labeled *evaluation research.* Such analyses currently address ". . . the need, implementation, and impact of interaction efforts" in terms of public policies and programs.[3] In its humble beginnings, however, evaluation research was much like the buzzard, attacking only dead programs. These postmortems were useful in developing a conceptual basis for evaluations but did little to improve policy formulation. The time involved in scholarly research, sometimes as much as five to seven years, made program improvements virtually impossible, since many of the federal programs chosen for such rigorous analyses were short-term pilot projects.

Even when programs continued, program managers were unlikely to utilize the results of these evaluations. This utilization problem stemmed from two factors: (1) program evaluators were "outsiders," often with different perceptions and opinions about the goals of the program; and (2) evaluators tended to focus on the negative aspects of a program and rarely offered constructive advice.[4] As Robert Clark suggests, unless evaluation is keyed to specific information requirements and decision-making needs in a timely fashion ". . . it risks being irrelevant—a monument to what might have been."[5]

The interface/timing problem is particularly acute in those policy areas that may have specific postaudit requirements but that have no formal mechanisms for translating the results into alternative plans. This situation is particularly perplexing, since much of the postaudit research is turning up intriguing and heretofore unknown information about second-order consequences and unintended impacts.[6] A clearer picture of these impacts should produce improved types of program and project designs, but at present the feedback loop is, at best, intuitive.

Emergence of Effectiveness-Oriented Evaluations

In the past, when the findings of evaluations have been used at all, the purpose has generally been to improve efficiency. Questions of efficiency often are defined and answered strictly in economic terms of least cost, with minimal consideration of priorities or of the relative worth of the programs pursued. It is possible to do things very efficiently, but if they are the wrong things to do they will have little impact on the problems at which the program is directed. An efficient transportation link may facilitate the movement of traffic from point A to point B with little or no waste, but this efficiency will be irrelevant if the real need is to get to point C. *Effectiveness* considers the relative worth of the point B versus point C with reference to specific values (goals and objectives) and variables (policy and fiscal constraints). Consideration of this relative worth— the actual impact of resource expenditures in terms of program performance— requires a clear articulation of program goals and objectives.

Some argue that the distinction between efficiency and effectiveness is artificial, and that, properly applied, a *criterion of efficiency* is sufficient to measure both dimensions of a program's activities.[7] The notion of a criterion of efficiency, as formulated by Herbert Simon, asserts that a choice among alternatives should be made in favor of the course of action that produces the largest result for a given application of resources.[8] This is the "biggest-bang-for-the-buck" approach that characterizes many military applications of cost-benefit analysis. To guide this choice, however, it is necessary to determine an appropriate level of goal attainment or level of program adequacy (for example, a desirable or minimum acceptable level of output). Unfortunately, misapplication or incomplete application of such criteria is more common than proper application. In the absence of definitive statements of program goals and objectives or identified levels of program adequacy, measures of efficiency cannot provide the insights necessary to make appropriate judgments about program achievements or benefits.

Improving efficiency may not require drastic changes in program strategies, but improving effectiveness often entails radical program adjustments. Thus, one reason that evaluations focused on effectiveness may not be fully utilized is that there are few opportunities to make the types of changes that they recommend. Nevertheless, increasing emphasis is being placed on effectiveness evaluations or on the assessment of results of policy implementation.

A case in point is the development of new auditing procedures by the General Accounting Office (GAO). Heretofore, audits focused on the question of *financial compliance,* "Did you spend the money in the way you said you would?" This is the traditional emphasis of the post-audit—an assessment of financial transactions for fidelity, legality, and accuracy. Gradually, more emphasis has been placed on *management audits* that ask: "Did you achieve your milestones in the most efficient and economical way possible?" Management audits involve an assessment of resource-utilization practices, including an examination of the adequacy of management information systems, administrative procedures, and organizational structure. More recently, however, the emphasis has expanded further to include an assessment of *program results,* addressing the question: "What difference did the program make?" An examination of program results seeks to determine whether the desired results or benefits were achieved, whether program objectives were met, and whether alternatives were considered that might yield the desired results in the future at a lower cost. Taken together, these three audit components constitute what the GAO has labelled a *performance audit*.[9] Such an audit is generally undertaken when a program or project has been completed or has reached a major milestone in its funding, whereas performance evaluations are often applied to ongoing programs.

The scale and time frame of performance evaluations must be such that the evaluation can assist in formulating program improvements. Moreover, such an evaluation must specify program problems in a way that provides clear indications of alternative courses of action.

The identification of new courses of action has received added impetus from the emergence of various *sunset laws,* which require periodic evaluations of programs and the termination of those that cannot justify their continuance. Although it may differ from place to place, most sunset legislation provides for the following:

1. Agencies, departments, and programs heretofore granted indefinite tenure are assigned a mandatory termination date.
2. If the governing body takes no action, the enterprise is concluded (the sun sets) on its termination date.
3. The agency or department is given the opportunity to justify its continued existence prior to termination. This justification may entail any number of evaluative indices, including the results of a performance audit, and may be undertaken in conjunction with the processes of zero-base budgeting.
4. The legislative body has the option to reinstate or "reconstruct" the agency or program or to terminate it.
5. Reinstatement may leave the agency unchanged, whereas reconstruction may significantly modify the agency's mandate and responsibilities.
6. If reauthorized or reconstituted, the agency or program will again be subject to review and possible termination at the end of the next cycle.[10]

Although evaluations may not have realized their full potential in the past, new techniques, coupled with sunset provisions, provide additional incentives for administrators to heed evaluations and to use them as vital tools in improving program performance.

Cost-Benefit and Cost-Effectiveness Analysis

Another major example of the shift in emphasis from efficiency to effectiveness is found in recent developments in cost-benefit analysis. A comprehensive cost-benefit analysis requires estimates of direct and indirect costs and of tangible and intangible benefits involved in a given program or program alternative. Once specified, the costs and benefits are translated into a common measure, usually although not necessarily a monetary unit. Comparisons are then made by computing either a benefit-cost ratio; net benefits (benefits minus costs); or some other value, such as internal rate of return, for summarizing the results of the analysis. Such evaluations focus on issues of efficiency, that is, the greatest benefits for the lowest cost.

Cost-benefit analysis is obviously appropriate to technical and industrial projects, where it is reasonable to place monetary values on benefits as well as costs; but the program outputs of many public activities cannot be measured in strict monetary terms. Recognition of this shortcoming in traditional cost-benefit techniques has led to the development of the procedures of cost-effectiveness analysis. While cost-effectiveness requires the quantification of program costs and benefits, only the costs have to be expressed in monetary terms. Program benefits or outputs are expressed in terms of the actual substantive performance associated with the program objectives; that is, the efficacy of a program in attaining specific objectives is assessed in relation to the monetary value of the resources or costs required by the program. A cost-effectiveness analysis permits comparisons and rankings of potential programs according to the magnitude of their effects relative to their costs.[11]

Cost-effectiveness analysis requires the construction of a model that can relate incremental costs to increments of effectiveness. A cost curve is developed for each program or alternative, representing the sensitivity of costs (inputs) to changes in the desired level of effectiveness (outputs). Costs may change more or less proportionately to the level of achievement, so that each additional increment of effectiveness desired will require the same units of expenditure. However, if effectiveness increases more rapidly than costs, then the particular alternative is operating at a level of increasing returns, represented by a positively sloped curve that accelerates at an accelerating rate If costs increase more rapidly than effectiveness, the alternative is operating in an area of diminishing returns. Increasing returns do not mean that an alternative should be automatically adopted or that an ongoing program should necessarily be expanded. Conversely, diminishing returns should not automatically disqualify a program alternative. It is useful to know, however, that an additional commitment of, say, $200,000 to one alternative will carry it 20 percent closer toward an established objective, whereas the addition of the same resources to another alternative will carry it only 5 percent closer.

For some types of problems, it is relatively easy to develop practical models; for other problems, cost curves can be approximated from historical data. Construction of cost curves and effectiveness scales should become increasingly more sophisticated as the input-output relationships associated with various program alternatives are better understood through analysis and evaluation.[12] Current studies suggest that the cost-effectiveness relationship in many social programs often approximates an S-curve. In the initial phases of a program, start-up costs are high in relation to the level of effectiveness achieved. As a "critical mass" of clients is reached, the increments of effectiveness may increase more rapidly than the increments of cost because, for example, certain economies of scale have been achieved. At some point, however, the hard-to-reach segments of the client group must be considered and diminishing returns may set in, with costs increasing more rapidly than the additional increments of service provided.

Planning for Better Evaluations

While it may be obvious that evaluations that seek to facilitate program improvements must be carefully designed and executed, many evaluations suffer from a lack of planning. This shortcoming is understandable, given the ex post facto nature of past evaluation efforts. Ex post and ex ante evaluations involve the same principles and methods, except that in a retrospective evaluation empirical data derived from program operations and achievements replace estimates and assumptions. Planning is necessary in developing a sound data base for empirical evaluations. As evaluations become more timely, however, it is possible to initiate evaluation planning at approximately the time at which a program alternative is chosen for implementation. The evaluation design may be an extension of the process applied in the analysis and selection of the program alternative. It may be reasonable to expect the evaluability of alternatives to affect program decisions, since knowing that a program will be effective may be closely linked to showing that it is. This does not imply that program managers should only do that which promises to be most demonstrative, but it does suggest that evaluation strategy is a vital consideration in program planning. As Rossi et al. have so aptly observed: ". . . the more formal aspects of systematic evaluations depend upon what transpires during planning and program development. As every sailor knows, the trick is not to navigate the seas but to get out of the harbor."[13]

Clarifying Program Objectives

Before the initiation of a systematic evaluation, the exact character of program goals and objectives must be clarified. Complete clarity rarely comes from merely examining the final statements of goals and objectives. Evaluators must attempt to retrace the policy-formulation and program-planning processes to determine what types of impacts are actually anticipated. The links between program planning and evaluation require mutual understanding of the tasks and processes involved on both sides.

Shortell and Richardson have provided the following list of criteria for clarifying program objectives:

1. *Nature or content of the objective:* It is important to determine the intended changes to be brought about by the program.
2. *Ordering of objectives:* Objectives should be clearly presented at each level of abstraction, with corresponding operational indicators to determine if the objective has been met.
3. *Target group:* The specific group (s) to which the program is directed should be identifiable in terms of age, sex, ethnic categories, geographic boundaries, and so forth.
4. *Short-term versus long-term effects:* It is important to document both the short-term and long-term effects of any program.
5. *Magnitude of effects:* It is necessary to determine how large or small an effect will be acceptable as a positive indicator of success.
6. *Stability of effects:* For many programs, the effects are meant to be lasting; but for others, particularly programs involving behavioral changes, additional exposure to the program may be necessary.
7. *Multiplicity of objectives:* It is important to clarify objectives to the point at which possible conflicts among them can be identified and dealt with.
8. *Interrelatedness of objectives:* Where a set of lower-order objectives may serve as an important component in the achievement of higher order objectives, such linkages should be identified in the statement of objectives.
9. *Importance:* Objectives will differ in importance, and individuals often may disagree on the relative importance of each objective; however, some attempt should be made to place objectives in some general priority order.
10. *Unintended and unanticipated "second order" consequences:* It is important to identify possible "side effects" of the program—effects not intended but anticipated—or even unanticipated—by the initiators of the program.[14]

Measuring Program Effectiveness

Following the clarification of objectives, evaluators should conduct a brief survey of existing systems of measuring program effectiveness and determine how best to augment these systems. The GAO has described this activity as a four step process:

1. Identify and document existing systems for measuring effectiveness.
2. Assess the validity and sufficiency of the performance indicators, that is, quantifiable expressions of program objectives.

3. Assess the accuracy of the performance-indicator data.
4. Determine the appropriateness of the performance standards, that is, desired levels of achievement for performance indicators.[15]

It is noteworthy that not all performance criteria (indicators and standards) will be expressed in quantitative terms. Other factors, however, are more important, such as that performance indicators accurately reflect the intent of the objectives, that they *not* merely correspond to workload measures, and that they avoid tie-ins with impacts that are obviously attributable to other phenomena. More will be said about these control factors in the next section.

Having checked out the existing evaluation apparatus, it may be necessary in some cases to circumvent existing systems altogether. This process has been labelled an *ad hoc system,* implying that it is only a temporary substitute for "built-in" evaluation systems.

> Generally, the measurements obtained from an ad hoc system are not as refined or comprehensive as would be possible from a permanently established and well designed effectiveness measurement system. Nonetheless, an ad hoc system provides the users of the program results review findings with more reliable effectiveness data than they had previously been provided and shifts the burden for fine-tuning the performance data back to program management.[16]

Regardless of the findings of ad hoc systems, program management should design and implement a more permanent evaluation system to continue to monitor program performance. Ad hoc systems and/or the involvement of elaborate one-shot outside research efforts are not as valuable as the development of a full-time evaluative capability. Permanent systems offer the greatest potential for improved program performance in the long run.

Strategies for Practical Program Improvement

As suggested above, program improvement depends on evaluation strategies for assessing ongoing activities, rather than on studies, no matter how comprehensive or rigorous, of dead or dying government programs. As Quade points out, in contrast to analyses of proposed programs or after-the-fact assessments, practical program evaluation must deal with on-going activities and with the people who participate in or are affected by these activities. "People interact with an evaluation in ways that must be taken into account by the analysts."[17] In application, policy analysis and policy evaluation must form an interactive cycle—analysis preceding policy and program commitments and evaluation assessing the impacts and effectiveness of these decisions and commitments.

Management Information and Program
Evaluation Systems (MIPES)

Evaluation reflects a shift in emphasis away from the "input orientation" of traditional public sector activities toward an "output orientation" that concentrates on an identification of *change impacts,* both positive and negative, resulting from government programs. The input focus was institutionalized by budgetary procedures such as the traditional line-item or object-of-expenditure budget, which emphasizes the resources necessary to support public programs. The focus on outputs was first widely discussed in connection with performance budgeting in the late 1930s and 1940s and has more recently become a principal component of program budgeting. Evaluation assists public officials in determining whether a policy or program should be continued as is or be expanded, modified, reduced, or eliminated. If a program is not performing as anticipated, the evaluation may indicate reasons for ineffectiveness and suggest actions that might remedy the situation.

Effectiveness status monitoring (ESM) or *performance measurement* represents a special type of program evaluation involving a regular assessment of the status of ongoing program areas. The objective of an ESM is to provide a more continuous basis—at least an annual basis—for the review and evaluation of the general effectiveness of the major program responsibilities of government—health, safety, fire protection, recreation, waste collection and disposal, and so forth. While program evaluation attempts to identify the specific effects attributable to a given public program, ESM concentrates on the related changes arising in the delivery of public services in general. Together, program evaluation and effectiveness status monitoring constitute the fundamental components of a Management Information and Program Evaluation System (MIPES).

Decision makers seldom deal directly with problems; rather, they deal almost exclusively with information about problems. In turn, the must make decisions that best satisfy not actual conditions, but information about these conditions. As Ross has observed: "The art of management has been defined as the making of irrevocable decisions based on incomplete, inaccurate, and obsolete information."[18]

Managerial accounting is that branch of accounting theory and practice concerned with providing information that is useful in making decisions related to the development of resources and the exploitation of program opportunities.[19] Unlike financial accounting, which focuses on the recording of fiscal transactions, managerial accounting is involved in the formulation of financial estimates of future performance (the planning and budgeting processes) and subsequently in the analysis of actual performance in relation to these estimates (program evaluation and performance auditing).

The objective of managerial accounting is to improve the effectiveness of planning, management, and control. Government does not require a grandiose master plan drawn in the abstract; what is important, rather, is the fundamental ability to know how much is being spent, where, and for what purposes. Building the planning process on one data base (program analysis) and the mechanisms of control on another (financial accounting) places too great a stress on the management system as the intermediary. Planning depends on the same data-reporting mechanisms that make central oversight possible and decentralized management feasible.[20] An important task of managerical accounting is to enlarge the circle of those familiar with the planning, budgeting, and implementation processes, through the communication of pertinent management information as well as of financial data.

Approaches to Practical Program Evaluation

Ideally, evaluation seeks to compare *what actually happened* to *what would have happened* or what conditions would have prevailed if the program or policy had not been introduced.[21] Since it is difficult, if not impossible, to determine exactly "what would have happened if . . . ," the problem is to develop and apply evaluative procedures that can approximate this state. In short, evaluation seeks to test the classical design of the scientific method—given A, B occurs; but without A, B does not occur.

As with the application of the scientific method, there are several standard approaches to the conduct of an evaluation, including: (1) before-and-after comparisons; (2) time trend data projections; (3) with-and-without comparisons; (4) controlled experimentation; and (5) comparisons of planned versus actual performance. Each of these methods of evaluation begins and ends with the same procedural steps. The first step is to identify the *relevant objectives* of the policy or program under evaluation and the corresponding evaluative criteria or effectiveness measures. The major purpose of evaluation is to identify changes in those criteria that can reasonably be attributed to the program or policy under study. A major problem, however, is that other factors, such as external events or the simultaneous introduction of other related programs, may have occurred during the time period covered by the evaluation. One of these other factors, and not the program or policy under evaluation, may have been the significant reason for the observed changes. The second, third, and fourth approaches listed above include explicit provisions for controlling for at least some of these exogenous factors. Nevertheless, in all cases the final step in the evaluation should include an explicit and thorough search for *other plausible explanations* for the observed changes and, if any exist, an estimate of their effects on the data.

Building on the work of Campbell and Stanley,[22] Rossi and his colleagues offer the following list of "competing processes" that may influence the outcome or program effects:

1. *Endogenous change:* The condition for which the program is seen as a remedy or enhancement may change of its own accord; in medical research, this phenomenon is known as "spontaneous remission."
2. *Secular drift:* Relatively long-term trends in the target population or broader community may produce changes that enhance or mask the effects of a program.
3. *Interfering events:* Short-term events may also produce enhancing or masking changes.
4. *Maturational trends:* Programs directed toward changing persons at various stages of the life cycle must cope with the fact that considerable changes also are associated with the process of maturation.
5. *Self-selection:* A serious obstruction to the assessment of impacts of a social program is the fact that those segments of the target population that are easiest to reach usually are those that are most likely to change in the desired direction for other reasons. Similar processes in the opposite direction may lead to differential attrition; dropout rates vary from project to project, but are almost always troublesome in evaluation.
6. *Stochastic effects:* Chance or random fluctuations in any measurement effort, termed stochastic processes, may make it difficult to judge whether a given outcome is, in fact, large enough to warrant attention. Sampling theory describes how much variation can be expected by chance.
7. *Unreliability:* Data collection procedures are subject to a certain degree of unreliability. A major source of unreliability may be the measurement instrument itself.
8. *Program-related effects.* The actual evaluation effort may result in contamination; this is the problem of the "uninvolved observer."[23]

The outcome of a program is a function of net program effects and these confounding elements. The isolation of these competing processes must be undertaken in each of the evaluation approaches described in detail in the following sections.

Before-and-After Comparisons. As the label suggests, this approach compares conditions in a given jurisdiction or target population at two points in time—immediately before a program or policy is introduced and at some appropriate time after its implementation. This method of evaluation is the simplest and least costly approach as well as the most common; it is, however, least capable of separating other influences from the effect of program activities.

The procedural steps in a before-and-after comparison are simple. After relevant objectives and corresponding evaluation criteria have been identified, values of these critiera are obtained for the periods before and after implementation of the program. The assumption is that any changes in the "after" data, as compared to that from "before," have occurred as a consequence of the new program or policy. As previously noted, particular attention should be given to any other plausible explanations for these changes.

This approach is valid only in those situations where program comparisons are not likely to reflect short-term fluctuations and where program-related changes are clearly measurable. Its effectiveness is increased if the evaluation is planned prior to program implementation so that appropriate data can be collected as a basis for the evaluation criteria. Reliance on data normally available in established collection procedures seldom provides an adequate basis for evaluation. Special data-collection procedures will increase the cost of the evaluation, but this approach is still the least expensive of the methods outlined.

Time Trend Data Projections. The second approach attempts to draw a comparison between actual postprogram data generated by the evaluation criteria and extrapolated data suggestive of conditions that would have prevailed without the policy or program. Data on each of the evaluative criteria should be obtained at several intervals before and after the initiation of the program or policy. By means of standard statistical methods, preprogram data are projected to the end of the time period covered by the evaluation; actual and projected estimates are then compared to determine the amount of change resulting from the introduction of the program or policy. This approach is most appropriate when there appears to have been an underlying trend over a period of time that would have been likely to continue if the new program had not been introduced. The objective of the program is to change the direction of this trend—to amplify some desirable change or to dampen some undesirable emerging conditions. If data for prior years are too unstable, however, such statistical projections may be meaningless. Likewise, if there is strong evidence that underlying conditions have changed in very recent years, data for prior years probably should not be used.

This approach adds two elements of cost to the first method: (1) the cost of technical expertise to undertake the statistical projections, and (2) the added data collection for prior years. This latter requirement may become problematic in assuring that preprogram data are compatible with postprogram or current data.

With-and-Without Comparisons. A third approach seeks to draw comparisons between a jurisdiction with a particular program and one or more other communities without comparable programs. This approach also can be used if some segment of the population within a community is to be served by a given program while others are not, as happens when a pilot program is tested. This method tests the "null hypothesis"—if the groups without the program show changes comparable to those experienced by the groups receiving benefits from the program, then it is likely that factors other than those introduced by the program have contributed to these changes.

Following the identification of relevant objectives and corresponding evaluation criteria, it is necessary to identify other similar jurisdictions (or populations within the target jurisdiction) where the program is not operating. Data are obtained on each of the criteria in each jurisdiction or for each of the population segments being compared from before the implementation of the program up to the time of evaluation. Changes in the values of the criteria (rates of change as well as amounts) for the "with" and the "without" groups are then compared.

The characteristics determining the choice of comparative groups will vary with the types of programs under evaluation. Ultimately, this choice is based on the judgment of the evaluator as to what non–program-related factors might influence the effectiveness of the program under study. Although this approach helps control for some important external factors, it is generally not a fully reliable measure of program effects; it is best applied in conjunction with other evaluative methods.

Considerable effort may be needed to identify comparable communities or populations within communities. If standard data categories are adequate (such as similar population size, proximity, and so forth), the cost may be reasonable. But if communities are selected for particular combinations of characteristics or to ensure that a similar program does not exist in the "without" communities, the costs may rise significantly. Since the type of data collected and the precision with which they are collected is likely to vary from community to community, the availability of comparable data may be severely limited. If special data-collection efforts are required, the cost will be considerably higher.

Controlled Experimentation. By far the most potent approach to program evaluation, controlled experimentation is unfortunately also the most difficult and costly to undertake. This approach attempts to assess the effectiveness of a program or policy by systematically comparing specific changes in two or more carefully selected and controlled groups—one in which the program is operational and another in which it is not. This approach also can be used to test different levels of applications of the same program or variations on a program theme to determine which is most effective.

The procedures of this approach may involve many technical steps of experimental design techniques which can become very complex with respect to a particular program evaluation. The basic steps, however, are as follows:

1. identification of relevant objectives and corresponding evaluation criteria (effectiveness measures)
2. assign members of the target population or a probability sample of that population in a "scientifically" random manner to control and experimental groups; it is important to select groups that have similar characteristics with respect to their likelihood of being effectively "treated" by the program
3. measurement of the preprogram performance of each group using the selected evaluation criteria
4. application of the program to the experimental group but not to the control group
5. continuous monitoring of the operation of the experiment to determine of any actions occur that might distort the findings (If appropriate and possible, such behavior should be adjusted, or, if not, at least identified and its impact on the eventual findings explicitly estimated.)
6. measurement of postprogram performance of each group using the selected evaluation criteria
7. comparison of pre- versus postprogram changes in the evaluation criteria of the groups
8. search for plausible alternative explanations for observed changes and, if any exist, estimates of their effects on the data.[24]

The controlled experimental approach has traditionally been advanced as most appropriate for the evaluation of programs directed toward specific individuals, such as health programs, manpower training, and so forth, and for a variety of treatment programs such as those for drug and alcohol abuse, correction and rehabilitation, or work-release. It is not likely to be appropriate, however, in situations where large capital investments in equipment or facilities are required.

An important variation on this approach for local government purposes involves the comparison of different geographical areas of a community. Many programs can be split geographically—introduced initially in some areas of the community and not in others. For the evaluation of state programs, a new approach might be introduced in some counties or cities and not in others. For example, new crime prevention programs, solid waste collection procedures, programs of traffic control, and so forth are often tried out and evaluated in a few areas before receiving widespread application. Areas with similar characteristics with respect to the program being introduced could be identified, and some of these areas could then be randomly designated as program recipients. If trends in the evaluation data before the new program was introduced were similar in all selected areas, and if, after the new program was in operation, improvements were considerably greater in those areas with the program, then a basis would be provided for attributing the change to the introduction of the program.

This fourth approach is not without its special problems—problems that can bring the observed results into question. Some of these are as follows:

1. Members of an experimental group may respond differently to a program if they realize that they are being observed as part of an evaluation. This problem is commonly known as the "Hawthorne effect," after the studies by Roethlisberger and Dickson in the late 1920s at the Western Electric Company's Hawthorne Works in Chicago, in which the productivity of the test groups increased even under adverse conditions as a consequence of their selection for evaluation. To help reduce this problem, it may be necessary to inform members of the control group that they too are part of an experiment.

2. If the experimental group is only one part of a community, the responses to the program may differ significantly from what would occur if all parts of the community were receiving the benefits. For example, a new crime control program introduced on a pilot basis in one part of a community may merely cause a shift in the incidence of crime to other parts of the community without any overall reduction in the crime rate.

3. In some situations, political pressures may make it impractical to provide a service to one group in the community but not to others. Such resistance is lessened when variations of a program are tested in several locations rather than program resources being allocated on an all-or-nothing basis.

4. Some people may consider it morally wrong to provide a government service temporarily if the service might cause dependency among clients and leave them worse off after the program is withdrawn.

5. As noted previously, if persons are permitted to volunteer to participate in the experimental group, the two groups are not likely to be comparable. A self-selected group will probably be more receptive to the program and thus may not be typical of the whole target population.

6. Problems may arise in the administration of the service. While the use of a trained research group may minimize evaluation problems by maintaining the intent of the experimental design, such a group may not be familiar with service delivery problems and may therefore introduce a bias into the program results.

7. On the other hand, a specially trained administrative staff may be able to deliver the pilot program at a level that cannot be met by those agency personnel who will be called on to administer the full-scale program.

The use of the controlled experiment approach generally costs considerably more than the other evaluation techniques because of: (1) the greater time required to plan and conduct the experiment and to analyze the data; and

(2) the higher level of analytical and managerial skill required. This approach also implies certain indirect costs arising from the temporary changes made in the way the program operates so that different types of program benefits will be attained by the experimental and control groups.

Innovative projects can be evaluated more readily by the controlled experiment approach because pools of "unexposed" potential targets usually are available. Established projects, on the other hand, often need to be evaluated by statistical methods that measure the effects in degrees of exposure as well as by reflexive controls that utilize time-series analysis.[25]

Comparisons of Planned versus Actual Performance. The final approach to be discussed involves a comparison of actual results against planned or targeted results. In spite of rather straightforward procedures, such after-the-fact comparisons are still surprisingly rare. This approach requires the establishment of specific measurable objectives or targets prior to the initiation of the program or policy. Targets should be established for specific achievement within specific time periods (for example: "reduction in the incidence of juvenile delinquency by 15 percent in two years," rather than: "the elimination of juvenile delinquency"). If program targets are expressed in terms of effectiveness measures, as in most applications of program budgeting, such evaluations can be readily undertaken. At the end of the established time period, actual performance is compared against the established targets.

Like the initial before-and-after approach, this approach provides no direct means of indicating the extent to which the changes in values of the effectiveness criteria can be attributed solely to the new program or policy. As with other evaluative techniques, an explicit attempt must be made to search for plausible explanations other than the proram under evaluation as to why the targets have been met, exceeded, or not met.

Most state and local governments occasionally use a variation of this approach, involving a comparison of actual program performance with *implied* rather than explicit targets. The after-the-fact approach can be applied more widely once provision is made for the regular collection of necessary data for measuring evaluation criteria (that is, effectiveness measures). Targets can readily be set each year for one or more future years. Consequently, this approach is particularly useful for annual evaluations of programs that have existed for a number of years, so that before-program data are not of much utility. Much can be learned from a careful, systematic examination of the immediate, short-term consequences of a program, even if a more elaborate evaluation method is not applied.

This approach requires the establishment of appropriate, realistic objectives or targets for the evaluation criteria. The setting of such objectives may not be taken seriously if the evaluations are not used seriously—a problem with all evaluation techniques. Targets may be overstated and therefore unattainable, or may be understated to make the program achievements look better. However, if the evaluation findings are used seriously by decision makers, a valuable spinoff of this approach is that the establishment of targets is likely to become an important issue. Higher-level officials, as well as program managers, should participate in the establishment of these operational objectives, and the targets should explicitly encompass all key program effects.

It is important that this approach not be used to encourage haphazard assessments of performance or to discourage the use of other approaches described previously. This evaluative technique is relatively inexpensive compared to other methods; costs depend primarily on the expenditures necessary to gather additional data for the evaluation criteria selected. The setting of appropriate (measurable) objectives is likely to entail relatively small costs, at least in dollar terms.

Additional Considerations. There can seldom be complete assurance that changes were brought about by a specific program. Even in a controlled experiment, it would not be feasible to control for all factors that might conceivably be important. Often it will not be possible to attribute the effects solely to the program or policy under evaluation. However, decisions about public programs are inevitably made under conditions of considerable uncertainty; evaluations can reduce this uncertainty but cannot eliminate it totally. Even though it may not be possible to isolate the effects of a program from other events occurring at about the same time, it may be unnecessary to be overly concerned if the evaluation indicates significant benefits to the community or target population.

While the selection of an appropriate approach will depend on the timing of the evaluation, the costs and resources available, and the desired accuracy, it should be evident that these approaches are not either-or choices; some or all of the first three methods are often used together. The before-and-after method is relatively weak when applied alone, but becomes much more useful in combination with other approaches. The after-the-fact approach, involving comparisons of planned versus actual performance, is likely to be used more extensively once the concept of MIPES becomes more widely accepted and implemented in the public sector. Although the experimental approach provides the most precise evaluation, its cost and special characteristics result in its being applied on a very selective basis.

Using More Sophisticated Techniques

In terms of scientific rigor, the controlled experimental design is the zenith to which many policy analysts and evaluators aspire. This aspiration is particularly evident among the newly minted analysts emerging from various schools of planning and public policy, such as those at the University of California, at Berkeley, the University of Michigan, and Duke University. This fascination with statistical techniques is not necessarily valuable in the real world of administrative analysis, although the rigorous thinking is certainly an asset. Moreover, certain statistical devices provide a shorthand method for simulating complex relationships and thereby facilitating more comprehensive evaluations than would otherwise be possible.

Statistical analysis is useful at several key junctures in the development of more rigorous methodology of evaluation. To begin with, a statistical randomization technique can be instrumental in establishing a *true experiment.* This technique involves the use of chance selection in the assignment of potential target participants to experimental and control groups. Rossi et al. have demonstrated the use of statistical analysis as a control for stochastic effects, or "measurement fluctuations attributable to chance."[26]

The more profound value of statistical analysis is manifested in those situations in which it is impossible to conduct an actual experiment. These situations involve what is known as the *quasi-experimental design.* Quasi-experimental techniques can be applied in nearly all the evaluative approaches discussed previously. For example, statistical analysis can be used in the pre- and postprogram, the with-and-without, and the planned-versus-actual-performance approaches to control for the influences of nonprogram factors, such as the differences between groups (in terms of income, race, age, sex, and so forth) and the unequal distribution of critical variables. Group differences can be adjusted based on categories derived by studying the relationship to target variables, and unequal distributions can be ironed out somewhat if measures of target variables are taken at several points in time.[27]

It may be possible to evaluate performance by predicting a certain level of program results through *linear extrapolation.*[28] A variety of techniques also are available for application to nonlinear or curvilinear relationships, that is, those relationships that diminish over time.

In general, these statistical techniques provide a means of testing intuitive assumptions or perceived relationships, while screening for extraneous factors that might be responsible for the perceived change. In this way, they greatly enhance the explanatory capabilities of the policy analyst. In turn, the use of these powerful statistical tools intensifies the search for ineffective program ingredients and may even permit the isolation of poor policy elements in the midst of relatively successful program packages. A final point is that the scientific rigor of these approaches forces policy analysts to think of their recommendations as *causal hypotheses* to be empirically tested. In an era of dwindling public resources in relation to demands, techniques that can document policy impacts or the lack thereof certainly seem to warrant more active application.

The Role of Evaluation
in the Policy-Making Process

The most comprehensive and rigorous evaluation is little more than an academic exercise if its findings have no impact on the processes by which policies are made and programs are developed. Much evaluative research, particularly that which has been undertaken on the grand scale of national programs, has filled pages of scholarly treatises, with only modest implications for the policies and programs toward which this research has been directed. As Rossi et al. have observed: "Evaluations cannot influence decision-making processes unless those undertaking them recognize the need to orient their efforts toward maximizing the policy utility of their evaluation activities."[29] To this observation might be added that the need for evaluation must be recognized and accepted by those who have responsibility for the implementation of programs and policies.

Major Types of Evaluation of Interest to Policy Makers

Generally speaking, there are three major types of evaluation studies of interest to policy makers: (1) program-impact evaluations, (2) demonstration projects, and (3) field experiments. Of these three basic types, the demonstration project would seem to have the best chance to influence decision makers.

Joseph Wholey has suggested that program-impact studies often do not provide the types of information that decision makers need to assist in the process: ". . . rarely if ever is evaluation preceded by an analysis of the decision-making process and the constraints on the options open to the decision-makers for whom the evaluation is being done."[30] Wholey cites two national program-impact evaluations—the Westinghouse-Ohio University evaluation of the Head Start program and the annual evaluations by the Department of Labor of its manpower programs—the findings of which have played almost no part in the ongoing administration of these programs.

The principal difference between the field trial and the demonstration project is that in the former, those responsible for the evaluation exercise greater control over input variables (objectives, staff, clients, program location, size of program, and so forth) and are therefore in a better position to measure the results (outputs) to determine the extent to which program objectives have been achieved. Unlike program-impact evaluations, which tend to be retrospective, the demonstration project and field trial evaluations may be introduced into public programs either before the major effort is launched or at the same time.

Demonstrations and field experiments provide an excellent opportunity to discover and document whether a particular program is going to produce the required results, especially if participants can be randomly assigned to test and control groups. These types of *internal validity* checks are difficult to implement, however, even in highly controlled experiments. Moreover, internal validity is no guarantee of *external validity,* or the ability to generalize to a wider population. In general, large-scale social experiments, even with the smaller field trials, are difficult to manage and are therefore very costly to conduct.

Taking these factors into consideration, Wholey concludes that, in terms of decisions actually influenced, the basic payoff may be in terms of evaluation conducted for and provided to program managers during the implementation cycle.[31] This type of evaluation is often referred to as *program monitoring,* another phrase that adds to the general methodological confusion. Rossi and his colleagues tend to concur with Wholey's conclusion, although they also allude to the fact that "quick and dirty" evaluations can be conducted at numerous points in the policy formulation and implementation enterprise. Thus, practical evaluations need not be synonymous with program monitoring. Rossi et al. see at least three major roles for evaluation in determining policy decisions:

1.   in decisions regarding technical planning and management questions, such as whether a program should take this form or another
2.   in the provision of definitive information on which the decision makers and program managers can act
3.   in the provision of some general impacts on decision making by changing the ground of political argumentation.[32]

Policy and Program Renegotiation

In the face of sunset legislation, the future seems to portend termination for many ineffective programs. However, the future has not yet arrived, and many programs continue to have a life of their own. The real art of program improvement will not be the bold guillotining of unpromising programs, but rather the reconstruction or *renegotiation* of the policy process. As the concept of evaluation as "hypothesis testing" suggests, evaluation is actually a reinitiation of the policy-formulation process. However, because of the commitment of resources as well as the various constraints that must be dealt with, policy development in the evaluation stage is very tightly circumscribed.

The concept of renegotiation emerges from the feedback phase of the systems model, wherein the initial policy or program outputs are modified in response to the reactions of affected groups and sources of support. Renegotiation suggests the refinement and retargeting of policies and programs, rather than the setting of totally new directions. In short, renegotiation involves a reintroduction of an abbreviated strategic planning process (see chapter 9 for a discussion of strategic planning).

Although program termination is rare, the concept is a highly useful one. Moreover, curtailment, if not out-and-out termination, is likely to become a fairly common phenomenon. To overcome organizational and sociopolitical inertia with respect to program longevity, it is first necessary to understand the problems associated with actually terminating a program. Some of these problems can be outlined as follows:

1. *Institutional permanence:* Policies and agencies are designed to endure; complex organizations have an uncanny survival instinct—they are ultrastable.
2. *Situational dynamics:* Programs constantly are being adapted to emerging situations to avoid termination.
3. *Intellectual reluctance:* Given the hard-fought battles necessary to obtain a policy or program in the first place, analyst and planners have a natural reluctance to consider the question of termination.
4. *Antitermination coalitions:* Significant political and clientele groups often support programs beyond their span of effectiveness.
5. *Legal obstacles:* Programs have certain rights of "due process."
6. *High start-up costs:* Mounting campaigns for termination often is costly, both monetarily and politically.[33]

With public programs, strategic renegotiations often are possible, particularly if they are profitable to entrenched interests. De Leon provides the following helpful hints for program modification:

1. Modification and/or termination should not be viewed as the end of the world; rather, it is an opportunity for policy improvement.
2. Modification and/or termination should coincide with systematic evaluation.
3. Policies and program have certain "natural points"—times and places in their lifespans—where reconsideration is more likely and more appropriate.
4. The time horizon for gradual change is a significant factor.
5. The structure of incentives might be changes to promote modification; for example, agencies might be permitted to retain a portion of the program funding that they voluntarily cut.
6. Agencies might employ a staff of "salvage specialists," trained in reallocating resources.[34]

Increasingly, government activities are constrained by impending fiscal crises, and thus terminations or at least serious renegotiations are becoming more viable. In the movement toward more innovative approaches in the implementation of policies and programs, strategic planning provides a tool for salvaging or scrapping particular programs.

Notes

1. D.N.T. Perkins, "Evaluating Social Interventions: A Conceptual Schema," *Evaluation Quarterly* 1(November 1977):642–645.

2. Carol Weiss, *Evaluation Research* (Englewood Cliffs, N.J. Prentice-Hall, 1972), p. 1.

3. Peter H. Rossi, Howard E. Freeman, and Sonia R. Wright, *Evaluation: A Systematic Approach* (Beverly Hills, Calif.: Sage Publications, 1979), p. 15.

4. See Rehka Agawala-Rogers, "Why is Evaluation Research Not Utilized?" in *Evaluation Studies,* vol. 2, ed. Marcia Guttentag (Beverly Hills, Calif.: Sage Publications, 1977), pp. 329–330; also note Carol Weiss and Michael J. Bucuvalas, "The Challenge of Social Research to Decision-Making," in *Using Social Research in Public Policy Making,* ed. Carol Weiss (Lexington, Mass.: Lexington Books, D.C. Heath and Company, 1977), pp. 213–234.

5. Robert Clark, "Policy Implementation: Problems and Potentials," paper presented at a meeting of the Southern Political Science Association (October 1976), p. 2; available from the U.S. Community Services Agency. Reprinted with permission.

6. For an example, see Wade Andrews and Dennis G. Geertsen, *The Social Dimensions of Urban Flood Control Decisions* (Logan, Utah: Institute of Social Research on Natural Resources, 1974).

7. Lennox L. Moak and Albert M. Hillhouse, *Concepts and Practices in Local Government Finance* (Chicago, Ill.: Municipal Finance Officers Association, 1975), pp. 380–391.

8. This concept was first proposed in Herbert A. Simon and C.E. Ridley, *Measuring Municipal Activities* (Chicago, Ill.: International City Managers' Association, 1938) and further expanded in Herbert A. Simon, *Administrative Behavior* (New York: The Macmillan Company, 1957), chap. 9.

9. U.S. General Accounting Office, *Standards for the Audit of Government Organizations, Programs, Activities, and Functions* (Washington, D.C.: U.S. Government Printing Office, 1972), p. 2.

10. See Bruce Adams, "Guidelines for Sunset," *State Government* (Summer 1976).

11. Rossi et al., *Evaluation,* p. 248.

12. For a further discussion of cost-effectiveness analysis, see Alan Walter Steiss, *Local Government Finance* (Lexington, Mass.: Lexington Books, D.C. Heath and Company, 1975), chap. 10.

13. Rossi et al., *Evaluation,* p. 120.

14. S.M. Shortell and W.C. Richardson, *Health Program Evaluation* (St. Louis, Mo.: Mosby, 1978), pp. 18–20.

15. U.S. General Accounting Office, *Comprehensive Approach for Planning and Conducting a Program Results Review* (Washington, D.C.: U.S. Government Printing Office, 1978), p. 31.

16. Ibid., p. 46.

17. E.S. Quade, *Analysis for Public Decisions* (New York: American Elsevier Publishing Company, 1975), p. 224.

18. Joel E. Ross, *Modern Management and Information Systems* (Reston, Va.: Reston Publishing Company, 1976), p. 133.

19. See Robert G. May, Gerhard G. Mueller, and Thomas H. Williams, *A Brief Introduction to the Managerial and Social Uses of Accounting* (Englewood Cliffs, N.J.: Prentice-Hall, 1975), pp. 1–2.; Robert J. Mockler, *The Management Control Process* (New York: Appleton-Century-Crofts, 1972), pp. 95–96; Robert N. Anthony, *Management Accounting Principles* (Homewood, Ill.: Richard D. Irwin, 1965), pp. 185–187, 243–245.

20. Robert Zemsky, Randall Porter, and Laura P. Oedel, "Decentralized Planning: To Share Responsibility," *Educational Record* 59, no. 3(Summer 1978):244.

21. Harry P. Hatry, Richard E. Winnie, and Donald M. Fisk, *Practical Program Evaluation for State and Local Governments* (Washington, D.C.: The Urban Institute, 1973).

22. D.T. Campbell and J.C. Stanley, *Experimental and Quasi-Experimental Designs for Research* (Chicago: Rand McNally Company, 1966).

23. Rossi et al., *Evaluation,* pp. 172–175.

24. Adapted from Hatry et al., *Practical Program Evaluation.*

25. Rossi et al., *Evaluation,* p. 224.

26. Ibid., p. 186.

27. See David Nachmias, *Public Policy Evaluation: Approaches and Methods* (New York: St. Martin's Press, 1979), pp. 51–56.

28. For further discussion of these applications, see L.A. Wilson, "Statistical Techniques for Analysis of Public Policies," in *Methodologies for Analyzing Public Policies,* ed. Frank P. Scioli, Jr. and Thomas J. Cook (Lexington, Mass.: Lexington Books, D.C. Heath and Company, 1975), pp. 107–109.

29. Rossi et al., *Evaluation,* p. 283.

30. Joseph Wholey et al., *Federal Evaluation Policy* (Washington, D.C.: The Urban Institute, 1975), p. 364.

31. Ibid., p. 365.

32. Rossi et al., *Evaluation,* p. 305.

33. These problems were distilled from Peter de Leon, "A Theory of Termination," paper presented at the American Political Science conference (September 1977); available as a publication of the Rand Corporation, Santa Monica, California.

34. Ibid.

12 Values and Public Administration

Whether explicitly or merely implicitly, all public administrators subscribe to certain moral or ethical viewpoints that guide their interpretations of that nebulous substance known as the "public interest." These values were of little apparent consequence when it was assumed that administrators blindly pursued the public interest as defined by the legislative process. As recognition of the influence of administrators on policy making grows, however, the values they hold be of critical importance.

Normative Issues and Meta-Ethics

Recently, this recognition has led to a resurgence of concern about normative issues among students of public administration. Proponents of the so-called "New Public Administration," for example, decried the "normative aridity" of traditional administrative theory and practice. Todd LaPorte explains the problem as follows:

> ... social values which firmly anchored Public Administration in its role as the keeper of the social order no longer have their traditional currency. At a time requiring great moral, ethical, and philosophical vision we fall back upon analysis sprung from weakened, atrophied philosophical roots and premises. An increasing crisis in meaning seems to underlie much in the study and actions of public organizations; a loss of direction; foreshortened vision and failure of nerve in exploring the consequences for public organizations and politics occasioned by new conditions, new aspirations, and new anger with the underfulfilled promises of abundance.[1]

Despite these admonitions, it is rare indeed to find public managers or policy analysts confronting their own evaluative presuppositions.

Of Facts and Values

Among other topics, contemporary studies in meta-ethics—the discipline that addresses the logic of moral reasoning—have been concerned with the adjudication of value conflicts. Basically, this concern is manifested in discussions of the relationship between factual and value judgments. John Dewey, for example, was vitally concerned with how individuals made ethical choices. Dewey's conceptual approach, known as *instrumentalism* or *pragmaticism,* is essentially a situational ethic; that is, value judgments become factual statements when the individual examines the consequences of his or her values.[2] This view is highly congruent with the precepts of modern science.

Holding that values are, at bottom, merely facts leads one to encounter some basic philosophical and methodological problems. For example, two alternatives might be in conflict although they would have equally favorable or equally negative consequences. In such cases, pragmatic analysis usually relies on a "utilitarian" assessment, that is, that which produces the greatest good for the greatest number. Here again, what is "good" is a normative judgment. Moreover, the ordering, interpretation, and weighting of facts often entail elaborate value judgments as well. Converting values to facts does not necessarily resolve all disputes.

At a more fundamental level, utilitarianism may fail to provide a clear exposition of ethical obligation. Pragmaticism merely assumes that everyone should promote the greatest good. The ultimate validity of this notion of good, however, generally derives from societal consensus, another assumed fact that may be difficult to measure. Is it a "fact" that this society abhors the taking of a human life? What about abortion? What about in time of war? Facts may indeed conflict with ethical imperatives.

Finally, the appeal to facts may render authentic moral argument impossible. The elimination of "ought" statements also eliminates ethical opposition and moral admonition. This problem was first identified by the British logician G.E. Moore, who attempted to reinstate ethical argumentation with his well-known "open question." He suggested that the reduction of values to facts is incorrect because it does not allow dissenting groups to ask: "But is that moral?"[3] For example, a fundamentalist religious sect (or anyone, for that matter) may wish to challenge the pervasive hedonism of American society. But, if it is a simple fact that whatever a given society practices at a given point in time is its morality, then it cannot be called immoral. It would seem, however, that these are precisely the types of arguments that moral theorists, religious leaders, community fathers, and social critics have been making for years. In other words, pragmaticism ultimately leads to a tautology (something true by definition): "that which is good in this society is that which the society defines as good" (*good* meaning to have acceptable consequences).

Normative Language

Moore began a revolution in ethical theory which soon spawned a range of theories, most of them concerned with the uses of normative language. These alternatives, collectively labelled *noncognitivism,* hold that values are unknowable in a scientific or factual sense and are concerned with maintaining the "performative force" and the "emotive meaning" of moral utterances—their ability to persuade, recommend, and admonish).[4] It should be pointed out that facts may have performative force and that impacts or consequences may persuade.

Generally speaking, the noncognitivists construct a deductive logic of normative justification similar to Dewey's instrumentalism. In this respect, they admit that most normative disputes are actually factual disputes involving a disagreement about fact rather than about value.

For the sake of argument, however, it can be assumed that polar dichotomies do exist. When a fundamental disagreement over the taking of a life, or some similar dispute such as those about environmental quality, equal employment opportunities, and so forth, can be determined, then this is where ethical analysis actually begins. At that point, moral assumptions can be traced backward to the set of principles from which they were logically deduced. For Hare and many other noncognitivists, the matter is now one of individual choice. However, this ontological view, similar to existentialism, is not very helpful in resolving moral conflicts. Hare contends that a golden rule of sorts can be applied to the adjudication of conflicting claims.[5] This rule implies that a choice of moral principle is justified if an individual is willing to have the implied consequences of that choice befall him or her. While noncognitivism raises ethics above the level of social convention, it is still highly relativistic and thus fails to provide sufficient grounding to the ethical system.

Justice as Fairness

To gain such a grounding, one must turn to a more "principlistic" approach—one that maintains the possibility of, or at least the conditional existence of, moral absolutes.[6] John Rawls, in *A Theory of Justice,* provides a point of departure in the quest for such a systematic foundation. Rawls's principal contribution is the notion of "justice as fairness" and an analytical system based on a logic of "original position" (similar to a "social contract" theory).[7] The logic of original position makes possible the assertion of ethical obligation that is vital to establishing a set of social norms. Stated simply, such a logic entails the notion that, if individuals were placed in a situation of forming a political community and were objective, in the sense that they were ignorant of the position or station they would have in this new community, they would rationally choose *distributive justice* (a system that benefits the least advantaged).[8]

Market Failures and Fair Public Policies

A unique facet of Rawls's theory is that it is nonutilitarian. It does not seek the greatest good for the greatest number at the expense of the individual. In this respect, it is an alternative to theories of economic efficiency that rely on a utility-maximization principle. As Rawls demonstrates, his focus on the individual is much more compatible with the market concept of economics and thus furnishes an analytic tool for addressing a variety of failures in market accommodations.

The interface between meta-ethics and economics may provide useful axioms for facilitating equitable arrangements in the absence of a free-market mechanism. The best example of market failure is environmental degradation. Specifically, with respect to water pollution a maximizing strategy in the form of the 1972 Water Pollution Control Act Amendments (the Muskie Act) has been pursued to offset market failures. From the economist's point of view, this act is administrative overkill; it does not place the full burden of technology on the individual polluters, and thus it may be inefficient and ineffective.[9] From Rawls's viewpoint, the social costs of water pollution have been distributed but not equitably; many may incur more or less than their fair share of these costs.

A more elaborate example of the application of Rawls's concepts to market failures is provided by Berry and Steiker. They have suggested the following use of the concept of justice as fairness:

> . . . a fair policy or plan . . . does not unduly favor or discriminate against any group as to the distribution of the costs involved. . . . parties have claims and . . . the measurement and consideration of the strength of these claims ought to reflect the degree to which the parties are affected.[10]

This perspective has several unique elements. The most intriguing is that it places emphasis on strength of claim rather than on empirical bargaining strength (money, prestige, and organizational capacity). Along these lines, a fair or equitable arrangement may achieve accommodations that are very different from those in market situations in which only the claims of those with considerable bargaining resources (bankers, lawyers, developers, and so forth) are articulated. Furthermore, calculating the individual distribution of costs (assuming this to mean social as well as economic costs) provides a useful way of augmenting the aggregate cost-benefit analyses now widely employed. This aspect of individual costs is often the issue at stake in attempts to challenge the planning process.

Another unique element of this perspective is that it does not automatically substitute a maximizing solution in the event of market failure. Although such maximizing solutions may improve the general community welfare, some individuals may have to incur more than their fair share of the costs in providing for their neighbors' benefits.

Berry and Steiker delineate a scheme for adjudicating claims that are *noncommensurable,* that is, not measured on a scale acceptable to all parties. In the example that they use, the following divergence of measures is presented: (1) recreationalists, whose strength of claim is measured in their willingness to pay for certain levels of water quality; (2) aquatic species, whose strength of claim is measured in terms of the total number of critically important species surviving under varied conditions of pollutions; (3) the steel mill owner, whose strength of claim is measured in his costs for pollution abatement; and (4) steel workers, whose strength of claim is measured in the number unemployed under production cutbacks required to meet various pollution standards. Weighting these claims becomes the important issue, according to Berry and Steiker, and to resolve this issue, the "objective" planner must use Rawls's logic of original condition and attempt to work out an accommodation that benefits the least advantaged and that distributes costs fairly evenly.

Justice and Administrative Policy

This type of armchair adjudication may not be much more conducive to the achievement of justice than the unbridled biases of individual administrators and/or community elites. Nevertheless, Rawls's concept of distributive justice and his logical justification of ethical commonalities provides a model for a set of administrative-process principles. David Hart alludes to the fact that theories like Rawls's may be what is necessary to reduce the discretionary scope of administrative policy making by fostering a universal set of administrative ethics.[11] In other words, if we accept the fact that administrators will continue to infuse their own values into the policy process, it may be prudent to impose a set of logical restrictions. The exact content of judgment will obviously differ in different situations; however, a common pattern of analysis will lead to similar evaluative conclusions and may be more easily monitored by a variety of internal and external mechanisms such as public interest groups and legislators.

As the *meta* in meta-ethics implies, logic does not necessarily dictate content. Under a system of common methods of ethical analysis and conflict adjudication, a myriad of value choices are possible. Just as a trial by jury does not guarantee an acquittal, a logic of moral inquiry does not dictate the same decision in all cases: it is more procedural than substantive. In this respect, a common logic may be compatible with numerous management styles.

A procedural approach of ethical introspection has many advantages. Initially, such an approach would permit adaptations to changing social institutions, while affirming certain basic principles such as human dignity. More important, a set of common procedures would force even the most myopic or mechanistic administrator to come to grips with his or her own evaluative reasoning and ultimately, his or her own rationale for public service.

Societal Values and Planned Change

In *Future Shock,* we are told that rapid change is endangering the very foundations of our society; that the human species is on the brink of its own self-made destruction. Nevertheless, change is inevitable in modern society. The question is not how to hold back change, but rather how to channel change effectively to produce positive results while minimizing its dysfunctional consequences. Change for the sake of change is not the appropriate objective; progress is not "our most important product" if we cannot define what we are progressing toward. Planned change, undertaken with full recognition of the byproducts and side effects of our actions, must begin with an understanding of the system—the society—and its values. Change must then be planned and regulated through effective mechanisms of public policy.

The Need for an Improved Metasystem

Three major issues confronting contemporary society give rise to the need for a true metasystem: (1) the need for institutional adjustments to the rapid growth of technology; (2) the absence of a common set of beliefs and attitudes binding society together for the achievement of some higher purpose; and (3) the decline of respect for temporal power and the loss of confidence in government. The term *metasystem,* as used in cybernetic theory, refers to a combination of systems or subsystems which, when connected, transcend the limitations of their own parameters; that is, the whole is greater than the sum of the parts.

Few would dispute the fact that our society is experiencing a technological revolution. It must be recognized, however, that the characteristic structure and operations of existing social institutions were conditioned primarily by older technologies. Had our major social institutions emerged under the formative influence of today's technology, it is likely that in many cases their structural configuration and modes of operation would be very different. However, because social institutions tend to resist any attempt to redefine their roles—because they are ultrastable—the full potential of contemporary technology has not been realized. There is a parallel concern that the rate of technological development is outstripping the ability of our present social institutions to control its applications. Increasingly, we are faced with moral questions or value issues for which our social institutions do not have readily available, consistent answers.

Religion once gave society a genuine metasystem that conveyed a broader ethic (set of values) to govern the operations of social institutions. Today, because the subsystems still appear to maintain their integrity, there is a tendency to continue to acknowledge the metasystem and to assume its sustained influence. Increasingly, the general public, especially its younger members, is not accepting the "binding influence" of this ethic. What is happening is not so much an outright rejection of the ethic as a questioning of the realities of contemporary practices in light of this ethic. The "back-to-basics" movements in various religious practices may be interpreted as a manifestation of the search for an improved metasystem.

As societies become more urban and more industrialized, nationalism frequently supplants traditional religious institutions, performing many of the important functions of societal integration. The flag may replace the symbols of the church, and nationalistic slogans may become the rallying cries of the society. With urbanization, a society often becomes more heterogeneous in its identifiable attitudes and values. Temporal power, vested in the government of the society, must serve as a mechanism for social cohesion and control. However, when this power is abused, when social injustices are sustained or even promoted by those in power, and when "credibility gaps" between government leaders and the people widen, then the spirit of nationalism can no longer function as the binding force of society.

Thus, established practices in contemporary society appear to be adrift in several dimensions at once. Social institutions have not been properly integrated with modern technology, and consequently, the full potential of technological advances has not been realized. At the same time, the genuine metasystem once provided by religion is rapidly disappearing along with its ethical language and authority. The metasystem of temporal power (government) that remains turns out to be spurious—no real metasystem at all. The society is faced with a set of outmoded social institutions, the modus operandi of which is governed by an anachronistic technology.[12] These social institutions are strung together, not in a true metasystem, but in accordance with rules which are themselves the product of a social institution—the social institution of the status quo.

Ultrastability and Planned Change

By adopting a general systems model, it is possible to view social institutions as interactive systems involving a variety of structural components that operate in partly stabilized but open-ended modes. Such systems include a number of nonsteady states and also exhibit the characteristics of equifinality, varifinality, and teleos.[13] These social institutions are composed of a number of esoteric, ultrastable subsystems. These subsystems are *esoteric* in that what goes on within them often is unintelligible to an outsider. They are *ultrastable* in that, if the subsystem is "disturbed" by some outside force that produces measurable changes in one or more of its variables, internal relationships are simply adjusted slightly so that the impact of the disturbance is offset and the subsystem continues to operate as it did before the disturbance.[14]

These characteristics of esoteric and ultrastable subsystems have an important bearing on efforts to improve the environment for public policy making. As Dror has observed, such improvements must reach a critical mass in order to influence the aggregative outputs of the system. Failing to reach this threshold, such improvements may be neutralized by countervailing adjustments of other components (what Ashby has called the ultrastability reaction).[15] It may be possible, however, to reach the impact threshold—and thus to achieve significant effects in the overall output of the system—through a combination of strategic, albeit incremental, changes in the component subsystems. As Dror observes:

> . . . a set of incremental changes may, in the aggregate, result in far-reaching system output changes. Furthermore, because we are speaking about changes in the policy-making system, there is a good chance that, under some conditions, a set of relatively minor and incremental changes . . . will permit—through multiplier effects—far-reaching innovations in the specific policies made by that system.[16]

One of the most important contributions derived from general systems theory is that any open system is rapidly dominated by its error-actuated feedback rather than by its inputs. The inputs to a system may be varied over a wide range; the functions that characterize the behavior of component elements within the system may be transferred over a broad spectrum; and the parameters of the system may change. As long as the systemic structure remains unchanged, however, the critical outputs of the system will be invariant. This conclusion is based on the assumption that the structure of a dynamic, open system is exceedingly complex, full of interaction, organized in a hierarchical fashion, and rich in negative feedback to permit self-correcting action. Therefore, systems reforms—planned change—must be directed primarily toward the introduction of new states or alternative responses within the structure of the system.

The optimism expressed by Dror regarding incremental changes in the components of the policy system must be examined in light of these conclusions. If these incremental changes operate on the existing structure without introducing new states (new structural conditions), there is little hope for any multiplier effects. In fact, such changes are likely to bring about even greater ultrastability among these subsystems. While the consequences of these changes may be greater organizational efficiency, policy effectiveness may show little improvement because inappropriate and ineffective policies may merely be implemented more efficiently. To achieve far-reaching changes in the output of the system will require structural innovations beyond the current institutional arrangements of most policy-making systems.

In the aftermath of Watergate, many contemporary policy-making systems are in a state of turmoil as a result of recent events and disclosures about national policy formulation processes and persons intimate to those processes. Therefore, perhaps Dror is correct in his assertion that ". . . the readiness to innovate is increasing as a result of the shock effect of readily perceived crisis symptoms."[17] Providing systematic responses to this readiness to innovate is the principal objective to which performance administration is dedicated.

Notes

1. Todd LaPorte, "The Recovery of Relevance in the Study of Public Organizations," in *Toward a New Public Administration*, ed. Frank Marini (Scranton, Pa.: Chandler Publishing, 1971), p. 20; also note Gregory A. Daneke, "Policy, Practicalities and Philosophy: Reflections on the State of the Art in Political Science," *Journal of Thought* (Fall 1976):190–198.

2. See John Dewey, *Theory of Valuation* (Chicago, Ill.: University of Chicago Press, 1939).

3. G.E. Moore, *Principia Ethica* (Cambridge: Cambridge University Press, 1903).

4. See, for example, Charles L. Stevenson, *Ethics and Language* (New Haven, Conn.: Yale University Press, 1944).

5. R. M. Hare, *Freedom and Reason* (Oxford: Oxford University Press, 1963).

6. For an elaboration of the principalistic approach, see Gregory A. Daneke, "Toward a Theory of Moral Instruction," *Theory Into Practice* 14, no. 4(October 1975):247–257.

7. John Rawls, *A Theory of Justice* (Cambridge, Mass.: Harvard University Press, 1971). The "social contract" forms the obligatory foundation of the Western tradition of jurisprudence and is found in Locke and Hobbes.

8. Ibid., pp. 118–194.

9. Note Allen Kneese and Charles Schultze, *Pollution, Prices, and Public Policy* (Washington, D.C.: The Brookings Institution, 1975), pp. 53–58.

10. David Berry and Gene Steiker, "The Concept of Justice in Regional Planning," *The Journal of the American Institute of Planners,* 40 (November 1974):415.

11. David Hart, "Social Equity, Justice and Equitable Administration," *Public Administration Review* 39 (January/February 1974): 3–10.

12. Stafford Beer, "The Cybernetic Cytoblast: Management Itself," *Progress of Cybernetics,* vol. 1 (London: Gordon and Breach Science Publishers, 1970), p. 80.

13. The concept of equifinality was first advanced by Ludwig von Bertalanffy as a result of his observations of the apparently purposeful, goal-directed (teleological) behavior that characterizes living or open systems. *Equifinality* means that the final state may be reached from different initial conditions and through different processes. The corollary of this open system characteristic is *varifinality,* which exists when different end states can be reached from the same initial conditions.

14. For a further discussion of these systemic characteristics, see Alan Walter Steiss, *Models for the Analysis and Planning of Urban Systems* (Lexington, Mass.: Lexington Books, D.C. Heath and Company 1974), chap. 10.

15. W. Ross Ashby, *Design for a Brain* (London: Chapman & Hall, 1960), pp. 56–64.

16. Yehezkel Dror, "From Management Sciences to Policy Sciences," in *Management and Policy Science in American Government,* ed. Michael J. White, Michael Radnor, and David A. Tansik (Lexington, Mass.: Lexington Books, D.C. Heath and Company, 1975)', p. 282.

17. Ibid., p. 282.

Indexes

Index of Subjects

Index of Names

About the Authors

Alan Walter Steiss is associate dean for research administration at Virginia Polytechnic Institute and State University. He received the A.B. in psychology and sociology from Bucknell University and the M.A. and Ph.D. in urban and regional planning from the University of Wisconsin. Dr. Steiss has served at Virginia Tech as director of the Center for Urban and Regional Studies, chairman of the Urban and Regional Planning Program and Urban Affairs Program, chairman of the Division of Environmental and Urban Systems, and associate dean for research and graduate studies of the College of Architecture and Urban Studies. He has been a guest lecturer at several universities, including Rider College, New York University, the University of Wisconsin, Georgia Institute of Technology, Virginia Commonwealth University, the University of British Columbia, and the University of Virginia. He was formerly the head of statewide planning for the State of New Jersey and has served as a consultant to the states of Wisconsin, New Jersey, Maryland, Virginia, South Carolina, New York, and Hawaii, the Trust Territory of the Pacific, and the Federal-State Land Use Planning Commission for Alaska. Dr. Steiss is the author of several books, including *Planning Administration: A Framework for Planning in State Government; Systemic Planning: Theory and Application* (with Anthony J. Catanese); *A Public Service Option for Architectural Curricula; Public Budgeting and Management; Models for the Analysis and Planning of Urban Systems; Urban Systems Dynamics; Dynamic Change and the Urban Ghetto* (with Michael Harvey, John Dickey and Bruce Phelps); *Local Government Finance; Capital Facilities Planning and Debt Administration;* and *Accounting, Budgeting and Control for Government Organizations* (with Leo Herbert and Larry N. Killough). He has contributed to numerous professional journals in the United States and abroad.

Gregory A. Daneke is associate professor of public policy, planning, and administration at the University of Arizona. He received the Ph.D. in 1976 from the University of California at Santa Barbara and has taught at several institutions, including the American University and the University of Michigan. Dr. Daneke has served as a Fellow with the U.S. General Accounting Office and as a consultant to other federal, state, and local government agencies. He is the author of numerous works in the areas of planning, policy analysis, and natural-resource management.

DATE DUE

2.26. '81	
1.22 '82	
8.19. '82	
9-9-82	
JUL 2 4 1996	
FEB 1 2 1998	
MAR 4 1998	
MAR 25	